ACHIEVEMENTS IN EUROPEAN RESEARCH ON GRID SYSTEMS

CoreGRID Integration Workshop 2006 (Selected Papers)

T0137761

ACHIEVEMENTS IN EUROPEAN RESEARCH
ON GRID SYSTEMS
CoreGRID Integration Workshop 2006
(Selected Papers)

October 19-20, Krakow, Poland

Edited by

Sergei Gorlatch
University of Muenster
Germany

Marian Bubak
ICS/ACC CYFRONET AGH
Krakow, Poland

Thierry Priol
IRISA / INRIA
Rennes, France

 Springer

Sergei Gorlatch
Universität Münster
FB Mathematik und Informatik
Institut für Informatik
Einsteinstr. 62
48149 Münster
GERMANY
gorlatch@math.uni-muenster.de

Marian Bubak
Academy Mining /Metallurgy
Inst. Computer Science, AGH
Al. A. Mickiewicza 30
30-059 KRAKOW
POLAND
bubak@uci.agh.edu.pl

Thierry Priol
IRISA / INRIA Rennes
Campus de Beaulieu
35042 RENNES CX
FRANCE
thierry.priol@irisa.fr

Achievements in European Research on Grid Systems
Edited by Sergei Gorlatch, Marian Bubak, Thierry Priol

ISBN-13: 978-1-4419-4450-4   e-ISBN-13: 978-0-387-72812-4

Printed on acid-free paper.

9 8 7 6 5 4 3 2 1

springer.com

Contents

Foreword

This volume is a selection of best papers presented at the CoreGRID Integration Workshop 2006 (CGIW'2006), which took place on 19–20 October 2006 in Krakow, Poland.

The workshop was organised by the Network of Excellence CoreGRID funded by the European Commission under the sixth Framework Programme IST-2003-2.3.2.8 starting September 1st, 2004 for a duration of four years. CoreGRID aims at strengthening and advancing scientific and technological excellence of Europe in the area of Grid and Peer-to-Peer technologies. To achieve this objective, the network brings together a critical mass of well-established researchers from forty institutions who have constructed an ambitious joint programme of activities.

The goal of the workshop is to promote the integration of the CoreGRID network and of the European research community in the area of Grid and P2P technologies, in order to overcome the current fragmentation and duplication of efforts in this area.

The list of topics of Grid research covered at the workshop included but was not limited to:

- knowledge and data management;
- programming models;
- system architecture;
- Grid information, resource and workflow monitoring services;
- resource management and scheduling;
- systems, tools and environments;
- trust and security issues on the Grid.

Priority at the workshop was given to work conducted in collaboration between partners from different research institutions and to promising research proposals that can foster such collaboration in the future.

The workshop was open to the members of the CoreGRID network and also to the parties interested in cooperating with the network and/or, possibly joining the network in the future.

The Programme Committee who made the selection of papers included:

Sergei Gorlatch, University of Muenster, Chair
Marian Bubak, ICS and ACC CYFRONET AGH
Artur Andrzejak, ZIB
Marco Danelutto, University of Pisa
Vladimir Getov, University of Westminster
Pierre Guisset, CETIC
Domenico Laforenza, ISTI-CNR
Norbert Meyer, Poznan Supercomputing and Networking Center
Ron Perrot, Queen's University Belfast
Thierry Priol, INRIA/IRISA
Uwe Schwiegelshohn, University of Dortmund
Domenico Talia, University of Calabria
Ramin Yahyapour, University of Dortmund
Wolfgang Ziegler, Fraunhofer-Institute SCAI

All papers in this volume were reviewed by the following reviewers whose help we gratefully acknowledge:

Martin Alt
Artur Andrzejak
Mark Baker
Briquet
Maciej Brzezniak
Marian Bubak
Mario Cannataro
Andrei Chernykh
Marco Danelutto
Patrizio Dazzi
Jan Dünnweber
Vladimir Getov
Pierre Guisset
Mikael Högqvist
Felix Hupfeld
Stavros Isaiadis
Gracjan Jankowski
Radek Januszewski
Ian Kelley
Raj Kettimuthu
Tobias Langhammer
Norbert Meyer
Jakub T. Moscicki

Nikos Parlavantzas
Kathrin Peter
Domenico Talia
Jeyarajan Thiyagalingam
Pawel Wolniewicz
Ramin Yahyapour
Wolfgang Ziegler

We gratefully acknowledge the support from the members of the Scientific Advisory Board and Industrial Advisory Board of CoreGRID, and especially the invited speakers Anssi Karhinen (Nokia) and Michal Turala (IFJ PAN). Special thanks are due to the authors of all submitted papers, the members of the Programme Committee and the Organising Committee, and to all reviewers, for their contribution to the success of this event. We are grateful to ACC Cyfronet AGH for hosting the Workshop and publishing its preliminary proceedings.

Muenster and Krakow, May 2007

Sergei Gorlatch and Marian Bubak (workshop organizers)
Thierry Priol (Scientific Coordinator of CoreGRID)

Contributing Authors

Davide Adami   CNIT Research Unit, Department of Information Engineering, University of Pisa, 56100 Pisa, Italy
(davide.adami@cnit.it)

Marco Aldinucci   Computer Science Department, University of Pisa, Largo Bruno Pontecorvo 3, 56127 Pisa, Italy
(aldinuc@di.unipi.it)

Gabriel Antoniu   Campus de Beaulieu, 35042 Rennes, France
(gabriel.antoniu@irisa.fr)

Filipe Araujo   CISUC, Department of Informatics Engineering, University of Coimbra, Portugal
(filipius@dei.uc.pt)

Alvaro E. Arenas   STFC Rutherford Appleton Laboratory, United Kingdom
(A.E.Arenas@rl.ac.uk)

Rosa M. Badia   Barcelona Supercomputing Center and Universitat Politècnica de Catalunya, Barcelona, Spain
(rosab@ac.upc.edu)

Ranieri Baraglia   Information Science and Technologies Institute, CNR, 56126 Pisa, Italy
(ranieri.baraglia@isti.cnr.it)

Francoise Baude   INRIA Sophia Antipolis, 2004, route des Lucioles, BP 93, France
(Francoise.Baude@inria.fr)

Olav Beckmann   Department of Computing, Imperial College London, 180 Queen's Gate, London SW7 2AZ, UK

Marian Bubak   Institute of Computer Science, AGH, al. Mickiewicza 30, 30-059 Kraków, Poland
Academic Computer Centre – CYFRONET, Nawojki 11, 30-950 Kraków, Poland
(bubak@agh.edu.pl)

Denis Caromel   INRIA Sophia Antipolis, 2004, route des Lucioles, BP 93, France
(denis.caromel@inria.fr)

Julita Corbalan   Barcelona Supercomputing Center, Universitat Politècnica de Catalunya (UPC), Spain
(julita.corbalan@bsc.es)

Natalia Currle-Linde   High Performance Computing Center (HLRS), University of Stuttgart, Germany
(linde@hlrs.de)

Marco Danelutto   Computer Science Department, University of Pisa, Largo Bruno Pontecorvo 3, 56127 Pisa, Italy
(marcod@di.unipi.it)

John Darlington   Department of Computing, Imperial College London, 180 Queen's Gate, London SW7 2AZ, UK
(jd@doc.ic.ac.uk)

Patrizio Dazzi   IMT (Lucca Institute for Advanced Studies), Lucca, Italy
ISTI/CNR, Pisa, Italy
(patrizio.dazzi@isti.cnr.it)

Marios Dikaiakos   Department of Computer Science, University of Cyprus, P.O. Box 537, CY-1678 Nicosia, Cyprus
(mdd@ucy.ac.cy)

Patricio Domingues   School of Technology and Management, Polytechnic Institute of Leiria, Portugal
(patricio@estg.ipleiria.pt)

Cătălin L. Dumitrescu   Mathematics and Computer Science Department, The University of Münster
(dumitres@uni-muenster.de)

Jan Dünnweber   Mathematics and Computer Science Department, The University of Münster
(duennweb@uni-muenster.de)

Dick H.J. Epema   Electrical Eng., Mathematics and Computer Science Department, Technical University of Delft
(d.h.j.epema@tudelft.nl)

Renato Ferrini   Information Science and Technologies Institute, CNR, 56126 Pisa, Italy
(renato.ferrini@isti.cnr.it)

Paraskevi Fragopoulou   Institute of Computer Science, Foundation for Research and Technology-Hellas, P.O. Box 1385, 71110 Heraklion-Crete, Greece
(fragopou@ics.forth.gr)

Włodzimierz Funika   Institute of Computer Science, AGH, al. Mickiewicza 30, 30-059 Kraków, Poland
(funika@agh.edu.pl)

Vladimir Getov   School of Computer Science, University of Westminster, Watford Rd, Northwick Park Harrow HA1 3TP, UK
(v.s.getov@westminster.ac.uk)

Stefano Giordano   Department of Information Engineering, University of Pisa, 56100 Pisa, Italy
(s.giordano@iet.unipi.it)

Sergei Gorlatch   Mathematics and Computer Science Department,
The University of Münster
(gorlatch@uni-muenster.de)

Francesc Guim   Barcelona Supercomputing Center, Universitat Politècnica
de Catalunya (UPC), Spain
(francesc.guim@bsc.es)

William Hoarau   LRI-CNRS 8623 and INRIA Grand Large, Université
Paris Sud XI, France
(hoarau@lri.fr)

Mikael Högqvist   Konrad-Zuse-Zentrum für Informationstechnik Berlin,
Takusstrasse 7, D-14195 Berlin-Dahlem, Germany
(hoegqvist@zib.de)

Fabrice Huet   INRIA Sophia Antipolis, 2004, route des Lucioles, BP 93,
France
(fabrice.huet@inria.fr)

Mathieu Jan   Campus de Beaulieu, 35042 Rennes, France
(mathieu.jan@irisa.fr)

Thilo Kielmann   Dept. of Computer Science, Vrije Universiteit, Amsterdam,
The Netherlands
(kielmann@cs.vu.nl)

Derrick Kondo   Laboratoire de Recherche en Informatique/INRIA Futurs,
France
(dkondo@lri.fr)

Elżbieta Krępska Dept. of Computer Science, Vrije Universiteit, Amsterdam,
The Netherlands
(e.krepska@gmail.com)

Krzysztof Kurowski   Poznan Supercomputing and Networking Center,
Poland
(kikas@man.poznan.pl)

Jesus Labarta Barcelona Supercomputing Center, Universitat Politècnica de Catalunya (UPC), Spain
(jesus.labarta@bsc.es)

Alexandros Labrinidis Department of Computer Science, University of Pittsburgh, Pittsburgh 15260, USA
(labrinid@cs.pitt.edu)

Domenico Laforenza Information Science and Technologies Institute, CNR, 56126 Pisa, Italy
(domenico.laforenza@isti.cnr.it)

Piotr Machner Institute of Computer Science, AGH, al. Mickiewicza 30, 30-059 Kraków, Poland
(machner@student.agh.edu.pl)

Evangelos P. Markatos Institute of Computer Science, Foundation for Research and Technology-Hellas, P.O. Box 1385, 71110 Heraklion-Crete, Greece
(markatos@ics.forth.gr)

Philippe Massonet Centre of Excellence in Information and Communication Technologies (CETIC), Belgium
(philippe.massonet@cetic.be)

Matthieu Morel INRIA Sophia Antipolis, 2004, route des Lucioles, BP 93, France
(matthieu.morel@inria.fr)

Jarek Nabrzyski Poznan Supercomputing and Networking Center, Poland
(naber@man.poznan.pl)

Syed Naqvi Centre of Excellence in Information and Communication Technologies (CETIC), Belgium
STFC Rutherford Appleton Laboratory, United Kingdom
(snaqvi@ieee.org)

Ariel Oleksiak Poznan Supercomputing and Networking Center, Poland
(ariel@man.poznan.pl)

Sofia Panagiotidi   Department of Computing, Imperial College London, 180 Queen's Gate, London SW7 2AZ, UK

Harris Papadakis   Institute of Computer Science, Foundation for Research and Technology-Hellas, P.O. Box 1385, 71110 Heraklion-Crete, Greece (adanar@ics.forth.gr)

Nikos Parlavantzas   Harrow School of Computer Science, University of Westminster, HA1 3TP, UK
(N.Parlavantzas@westminster.ac.uk)

Marcelo Pasin   Dept. Computer Science, Univ. of Pisa, Italy & CoreGRID Programming Model Institute
EIA/FR, Fribourg, Switzerland
(marcelopasin@gmail.com)

Luigi Presti   IMT (Lucca Institute for Advanced Studies), Lucca, Italy (luigi.presti@imtlucca.it)

Michael Resch   High Performance Computing Center (HLRS), University of Stuttgart, Germany
(resch@hlrs.de)

Ivan Rodero   Barcelona Supercomputing Center, Universitat Politècnica de Catalunya (UPC), Spain
(ivan.rodero@bsc.es)

Nuno Rodrigues   Dep. Engenharia Informática, University of Coimbra, Polo II, 3030–Coimbra, Portugal

Katarzyna Rycerz   Institute of Computer Science, AGH, al. Mickiewicza 30, 30-059 Kraków, Poland
Academic Computer Centre – CYFRONET, Nawojki 11, 30-950 Kraków, Poland
(kzajac@agh.edu.pl)

Luis Moura Silva   CISUC, Department of Informatics Engineering, University of Coimbra, Portugal

Dep. Engenharia Informática, University of Coimbra, Polo II, 3030–Coimbra, Portugal
(luis@dei.uc.pt)

Raül Sirvent   Barcelona Supercomputing Center and Universitat Politècnica de Catalunya, Barcelona, Spain
(rsirvent@ac.upc.edu)

Peter Sloot   Faculty of Sciences, Section Computational Science, University of Amsterdam, Kruislaan 403, 1098 SJ Amsterdam, The Netherlands
(sloot@science.uva.nl)

Décio Sousa   Dep. Engenharia Informática, University of Coimbra, Polo II, 3030–Coimbra, Portugal

Domenico Talia   DEIS, University of Calabria, Via Pietro Bucci 41C, 87036 Rende (CS), Italy
(talia@deis.unical.it)

Jeyarajan Thiyagalingam   School of Computer Science, University of Westminster, Watford Rd, Northwick Park Harrow HA1 3TP, UK

Sébastien Tixeuil   LRI-CNRS 8623 and INRIA Grand Large, Université Paris Sud XI, France
(tixeuil@lri.fr)

Nicola Tonellotto   Information Science and Technologies Institute, CNR, 56126 Pisa, Italy
(nicola.tonellotto@isti.cnr.it)

Paolo Trunfio   DEIS, University of Calabria, Via Pietro Bucci 41C, 87036 Rende (CS), Italy
(trunfio@deis.unical.it)

Marco Vanneschi   Dept. Computer Science, Univ. of Pisa, Italy & Core-GRID Programming Model Institute
(vannesch@di.unipi.it)

Philipp Wieder   Central Institute for Applied Mathematics, Research Centre Jülich, 52425 Jülich, Germany
(ph.wieder@fz-juelich.de)

Oliver Wäldrich Department of Bioinformatics, Fraunhofer Institute SCAI, 53754 Sankt Augustin, Germany
(oliver.waeldrich@scai.fraunhofer.de)

Ramin Yahyapour   Robotics Research Institute, University of Dortmund, 44221 Dortmund, Germany
(ramin.yahyapour@udo.edu)

Jingdi Zeng   DEIS, University of Calabria, Via Pietro Bucci 41C, 87036 Rende (CS), Italy
(zeng@si.deis.unical.it)

Wolfgang Ziegler   Department of Bioinformatics, Fraunhofer Institute SCAI, 53754 Sankt Augustin, Germany
(wolfgang.ziegler@scai.fraunhofer.de)

DIVIDE ET IMPERA: PARTITIONING UNSTRUCTURED PEER-TO-PEER SYSTEMS TO IMPROVE RESOURCE LOCATION

Harris Papadakis, Paraskevi Fragopoulou*, Evangelos P. Markatos
Institute of Computer Science
Foundation for Research and Technology-Hellas
P.O. Box 1385, 71 110 Heraklion-Crete, Greece
(adanar | fragopou | markatos)@ics.forth.gr

Marios Dikaiakos
Department of Computer Science
University of Cyprus
P.O. Box 537, CY-1678 Nicosia, Cyprus
mdd@ucy.ac.cy

Alexandros Labrinidis
Department of Computer Science
University of Pittsburgh
Pittsburgh, PA 15260, USA
labrinid@cs.pitt.edu

Abstract   Unstructured P2P systems exhibit a great deal of robustness and self-healing at the cost of reduced scalability. Resource location is performed using a broadcast-like process called flooding. The work presented in this paper comprises an effort to reduce the overwhelming volume of traffic generated by flooding, thus increasing the scalability of unstructured P2P systems. Using a simple hash-based content categorization method the Ultrapeer overlay network is partitioned into a relatively small number of distinct subnetworks. By employing a novel index splitting technique each leaf peer is effectively connected to each different subnetwork. The search space of each individual flooding is restricted to a single partition, and is thus considerably limited. This reduces significantly the volume of traffic produced by flooding without affecting at all the accuracy of the search method. Experimental results demonstrate the efficiency of the proposed method.

Keywords: Peer-to-peer, resource location, flooding, overlay network, network partition.

*Paraskevi Fragopoulou is with the Department of Applied Informatics and Multimedia, Technological Educational Institute of Crete, Heraklion, Greece.

1.   Introduction

Peer-to-peer (P2P) systems have recently gained much popularity in the research community as well as among the general public. Researchers show increasing interest in this paradigm because of its inherent scalability and robustness, which promises to enable the development of global-scale, cooperative, distributed applications. Different entities, under different authoritative control, interconnect and cooperate to offer services to each other, each of them acting both as a server and as a client, thus the term *peers* for the participating entities.

Existing P2P systems fall into two main categories. *Structured* P2P systems impose a certain order on the connectivity of the participating peers which is reflected in the structure of the overall network. All files stored in the system are indexed in a distributed manner by employing a Distributed Hash Table (DHT), thus enabling efficient resource location in time usually logarithmic to the number of peers. The drawback of this method however is that the maintenance of such a rigid structure limits the ability of P2P systems to heal themselves efficiently in the face of failures and thus render them less robust, albeit more scalable.

On the other hand, *unstructured* P2P systems do not impose a certain structure to the network. Those systems are aptly named unstructured since each peer is directly connected to a small set of other peers, called *neighbours*, making the network more ad-hoc in nature. The absence of a structure makes such systems much more robust and highly self-healing compared to structured systems, however, at the cost of reduced scalability. To exploit peer heterogeneity to the system's benefit, in [13, 4] a distinction between peers was introduced and a two level hierarchy of peers was constructed. High bandwidth peers, the *Ultrapeers* (also known as *Superpeers*), form an unstructured overlay network, while peers with low bandwidth, the *Leaves*, are connected only to Ultrapeers. Each Ultrapeer has an index of all the files contained in its Leaves. This modification allows the system to retain its simplicity while offering improved scalability.

Due to the lack of a particular file indexing method, unstructured P2P systems employ a broadcast-like process called *flooding* for resource location. A peer looking for a file issues a query which is broadcast in the network, until all peers have received the request or until the query propagates a predefined maximum number of hops away from its source (Time-To-Live hops or TTL). Flooding generates a large number of messages, reducing the scalability of the method. Due to the completely decentralized nature of flooding, each peer may receive the same request through a number of different neighbours. Those duplicate messages often exceed in number the non-duplicate ones. For a flood targeting the entire network, the number of duplicate messages is $d - 2$ times the number of non-duplicate messages, where d is the degree of the overlay network (average number of peers neighbours). Recent work was carried out in P2P systems with the aim of reducing the number of duplicates generated [8]. However, even if all duplicate messages are eliminated, flooding would still not scale well, since the cost of flooding a request to the entire network is relative to the total number of peers. On the other hand, limiting the number of hops a query propagates, achieves improved scalability at the cost of reduced *network coverage* (defined as the percentage of peers that receive a request). When a two level hierarchy of peers is involved, any request originating at a Leaf peer is forwarded through the Ultrapeers it is connected to, while flooding is performed only at the Ultrapeer overlay network.

The aim of the work presented in this paper is to improve the scalability of flooding by reducing the number of peers that need to be contacted on each request, without decreasing the probability of query success (accuracy of the search method). The proposed method partitions the Ultrapeer overlay network into distinct subnetworks. Using a simple hash-based categorization of keywords the Ultrapeer overlay network is partitioned into a relatively small number of distinct subnetworks. By employing a novel index splitting technique each Leaf peer is effectively connected to each different subnetwork. The search space of each individual flooding is restricted to a single partition, thus the search space is considerably limited. This reduces the overwhelming volume of traffic produced by flooding without affecting at all the accuracy of the search method. Experimental results demonstrate the efficiency of the proposed method.

The remainder of this paper is organized as follows: Following the related work section, the method used to partition the overlay network is presented in Section 3. In Section 4 the simulation details along with the experimental results are presented. We conclude in section 5.

2. Related Work

In an effort to alleviate the large volumes of unnecessary traffic produced during flooding several variations have been proposed. Schemes like Directed Breadth First Search (DBFS) [12] forward requests only to those peers that have often provided results to past requests, under the assumption that they will continue to do so. Interest-based schemes, like [10] and [5] aim to cluster together (make neighbours of) peers with similar content, under the assumption that those peers are better suited to provide each other's needs. Both those systems try to contact peers that have a higher probability of containing the requested information. Such schemes usually exhibit small gains over traditional flooding.

Another technique widely used in unstructured P2P systems today, is 1-hop replication. One-hop replication dictates that each peer should send to all of its

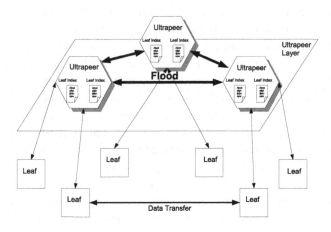

Figure 1.   The Gnutella 2-tier architecture.

immediate neighbours the index of the files it contains. Using this information during the last hop propagation of a request at the Ultrapeer level, the request is forwarded exclusively to those last hop Ultrapeers that contain the requested file. One-hop replication reduces the number of messages generated during the last hop of flooding [7], which constitutes the overwhelming majority of the traffic generated during the entire flooding. Simple calculations show that 1-hop replication requires d times fewer messages to spread to the whole network compared to naive flooding, where d is the degree of the network. It is easy to prove that in order to flood an entire, randomly constructed, network that employs 1-hop replication, one need only reach $3/d$ of the peers during all hops but the last. In today's Gnutella, where the average degree is 30, one would need to reach 10% of the peers and then use 1-hop replication to forward the query to the appropriate last hop peers, in order to reach the entire network.

Unstructured P2P systems implement 1-hop replication by having peers exchange bloom filters of their indices. A Bloom filter [3] is a space efficient way to represent a set of objects (keys). They employ one or more uniform hash functions to map each key to a position in an N-sized binary array, whose bits are initially set to 0. Each key is mapped through each hash function to an array position which is set to 1. To check for the participation of some key in the set, the key is hashed to get its array position. If that array position is set to 1, the bloom filter indicates key membership. Bloom filters require considerably less space than the actual set, which is accompanied by some loss of precision translated in the possibility of *false positives*. This means that a bloom filter may indicate membership for some key that does not belong to the set (more than one keys mapped to the same position). It cannot however indicate absence of a key which is in the set (false negative).

In Gnutella 2 [1] which uses a 2-tier architecture, each Leaf node sends its "list of keywords" in the form of a bloom filter to all Ultrapeers it is connected to. Each Ultrapeer produces the OR of all the bloom filters it receives from its Leaves (approximately 30 Leaf nodes per Ultrapeer) and transmits this collective bloom filter to all its neighboring Ultrapeers to implement the 1-hop replication. Ultrapeers flood queries to the overlay network on the Leave's behalf. Flooding is only performed at the Ultrapeer level where 1-hop replication is implemented. Whenever an Ultrapeer receives a request this is targetedly forwarded only down to those Leaves that contain the desired information (except in the case of false positives). Fig. 1 shows a schematic representation of the 2-tier architecture.

Another approach that has been used in the literature to make resource location in unstructured P2P systems more efficient is the partitioning of the overlay network into subnetworks using content categorization methods. A different subnetwork is formed for each content category. Each subnetwork connects all peers that posses files belonging to the corresponding category. Subnetworks are not necessarily distinct. A system that exploits this approach is the Semantic Overlay Networks (SONs) [6]. SONs use a semantic categorization of music files based on the music genre they belong to. The main drawback of this method is the semantic categorization of the content. In file-sharing systems for instance, music files rarely contain information about the genre they belong to and when they do so, each of them probably uses a different categorization of music. In SONs, an already existing, online, music categorization database is used. This database adds a centralized component in the operation of the network. Notice that 1-hop replication can be employed in conjunction with this scheme, inside each subnetwork. However, the fact that each peer may belong to more than one subnetwork, reduces the average degree of each subnetwork and thus, the efficiency of the 1-hop replication.

3.   The Partitions Design

The system we propose in this paper allows for the partitioning of any type of content. More specifically, we propose the formation of categories based on easily applicable rules. Such a simple rule is to apply a uniform hash function on each keyword describing the files. This hash function maps each keyword to an integer, from a small set of integers. Each integer defines a different category. We thus categorize the keywords instead of the content (files names) itself. Given a small set of integers, it is very likely that each peer will contain at least one keyword from each possible category.

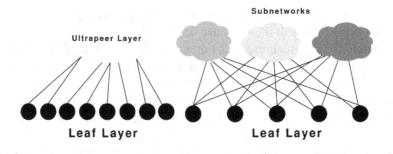

Figure 2. Illustration of the Gnutella network and the Partitions design.

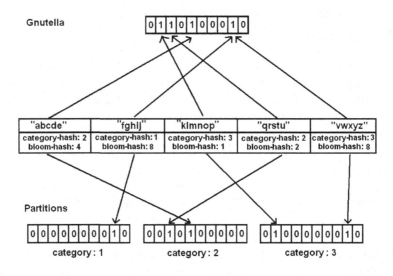

Figure 3. Gnutella and Partitions bloom filters.

In the Partitions design, each Ultrapeer in the system is randomly and uniformly assigned responsibility for a single keyword category, by randomly selecting an integer from the range set of the hash function used to categorize the keywords. Ultrapeers responsible for the same category form a distinct subnetwork. Leaves connect to one Ultrapeer per subnetwork and send to it all the keywords belonging to that category. Thus, an innovative index splitting technique is used. Instead of each Leaf sending its entire index (in the form of a bloom filter) to an Ultrapeer, each Leaf splits its index (keywords) based on the defined categories and distributes it to one Ultrapeer per category. Notice that peers operating as Ultrapeers also operate as Leaves at the same time (have a dual role). Even though in this design each Leaf connects to more than one

Ultrapeers, the volume of information it collectively transmits is roughly the same since each part of its index is send to a single Ultrapeer. Each Ultrapeer sends to its neighboring Ultrapeers all the aggregate indices of its Leaf nodes to implement 1-hop replication. In Fig. 2 we can see a schematic representation of the Partitions design. Fig. 3 illustrates the difference between the Gnutella and the Partitions bloom filters.

This separation of Ultrapeers from content has the benefit of allowing them to be responsible for a single keyword category. The benefit of this is two-fold. First, it reduces the size of the subnetworks since they are completely discrete (at the overlay level). Secondly, it allows each Ultrapeer to use all its Ultrapeer connections to connect to other Ultrapeers of the same subnetwork, increasing the efficiency of 1-hop replication at the Ultrapeer level.

There are, however, two drawbacks to this design. The first one is due to the fact that each Leaf connects to more than one Ultrapeers, one per content category. Even though each Leaf sends collectively the same amount of index data to the Ultrapeers upon connection as before, albeit distributed, however it requires more keepalive messages to ensure that its Ultrapeers are still operating. Keepalive messages however are very small compared to the average Gnutella protocol message. In addition, query traffic is used to indicate liveliness most of the time, thus avoiding sending keepalive messages. The second drawback arises from the fact that each subnetwork contains information for a specific keyword category. Requests however may contain more than one keywords and each result should match all of them. Since each Ultrapeer is aware of all keywords of its Leaves that belong to a specific category, it may forward a request to some Leaf that contains one of the keywords but not all of them. This reduces the efficiency of the 1-hop replication at the Ultrapeer level and at the Ultrapeer to Leaf query propagation. This drawback is balanced as follows. Even though the filtering is performed using one keyword only, Leaves' bloom filters also contain one category of keywords only, making them more sparse and thus reducing the probability of a false positive. Furthermore, the most rare keyword can be used to direct the search, thus further increasing the effectiveness of the search method. Finally, we also experimented with sending the bloom filters with all keyword types to every Ultrapeer, regardless of category, although Ultrapeers still extract and use only keywords of the same category they belong to form their aggregate bloom filter in order to implement 1-hop replication.

4. Experimental Results

In this section, we shall present the results from the simulations we conducted, in order to measure both the efficiency of the Partitions scheme in terms of cost of flooding (in messages) and maintenance costs.

We assumed a peer population of 2 million, a number reported by LimeWire Inc [2]. Each Ultrapeer in the Gnutella network serves 30 Leaves, a number obtained from real-world measurements [11]. In addition, each peer contains a number of files (and hence keywords) derived from a distribution also obtained from real-world measurements in [9].

Each Ultrapeer in the Partitions design serves 300 Leaves since we assume a number of 10 content categories and thus subnetworks. We perform a large number of floods, each designed to return at least a thousand query results before terminating. Table 1 shows the ratio of the average number of messages per flood for the Partitions design over the average number of messages per flood in Gnutella. Replication means that each Leaf sends all its keywords to all Ultrapeers it is connected to, regardless of category. For example, in the case of replication, flooding in the Partitions design generates 5.5 times less messages than flooding in Gnutella, in order to return the same number of results per query. We should emphasize that the drawback of filtering using only one keyword is balanced by the fact that Leaf indices are sparser (since they contain only one keyword category),thus produce less false positives. The main benefit comes from the message reduction due to the partitioning of the network and therefore the reduction of the search space. Each Partitions bloom filter (i.e. containing keywords of a certain category) has the length of a Gnutella bloom filter. Thus, one can roughly think of all the bloom filters of a single Partitions leaf as a (distributed) Gnutella bloom filter of 10 times the length (due to the 10 category types). However the bandwidth needed to transfer such a bloom filter is not 10 times that of a Gnutella bloom filter, mainly because sparser bloom filters are compressed more efficiently.

Table 1.   Flooding efficiencies.

	Ratio
No replication	4.2
Replication	5.5

In order to measure the maintenance cost of Gnutella and Partitions, we focus on the operation of a single Ultrapeer, because the load of Leaves is negligible in both systems compared to Ultrapeers load since flooding is performed at the Ultrapeer overlay. In both cases we simulated three hours in the life of a single Ultrapeer, with Leaves coming and going. Leaves have an average lifetime of 10 minutes, whereas Ultrapeer neighbours have an average lifetime of 1 hour. Each time a Leaf is connecting to the Ultrapeer, it sends its index information, which is propagated by the Ultrapeer to its thirty Ultrapeer neighbors. In addition, we assumed that, periodically , each Ultrapeer receives

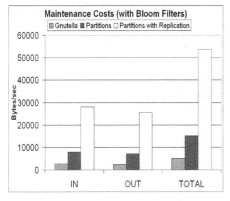

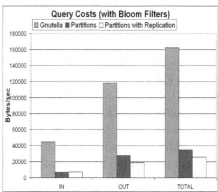

Figure 4. Maintenance traffic load for Gnutella and Partitions using Bloom Filters. Incoming, Outgoing and Total traffic.

Figure 5. Query traffic load for Gnutella and Partitions using Bloom Filters. Incoming, Outgoing and Total traffic.

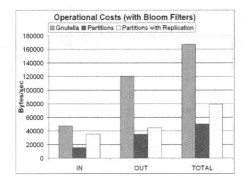

Figure 6. Operational traffic load for Gnutella and Partitions using Bloom Filters. Incoming, Outgoing and Total traffic.

a small keep-alive message from each Leaf and replies with a similar message to each one of them, unless a query and a reply were exchange during the specified period. For each communication taking place, we measured the incoming or outgoing traffic in bytes, in order to estimate the bandwidth requirements.

There are two modifications in this scenario, between Gnutella and Partitions. In Partitions, the number of Leaves per Ultrapeer is 300. In addition, the process of computing the size of the index information sent to the Ultrapeer differs greatly. For Gnutella, we have used the code by LimeWire [2], the most popular Gnutella client, to construct the bloom filter of each Leaf. We randomly decided on the number of files shared by each Leaf, based on the file sharing distribution per peer presented in [9]. We then extracted this number of files from a list of filenames obtained from the network by a Gnutella crawler developed in out lab. Those filenames were fed to the LimeWire bloom filter generation code, which produced the corresponding bloom filter in compressed form, i.e., the way it is sent over the network by LimeWire servents. Thus we constructed the actual bloom filter, although what we really need in this case is just its size. In the case of Partitions, we likewise computed the number of files to be shared by each Leaf. We extracted again the same number of filenames from the list of available filenames.

In addition to simulations for the Partitions scheme, we also run simulations for a modified version called Replication. In the Partitions scheme, each bloom filter sent to an Ultrapeer only contained appropriate keywords (of the same category as the corresponding Ultrapeer). In the Replications scheme, we used replication, i.e. each bloom filter contained all the keywords of the Leaf, regardless of category. In addition, positions of keywords of the corresponding category as the Ultrapeer were set in the bloom filter to the value of two instead of one. (This bloom filter essentially distinguishes between keywords of the appropriate category and the rest of the categories).

Fig. 4 shows the results of the simulation for the cost of maintaining the structures of Gnutella and Partitions, without any query (flood) traffic. From this figure it is obvious that, as expected, the maintenance cost of partitions is higher than that of Gnutella, but not that much. As we will see in the next paragraph the gains incurred during the operational phase of the two systems outweighs the increased maintenance costs.

We then focused our attention to the query traffic load. Measurements conducted in our lab showed that, on the average, each Ultrapeer generates 36 queries per hour (i.e., queries initiated by itself or its Leaves). This adds up to approximately 2000 queries per second generated anywhere in the Gnutella network. In addition, we observed a large number of Gnutella queries in order to find the distribution of the number of keywords in each query. Thus, according to those observations, during the simulations we assumed that 20% of the queries contain 1 keyword, 30% contain two, another 20% contain three and finally a 30% contain 4 keywords.

In our simulation, we assumed that the aim of each flood (both in Gnutella and Partitions) is to reach the entire network, or produce a fixed number of results, whichever comes first. As we mentioned before, such a flood that aims to reach the entire network would need to reach $\frac{1}{10}$th of the Gnutella's network (or a Partitions' subnetwork) during all hops of flooding except the last. This means that the Ultrapeer in our simulations has a probability of 0.1 to receiving each query. In addition, every time this does not occur, it has another opportunity to receive the query during the last hop, depending on its bloom filter (in case the searched keywords match in the bloom filter). Should the Ultrapeer receive a query, it is assumed to propagate it to its Leaves, again depending on their bloom filters or index (again depending on a possible keyword match by the bloom filter). Fig. 6 shows the comparison in the traffic load of Gnutella and Partitions, including maintenance and query traffic. We used a size of 40 bytes for each query. In reality, the size of a query can be up to a few hundred bytes, if XML extensions are used. This means that the performance gains described here are smaller compared to the ones we expect to see in the real world. In addition, for every 1400 bytes for each message sent, we added 40 bytes for the TCP and IP header. From these figures it is evident that Partitions outperform Gnutella in operational costs, in every case. Finally in Fig. 5 one can see the query traffic load alone (without the maintenance traffic) for both the Gnutella and the Partitions Ultrapeer.

5.   Conclusions

In this paper, we have described a novel approach to reducing the message cost of querying an unstructured P2P ork. A simple model has been described to illustrate that the benefits obtained from our scheme can be as high as an order of magnitude. Work is being carried out to measure the performance of our scheme, while varying the number of partitions. Furthermore, the benefit of Leaves communicating their full index (actual keywords) to Ultrapeers instead of bloom filter is currently exploited.

Acknowledgments

This research work was carried out under the FP6 NoE CoreGRID funded by the EC (IST-2002-004265) and was supported by project SecSPeer (GGET USA-031) funded by the Greek Secreteriat for Research and Technology.

References

[1] Gnutella 0.6 protocol specification.
    http://rfc-gnutella.sourceforge.net/developer/stable/index.html

[2] Limewire Inc. http://www.limewire.com

[3] B.H. Bloom. Space/time trade-offs in hash coding with allowable errors. *Communications of the ACM*, 13(7):422–426, 1970.

[4] Y. Chawathe, S. Ratnasamy, L. Breslau, N. Lanham, and S. Shenker. Making Gnutella-like P2P Systems Scalable. *Proc. ACM SIGCOMM 2003 Conf. on Applications, Technologies, Architectures, and Protocols for Computer Communication*, pp. 407-418, 2003.

[5] V. Cholvi P. Felber, and E. Biersack. Efficient search in unstructured peer-to-peer networks. *Proc. 16th ACM Symposium on Parallelism in Algorithms and Architectures*, 2004.

[6] A. Crespo and H. Garcia-Molina. Semantic overlay networks for p2p systems. Technical report, 2002.

[7] C. Gkantsidis, M. Mihail, and A. Saberi. Hybrid search schemes for unstructured peer-to-peer networks. *Proc. of INFOCOM*, 2005.

[8] C. Papadakis P. Fragopoulou E. Athanasopoulos M. Dikaiakos, A. Labrinidis, and E. Markatos. A feedback-based approach to reduce duplicate messages in unstructured peer-to-peer networks. *Proc. of the CoreGRID Integration Workshop*, 2005.

[9] R. Rejaie, Shanyu Zhao, and D. Stutzbach. Characterizing files in the modern Gnutella network: A measurement study. *Proc. SPIE/ACM Multimedia Computing and Networking*, 2006.

[10] K. Sripanidkulchai, B. Maggs, and H. Zhang. Efficient content location using interest-based locality in peer-to-peer systems. *Proc. of INFOCOM, 2003*.

[11] D. Stutzbach and R. Rejaie. Characterizing the two-tier gnutella topology. *Proc. of the ACM SIGMETRICS, Poster Session*, 2005.

[12] B. Yang and H. Garcia-Molina. Improving search in peer-to-peer networks. *Proc. of the 22nd International Conference on Distributed Computing Systems (ICDCS02)*, 2002.

[13] B. Yang and H. Garcia-Molina. Designing a Super-Peer Network. *Proc. Int. Conference on Data Engineering (ICDE 2003)*, pp. 49-60, 2003.

[14] Fisk, A. Gnutella Ultrapeer Query Routing, v. 0.1. LimeWire Inc. 2003

VALIDATING DESKTOP GRID RESULTS BY COMPARING INTERMEDIATE CHECKPOINTS*

Filipe Araujo
CISUC, Department of Informatics Engineering, University of Coimbra, Portugal
filipius@dei.uc.pt

Patricio Domingues
School of Technology and Management, Polytechnic Institute of Leiria, Portugal
patricio@estg.ipleiria.pt

Derrick Kondo
Laboratoire de Recherche en Informatique/INRIA Futurs, France
dkondo@lri.fr

Luis Moura Silva
CISUC, Department of Informatics Engineering, University of Coimbra, Portugal
luis@dei.uc.pt

Abstract   We present a scheme based on the comparison of intermediate checkpoints that accelerates the detection of computing errors of bag-of-tasks executed on volunteer desktop grids. Currently, in the state-of-the-art, replicated task execution is used for result validation. Our method also uses replication, but instead of only comparing results at the end of the replicated computations, we validate ongoing executions by comparing checkpoints of their intermediate execution points. This scheme significantly reduces the time to detect a computational error, which we show with both theoretical analysis and simulation results. In particular, we develop a model that gives the benefit of intermediate checkpointing as a function of checkpoint frequency and error rate, and we confirm this model with simulation experiments. We find that with an error rate of 5% and checkpoint frequency of 20 times per task, the gain is as high as 35% compared to the case where error detection is done only at the end of task execution; for higher checkpoint frequencies or high error rates, the benefits are even greater. In addition, when an erroneous computation is detected at an intermediate execution point, we propose the immediate replacement of that computation with a correct replica from another worker. In this way, useful execution and further validation can continue from that point onward instead of being delayed.

Keywords: Desktop grid, error detection, checkpointing, redundancy

---

*This work was supported by the CoreGRID Network of Excellence, funded by the European Commission under the Sixth Framework Programme. Project no. FP6-004265.

1.   Introduction

Desktop grids, which harvest volunteer computing resources, have gained tremendous momentum in recent years attracting hundreds of thousand of volunteers. Currently, more than a dozen large-scale projects exist, and new ones are being created regularly [6]. The advent of open source and easy-to-setup middleware frameworks like BOINC [4] and XtremWeb [10] have lowered the requirements and skills needed to exploit volunteered resources. To encourage volunteers, projects publish online rankings of contributed work. Interestingly, these rankings cause fierce competition, and attract even more dedicated volunteers [11].

Although desktop grids have a high return-on-investment, they also have major limitations, namely resource volatility and result correctness. The volatility of desktop grids is caused not only by hardware and software faults of computing systems, but also by resource owners who retain full priority in accessing and managing their desktop. Thus, owners reclaiming their resources might force hosted applications to be interrupted. Checkpointing is a common solution to cope with volatility, and some support exists for application-level checkpointing in desktop grid middleware, such as BOINC and XtremWeb [15].

Result correctness of computations performed on volunteer resources is an important issue, since interpreting incorrect results as correct can be worse than no results at all. A major source of result incorrectness is faulty hardware. In [4], Anderson cites *overclocking* as a significant cause of faulty computations in projects that resort to the BOINC framework. The fierce competition and rivalry among volunteers sometimes may also cause unhealthy behavior. Some users try to increase, not always by honest means, their credits. In some extreme cases, users resort to dishonest tricks to collect undue credits, like fabricating results that require much less computation than the real ones [12]. These users are known as *lazy cheaters*. Finally, another type of malicious user – saboteur – might simply act for the sole purpose of ruining the computation, without concern for credits [14]. In contrast to lazy cheaters, saboteurs may be difficult to counter since they may be resourceful and committed to perform everything they can to disrupt the computation.

Commonly, desktop grid projects resort to redundancy as a sabotage-tolerance technique [8]. Under this approach, the same task is distributed to r different worker machines (hopefully unrelated) to avoid collusion. When completed, results are compared and there is a majority vote. If a result has majority, that is, more than $r/2$ tasks return this result or an equivalent one [1], it is interpreted as the correct one and the task is flagged as completed. On the

---

[1] Some projects dependent on floating-point operations might have slightly different results when executed in different platforms, but yet equivalent from the project point-of-view [17].

contrary, if no consensus can be found, all results are discarded and the task is marked for rescheduling.

In this paper, we present a checkpoint and replication-based error detection technique that exploits checkpointing and redundancy. The technique compares intermediate checkpoint digests of redundant instances of a same task. If differences are found, the conclusion is that at least one execution is wrong. In contrast to the simple redundancy mechanism, where diverging computations can only be detected after a majority of tasks have completed, intermediate checkpoint comparison allows for earlier and more precise detection of errors, since execution divergence can be spotted at the next checkpoint following any error. This allows one to take proactive and corrective measures without having to wait for the completion of the tasks, therefore permitting faster task completion, since faulty tasks can immediately be rescheduled.

To complement the checkpoint-based comparison methodology for error detection, we propose a checkpoint-based replication technique whose goal is to promote fast completion of redundant instances of a same task, in order to speed up validation of results. Specifically, under the proposed technique, the replication of a redundant instance is scheduled as soon as the instance is determined to be erroneous or lagging behind. To minimize the computation to be redone, the technique tries to initialize the replica from a validated intermediate checkpoint. The technique extends the checkpoint-based verification, promoting a balanced execution of redundant instances, since validation can only occur when a majority of results have been completed. Moreover, since credits are given to workers only after results have been validated, this also accelerates validation and proper credit assignment, which is an important issue for a considerable percentage of volunteers [11].

Specifically, the contributions of the paper are as follows. First, we construct a model that estimates the benefit of comparing intermediate checkpoints as a function of the probability of task error and checkpoint frequency. Second, we propose the use of immediate replacement of erroneous or slowly executing tasks to prevent delays of task execution and validation. Third, we conduct simulations and analysis of results using our novel approach, which confirms the benefits estimated by our theoretical model.

The remainder of this paper is organized as follows. In Section 2, we define the assumptions used by the comparison techniques that are based on checkpointing and replication. In Section 3, we present our technique for error detection through checkpoint comparison and our theoretical model, while in Section 4, we introduce checkpoint-based task replication. In Section 5, we describe our simulation setup and results. In Section 6, we discuss related work. Finally, in Section 7, we summarize the conclusions and describe future work.

2.   Assumptions and Definitions

We assume a large-scale computing project, where a central supervisor co-ordinates the whole computation, by distributing tasks to requesting volunteer worker machines (henceforth *workers*). The tasks that comprise an application are sequential and independent from each others. Furthermore, we assume that all communications occur exclusively between workers and the supervisor. To circumvent Internet asymmetries [16] caused by NAT and firewall schemes, communications are worker-initiated. Thus, the supervisor is passive in the sense that it can only answer to worker requests. Note that this communication model is the one adopted by several desktop grid frameworks [10, 4].

At the worker level, fault-tolerance is achieved through application-level checkpointing [15]. We only consider tasks which can individually be broken into m temporal segments $S_t = \{S_{t_1}, \ldots, S_{t_m}\}$. The intermediate computational states can be checkpointed at the end of each temporal segment, yielding the checkpoint set $C = \{C_1, \ldots, C_m\}$, with C_m taken at the end of the computation. Projects with long duration tasks (weeks or months long), such as for example the climateprediction.net, whose tasks last for months on state-of-the-art machines, can benefit most from checkpointing. Whenever a task is interrupted (because the user switches the machine off, or for some other reason), its execution can be resumed from the last stable checkpoint C_j.

Depending on the application, checkpoints can get quite large, in the range of tens to hundreds of megabytes in size, and thus it might be inefficient to transfer and compare them. (For the purpose of comparison, all checkpoints need to be on the machine that effectively performs the comparison; thus at least one of them has to be transferred.) For comparison purposes, we assume that message digests of checkpoints (provided by the MD5 [13] and the SHA-family [9] algorithms, for example) can be used. Due to their reduced and predictable dimensions, message digests can be easily exchanged and compared. Furthermore, an application-specific pre-processing function might be deployed to normalize checkpoints (for instance, for removing task-dependent identifiers) prior to the use of a generic digest algorithm. For the purpose of comparison, checkpoint C_j is represented by the message digest $\text{MD}(C_j)$. Additionally, the comparison of checkpoints needs to be executed between what we term as *equivalent checkpoints*, that is, checkpoints from different replicas of a task that represent a same execution point of the task.

Regarding redundancy, we assume that the system executes each task r times, by r independent workers, with the supervisor applying majority voting to validate results, electing the so-called *canonical result* [4]. Afterwards, when the result verification is completed, the system assigns the proper credits to the workers which have returned correct results.

3.   Comparison of Equivalent Checkpoint Digests

For the comparison of equivalent checkpoint digests, a worker is requested to return, along with the results of the task that it computed, a selected set of message digests of the checkpoints saved during the task computation. The list of checkpoints whose message digests are requested is defined at task creation time so that redundant instances of a task share the same set of requested checkpoint digests.

When a majority of redundant executions are completed, and the supervisor holds enough results for meaningful comparisons, the checkpoint digests from equivalent execution points are compared to each others. If the digests are different, the execution point where the differences were detected is marked as suspicious. Comparatively to the sole result comparisons, the selective digests technique permits a finer grain detection level, since an erroneous computation can be located right after the first divergent checkpoint.

3.1   Reducing the Time to Detect an Error

Although the selective digests strategy allows for a more precise location of error occurrence, it does not speed up the detection of incorrect computations, since error detection can only occur after, at least, two redundant instances have terminated.

A more proactive variant is to have workers returning available checkpoint digests during the computation. Ideally, from a detection point-of-view, the worker should send to the supervisor a checkpoint digest immediately after its computation. This way, an error can be spotted by the supervisor as soon as a majority of checkpoint digests is available for the considered execution point. Thus, upon detection of a divergent computation, corrective measures can immediately be triggered by the supervisor. For instance, an additional instance of the task can be scheduled. Additionally, the thought-to-be faulty worker can be marked as a suspect and further probed to assess its computational honesty, or, if repeating a faulty behavior it can be blacklisted altogether [14].

3.2   Theoretical Analysis

In this section, we conduct an initial analysis of the advantage of detecting erroneous computations at intermediate checkpoints. The goal of this analysis is to estimate the potential advantages of our approach.

We assume that a task is segmented into m fragments. Additionally, we make the following simplifying assumptions: (1) machines and segments are homogeneous: a segment always takes t time to complete and the entire task requires $T = m \times t$. Hence, the number of segments, m, determines the computational effort of the task. The probability of obtaining a wrong checkpoint is the same for all the workers and for all checkpoints of the same task; (2) all the replicas of a task start at the same time across all workers; (3) the errors are independent of each others, and thus, no contamination of replicas occur, meaning that comparison of replicas is enough to catch all the errors.

Although these assumptions may seem too restrictive, we show experimentally in Section 5 that our analysis also holds for other more heterogeneous scenarios. We will focus on two variables that affect the system: the probability, p_e, of having a computational error in any of the checkpoints (either due to a computational mishap or malicious behavior) and the number of checkpoints of the task. We consider that results are validated through r-replication. (All the replicas must compute the same equivalent checkpoint digest.) However, comparison of intermediate checkpoint digests permits partial validation at point j as soon as the r replicas of a task have sent back their respective message digests of checkpoint j, that is, $MD(C_j)$. We compare this new and improved approach against the state-of-the-art method, which can only detect an error at the end of the execution.

When the computational error occurs before the first validation checkpoint (C_1), the checkpoint comparison method will permit a detection $T \cdot \frac{m-1}{m}$ time units sooner than the regular methodology. This case occurs when there is one or more errors in the computation of all the r replicas. It is easy to see that the probability of this event is $1 - (1 - p_e)^r$, which we denote as p to simplify. For the next checkpoint, the comparison of equivalent checkpoints saves $T \cdot \frac{m-2}{m}$ time units, relative to the normal validation method. This occurs with probability $p \cdot (1 - p)$. Extending this reasoning to checkpoint i yields a saving of $T \cdot \frac{m-i}{m}$ with probability $p \cdot (1 - p)^{i-1}$. (In the last segment, when $i = m$, or if there is no error for the whole computation, our approach brings no benefit.) We let W be a random variable to represent the error detection time, that is, the time elapsed from the occurrence of an error up to its detection. In other words, if we reschedule the task as soon as the error in the checkpoint is detected, W represents the maximum time that we can save, relatively to the compare-at-end approach, with a single error detection. However, in the regular strategy, the computation time can be even worse than $T + W$, because other errors can delay the task even further. Hence, if we are able to calculate W, we can have a measure of the advantage of detecting errors by comparing intermediate checkpoints. To calculate the expected value of W, we proceed as follows (we omit the probability of not having any error, as there is no gain in that case):

$$E[W] = \sum_{i=1}^{m} \left(pq^{i-1} \cdot \frac{m-i}{m} T \right) = Tp \left(\sum_{i=1}^{m} q^{i-1} - \frac{1}{m} \sum_{i=1}^{m} i \cdot q^{i-1} \right) \quad (1)$$

Where $q = 1 - p$. Since $\sum_{i=1}^{m} q^{i-1}$ is a sum of terms of a geometric sequence, its sum is $S_{m-1} = \frac{1-q^m}{1-q}$. We can use standard techniques to compute the second term of the difference. Consider that $S'_{m-1} = \sum_{i=1}^{m} i \cdot q^{i-1}$. By multiplying S'_{m-1} by q and taking the difference $(1-q)S'_{m-1}$, we get $S'_{m-1} = \frac{S_{m-1}-mq^m}{1-q}$. Since $p = 1 - q$, this yields:

$$E[W] = TpS_{m-1} - \frac{Tp}{m}S'_{m-1} = T\left(1 - \frac{1-q^m}{mp}\right) \qquad (2)$$

In Figures 1(a) and 1(b) we depict the time that we can save relative to T ($E[W]/T$), considering Equation 2. In Figure 1(a), we set $m = 20$, while in the other figure we set $p = 0.05$. From Eq. 2 we conclude that the maximum time that a checkpoint comparison can save converges to T, when $m \to \top$. When $p \to 1$, the time that we can save approaches $T \cdot \frac{m-1}{m}$ as we would expect. For example, we find that with only an error rate of 5% and checkpoint frequency of 20 times per task, the gain is as high as 35% compared to the case where error detection is done only at the end of task execution. Note that this is a conservative estimate of the benefit as many projects (such as Einstein@home and SIMAP [2–3]) checkpoint more often in a given work unit. In particular, in the BOINC project climateprediction.net [7], a work unit requires around 3 months of CPU time in a fast PCs, being checkpointed 72 times during the whole execution. In conclusion, for even conservative estimates of error rates and checkpoint frequencies, the benefit of comparing digests of intermediate checkpoints is significant, and is even greater for higher probabilities of error or for longer computations with checkpoints.

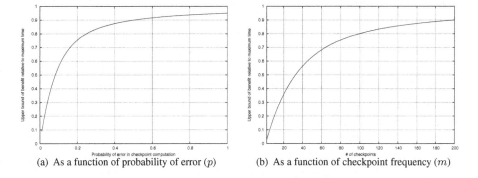

(a) As a function of probability of error (p)   (b) As a function of checkpoint frequency (m)

Figure 1.   Benefit (W) relative to maximum time (T).

4.   Checkpoint-based Task Replication

Some (BOINC-based) desktop projects increase, at least for specific period of times, the redundancy level to foster the chance of fast completion of tasks. Surprisingly, one of the main motivation for this important decision is not directly related to the gain of an higher confidence level for the results, but the need to quickly rewards worker with the proper amount of credits. In fact, credits are only committed to workers after validation of the sent results. These credits are determined by the supervisor, based on the credit claims made by the intervening workers (jointly with the completed results, the worker sends a claim with the amount of credits it believes it deserves). To circumvent the high volatility of volunteers, a number of instances higher than what is required for majority voting is scheduled for execution. This provides timely assignment of credits even in the presence of sluggish and drop-out workers. However, this approach wastes resources, and slows down the whole computation.

To speed up completion and validation of individual tasks, promoting fast credit assignment, we propose to combine the comparison of intermediate checkpoint digests with task replication. To prevent lengthy re-computations due to the replication of task, we resort to validated checkpoints to load execution state in tasks to replicate, avoiding to restart from scratch.

The task replication works by loosely coupling the execution of the redundant instances of a same task, which are configured for reporting selective checkpoint digests. Note that workers processing instances are not aware of each other (otherwise the risk of collusion would increase). The supervisor follows the progress of the coupled instances of a task through the messages holding the checkpoint digests sent back by these instances, validating the received checkpoint digests of the selected execution point through comparison as soon as a majority of results has been received.

Whenever a worker lags behind its instance partners by more than a specified threshold – the threshold takes into account the relative speed of the workers – the supervisor initiates a replace operation, with the goal of substituting the behind-schedule worker. To further speed up substitution, the substitute task should start from the last validated checkpoint, if available. To prepare for the instance substitution, the supervisor requests, upon the next communication of a paired-worker, the last validated checkpoint from this worker (not the digest, the entire checkpoint file). Upon receiving it, it checks its validity through message digest comparison, and creates a task which integrates the validated checkpoint file. This *replace task* is then scheduled to a requesting worker, which starts the computation from the checkpoint execution point, thus skipping the computation up to this point. From the point of view of the supervisor, the newly scheduled task replaces the lost/delayed one, and thus the monitoring of execution proceeds as previously explained. Note that, in order to prevent excessive replicas, replication should only be performed if the number of instances is below a predefined threshold.

5. Experimental Results

In this section, we confirm and extend the theoretical results obtained in Section 3.2 through simulation. Specifically, we assign a number of tasks to a set of workers, setting the duration of these simulated tasks beforehand. Whenever a worker computes a checkpoint, it randomly determines whether that computation is wrong or correct (once a checkpoint is wrong, all the remaining checkpoints from that worker are also considered as wrong.) The total time of the computation, T, is the time at which the last replica finishes its last checkpoint, regardless of whether it is correct or wrong. Assume that checkpoint C_j was the first one to be wrong and that the last replica finished C_j at time T_W. We are interested in the random variable $W = T - T_W$, which represents the benefit of using intermediate checkpoints relative to the state-of-the-art. In particular, the metric we use to quantify the gain compared to the state-of-the-art is the relative value W/T.

We started by considering the same parameter settings that were used to generate Figure 1(b). So, we set an uniform $p_e \approx 0.0253$ for all execution segments, considering homogeneous segments, and a two-replica scheme, which corresponds to $p = 0.05$. As expected, we got a curve that closely follows the theoretical prediction. Then, we studied the impact of considering different durations for the checkpoints and different error probabilities for each of the computed checkpoints. We used two different random distributions for this: uniform and truncated Gaussian. To maintain consistency, the average values for the error probability and for the segment duration were the same as for the fixed case, p_e and T, respectively. In the uniform distribution, the actual error probability was chosen uniformly from the interval $[0.5p_e, 1.5p_e)$ (which is always inside the interval $[0, 1]$), while the duration was chosen using the same distribution in the interval $[0.5T, 1.5T)$. For the Gaussian distribution, we considered averages of p_e and T, and standard deviations of 30% of the average. Additionally, we truncated the values of p_e and T to be inside the ranges $[0.5p_e, 1.5p_e]$ and $[0.5T, 1.5T]$, respectively. In Figure 2, we show the average result of varying the number of checkpoints for 300 different trials. As we can see, the curves overlap.

The most interesting conclusion from these results is that the particular random distribution that controls the duration and the errors of the checkpoints does not seem to make any significant difference, at least for the same averages. This would not be true if, for instance, the average duration of checkpoints

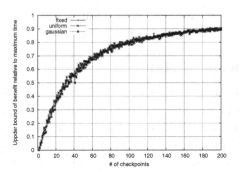

Figure 2.   Benefit (W) relative to expected maximum time (T) (obtained experimentally).

i and j was different for checkpoints i and j[2]. We believe that there is a simple and intuitive reason for this; on average the slowest replica should finish checkpoint i around time $i \cdot \frac{T}{m}$, where T is the time at which the slowest replica finishes the task. Although some particular cases may not follow this trend, our experimental results confirm this intuition for the average case.

6.   Related Work

Antonelli et al. [5] propose a distributed checkpoint-based technique for sabotage tolerance addressing sequential computation split in multiple consecutive temporal segments. To certify a given checkpoint C_j, the supervisor creates a verification task that references the checkpoint to verify and holds the network contact details of the worker which performed the computation. The task is then assigned to a worker node (*verifier*), which requests the checkpoint from the worker being scrutinized, and loads it upon reception, executing the task up to the next checkpoint, that is, C_{j+1}. It then sends the message digest of the this checkpoint to the supervisor. Finally, the supervisor compares the digest to the other equivalent digests. The scheme is appealing since it distributes the computation needed for verification of checkpoints through the workers. However, some major issues like asymmetrical communications and node availability are not addressed by the authors. Furthermore, workers need to keep some of the checkpoints of the computed tasks and transfer them when requested, a demand that might require meaningful space storage and network bandwidth, especially with large individual checkpoints. On top of that, promoting direct contact between workers may ease collusion.

---

[2]However, note that it would not make much sense to consider different average durations for different checkpoints, unless we were targeting a particular application with a well-known behavior.

Agbaria and Friedman [1] propose a replication and checkpoint-based scheme to detect intrusions through anomaly spotting. They resort to checkpoint comparison for the purpose of identifying intrusions in a Byzantine environment. Similarly to our approach, the execution is split in n sequential phases, with a checkpoint being taken by each worker node at the end of each phase. For supporting a maximum of t intruded nodes (each node executes a replica), the proposed scheme requires $t + 1$ replicas when no intruded node exists. However, when intrusion exists, the protocol needs additional stages, involving more than the $3t + 1$ replicas which would be required by a straight Byzantine agreement protocol. The unbalance is supported by the fact that intrusions are rare and thus it compensates to have a lightweight scheme which is only penalized when intrusions do occur. The protocol distinguishes between *workers* (nodes that perform the computation and which can get intruded) and *auditors*, which are responsible for assessing the integrity of the workers. Specifically, the auditors are used to agree that all the $t + 1$ replicas match. A major requirement of the protocol lies in the required synchronization, with workers having to send their checkpoints to the auditors within a given time frame. This requires that the replica execution occurs simultaneously, a premise that might hard to fulfill in a volatile environment such as desktop grids. Furthermore, the checkpoints (or equivalently, a message digest) need to be sent to the auditors at the end of every stage, an operation that requires communication resources and might be difficult if auditors are not directly addressable [16]. Relatively to the solution that we propose, our emphasis is more on the practicality of the error detections schemes and its integration with current desktop grid frameworks.

7.   Conclusion

We proposed a strategy for early detection of errors by comparing checkpoints of redundant tasks executed over desktop grid resources. We developed a theoretical model that estimates the benefit of using intermediate checkpoints given a task length and task segment error rate. We confirmed this theoretical analysis with simulation results. We find that with only an error rate of 5% and checkpoint frequency of 20 times per task, the gain is as high as 35% compared to the case where error detection is done only at the end of task execution. For higher checkpoint frequencies or high error rates, the benefits are even greater.

For future work, we plan to extend the study the case where segments are completed with non-uniform execution times. In addition, we will study and characterize work unit error rates in a real BOINC project, namely Xtrem-Lab [18], and then instantiate our model with such error rates. Finally, we intend to study the use of trickle messages [7] to regularly send the checkpoint digests to the central supervisor, without incurring any additional communication costs.

References

[1] A. Agbaria and R. Friedman. A replication-and checkpoint-based approach for anomaly-based intrusion detection and recovery. *Distributed Computing Systems Workshops, 2005. 25th IEEE International Conference on*, pages 137–143, 2005.

[2] D. Allen. Personal communication, June 2006.

[3] C. An. Personal communication, March 2006.

[4] D. Anderson. BOINC: A system for public-resource computing and storage. In *5th IEEE/ACM International Workshop on Grid Computing*, Pittsburgh, USA, 2004.

[5] D. Antonelli, A. Cordero, and A. Mettler. Securing Distributed Computation with Untrusted Participants. 2004.

[6] J. Bohannon. Grassroots supercomputing. *Science*, 308(6 May):810–813, 2005.

[7] C. Christensen, T. Aina, and D. Stainforth. The challenge of volunteer computing with lengthy climate model simulations. In *1st IEEE International Conference on e-Science and Grid Computing*, pages 8–15, Melbourne, Australia, 2005. IEEE Computer Society.

[8] W. Du, J. Jia, M. Mangal, and M. Murugesan. Uncheatable grid computing. *Distributed Computing Systems, 2004. Proceedings. 24th International Conference on*, pages 4–11, 2004.

[9] D. Eastlake and P. Jones. RFC 3174: US Secure Hash Algorithm 1 (SHA1). *Request for Comments, September*, 2001.

[10] G. Fedak, C. Germain, V. Neri, and F. Cappello. Xtremweb: A generic global computing system. In *1st Int'l Symposium on Cluster Computing and the Grid (CCGRID'01)*, pages 582–587, Brisbane, 2001.

[11] A. Holohan and A. Garg. Collaboration Online: The Example of Distributed Computing. *Journal of Computer-Mediated Communication*, 10(4), 2005.

[12] D. Molnar. The SETI@home Problem. *ACM Crossroads Student Magazine*, september 2000.

[13] R. Rivest. RFC-1321 The MD5 Message-Digest Algorithm. *Network Working Group, IETF*, April 1992.

[14] L. Sarmenta. Sabotage-tolerance mechanisms for volunteer computing systems. In *1st International Symposium on Cluster Computing and the Grid*, page 337, 2001.

[15] L. M. Silva and J. G. Silva. System-level versus user-defined checkpointing. In *Symposium on Reliable Distributed Systems*, pages 68–74, 1998.

[16] S. Son and M. Livny. Recovering Internet Symmetry in Distributed Computing. *Cluster Computing and the Grid, 2003. Proceedings. CCGrid 2003. 3rd IEEE/ACM International Symposium on*, pages 542–549, 2003.

[17] M. Taufer, P. J. Teller, D. P. Anderson, and I. Charles L. Brooks. Metrics for effective resource management in global computing environments. *e-science*, 0:204–211, 2005.

[18] XtremLab. http://xtremlab.lri.fr.

INTEGRATION OF THE ENANOS EXECUTION FRAMEWORK WITH GRMS*

Ivan Rodero, Francesc Guim, Julita Corbalan and Jesus Labarta
Barcelona Supercomputing Center, Universitat Politecnica de Catalunya (UPC), SPAIN
ivan.rodero@bsc.es
francesc.guim@bsc.es
julita.corbalan@bsc.es
jesus.labarta@bsc.es

Ariel Oleksiak, Krzysztof Kurowski and Jarek Nabrzyski
Poznan Supercomputing and Networking Center
ariel@man.poznan.pl
kikas@man.poznan.pl
naber@man.poznan.pl

Abstract   The eNANOS is an execution framework developed in the Barcelona Supercomputing Center. One of its main objectives is to provide a framework to execute multilevel parallel applications with low-level support. It is also able to provide information about the execution behavior of applications in run time. This information can be used by a Grid Resource Broker or metascheduler to improve its scheduling and resource strategies and the execution platform can improve the execution time of applications and resource usage as well. In this paper we discus the steps that we have to follow to integrate the eNANOS execution environment into the GRMS infrastructure, developed by PSNC. In particular we are interested in the mechanisms to allow the integration of the different components and how to use the information provided by eNANOS to improve the scheduling strategies in the GRMS system.

Keywords: Grid resource management, scheduling strategies, application performance, eNANOS, GRMS.

*This work has been supported by the CoreGRID European Network of Excellence (FP6-004265) and by the Spanish Ministry of Science and Technology under contract TIN2004-07739-C02-01.

1.   Introduction

The eNANOS is an execution framework developed in the Barcelona Super-computing Center. One of its main objectives is to provide a framework to execute multilevel parallel applications with low-level support. Furthermore the eNANOS architecture is based on the idea of coordination between the different layers [9]. Currently the eNANOS Execution platforms uses the eNANOS Grid Resource Broker [8] which manages the jobs from the Grid layers in coordination with the local resource environments.

The eNANOS System is also able to provide information about the execution behavior of applications in run time, such as its progress or the obtained performance in a given moment. This information can be used by a Grid Resource Broker or metascheduler to improve its scheduling and resource strategies and the execution platform can improve the execution time of applications and resource usage as well.

The main effort of the PSNC in the Grid resource management is the GRMS resource broker [2]. GRMS is an open source meta-scheduling system for large scale distributed computing infrastructures. Based on the dynamic resource selection, mapping and advanced grid scheduling methodologies, it has been tailored to deal with resource management challenges in Grid environments, e.g. load-balancing among clusters, setting up execution environments before and after job execution, remote job submission and control, files staging, workflow management and more.

In this paper we discus the steps that we have to follow to integrate the eNANOS execution environment into the GRMS infrastructure. In particular we are interested in the mechanisms to allow the integration of the different components and how to use the information provided by eNANOS to improve the scheduling strategies in the GRMS system.

In section 2 we present the eNANOS approach and its main characteristics and in section 3 we introduce the GRMS system. In section 4 we study the possibilities of integration between the eNANOS and GRMS systems, and, finally, in section 5 we present the conclusions and future lines of work.

2.   eNANOS Execution Environment

The eNANOS project aims at developing an execution platform for parallel applications on Grids. The objective of this platform is to provide support to implement and evaluate resource management and scheduling policies on a computational Grid. The eNANOS project is based on the idea of having a good low level support for performing a good high level scheduling taking into account these ideas: a fine grain control between scheduling levels, dynamic allocation (MPI+OpenMP jobs) to improve system performance, detailed information about current scheduling and performance to improve future scheduling decisions, and, based on this accurate information, efficient scheduling (in terms of slowdown) based on performance prediction.

The scheduling strategies are based in the coordination between the different layers involved in the execution of a job: Grid scheduling, cluster scheduling and processor scheduling. The scheduling decisions are known by the other elements in the system and are taken based on direct information, not based neither on estimations nor just observations.

The idea is providing well defined API between levels to both forcing the scheduling decisions (for instance specific allocations) and getting detailed information (for instance the real performance reached by a job in run time). A general overview of the system architecture is shown in Figure 1.

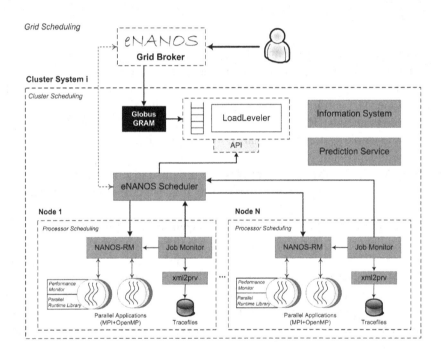

Figure 1. eNANOS Overall Architecture.

The Grid jobs are managed by the eNANOS Resource Broker and submitted to the local HPC resources through the Globus infrastructure. The eNANOS Resource Broker is developed on top of Globus Toolkit 3 as a Grid service and it is compatible with both GT2 and GT3 services. It implements the resource discovery, selection and monitoring, the job submission, and the job monitoring. Moreover, the eNANOS Broker provides a set of Grid Service interfaces and a Java API that can be used from command-line clients, applications or portals. The eNANOS broker has been extended to provide more functionality and supporting JSDL 1.0 with a gateway implemented as a GT3 Grid service as well. More detailed information about this broker can be found in [8].

For the cluster management eNANOS uses LoadLeveler as a queuing system and the eNANOS Scheduler as an external scheduler to manage the local jobs. It implements scheduling policies based on FCFS and backfilling (in progress) guided by the information regarding the behavior of applications and performance obtained in runtime from the processor scheduler. So, the scheduler centralizes the information from the runtime about the allowed multiprogramming level of multiple computational nodes and also some information regarding the applications and hardware (e.g. load of nodes or CPUs used by each job). It also communicates with the eNANOS Broker in order to provide information to the upper level.

The CPU scheduling is performed by the NANOS-RM. Its main goal is to efficiently distribute a set of processors between a set of applications that are under its control. It implements scheduling policies based on dynamic allocation in a two-phase fashion (multilevel). The first phase is between applications and implements a FIFO policy, and the second phase is between processes of a MPI+OpenMP application and implements Equipartition [7] and Dynamic Processor Balancing [3]. The idea is sharing the required information for improving the whole system performance without penalizing the applications performance independently.

The NANOS Job Monitor provides the monitoring information about the execution of workloads in XML that can be translated to trace files format to visualize and analyze them [1].

The information system (Palantir) can be seen as a meta-information system that can collect a very large kind of different information, providing a uniform access to it. The Predictor service provides predictions about the job performance that can be used by both the eNANOS Scheduler and the eNANOS Broker. It implements two kinds of prediction techniques: those that are based on statistical approaches that use estimators; and those that are based on data mining algorithms. Both information and predictor systems are not integrated yet but their services are available.

3.   Grid Resource Management System (GRMS)

GRMS is an open source meta-scheduling system for large scale distributed computing infrastructures. Based on the dynamic resource selection, mapping and advanced grid scheduling methodologies, it has been tailored to deal with resource management challenges in Grid environments, e.g. load-balancing among clusters, setting up execution environments before and after job execution, remote job submission and control, files staging, and more. For our tests we have used version 2.x of GRMS, which is based on the GT4 and makes use of low-level Globus Services deployed on resources located in various academic institutions in Europe and USA. GRMS connects to the core services through a set of Java and C APIs. In particular, GRMS uses GRAM, GridFTP and GRIS/GIIS services. As a persistent service, GRMS provides a set of well-defined GSI-enabled Web Service interfaces for various clients, e.g. applications, command-line clients or portals. Moreover, GRMS is able to take advantage of middleware services, e.g. the GridLab Authorization Service or Replica Management Services as well as to interoperate with the infrastructure monitoring tools such as the Mercury Monitoring System. Therefore GRMS is in fact one of the main components of a grid middleware layer that can be organized in many different ways depending on particular infrastructure and applications.

The architecture of GRMS together with a set of its internal modules, namely Job Queue, Job Registry, Job Manager, Resource Discovery and a central unit called Broker Module is presented in Figure 2. The aim of the Broker Module is to control the whole process of resource and job management. The broker was designed in such a way that it allows us to implement various scheduling and policy plug-ins. One of plug-ins, called Reschedule plug-in, is responsible for jobs migration and rescheduling within GRMS. Worth mentioning is also the Resource Discovery Module, that monitors a status of distributed resources. It uses a flexible hierarchical access to both central (GIIS) and local information services (GRIS).

GRMS uses the multicriteria decision support methods for scheduling. Based on user preferences it evaluates and selects convenient resources. The multicriteria techniques used in Grid resource management were described in details in [4]. Examples of use of this model for specific Grid resource management problems were presented in [5] [6].

4.   Integration Issues

To start with the integration of the eNANOS execution environment with the GRMS system we need to identify the common features and what are the functionalities provided by eNANOS that can be useful for the GRMS.

Currently, in the complete infrastructure of the eNANOS Execution Framework the Grid resource management is performed by the eNANOS Resource Broker. The idea was to implement a customized environment to execute efficiently multilevel parallel applications, but one of the desirable features for one of this kind of systems is to provide generic interfaces. Therefore, the local execution system should be able to be integrated to other Grid Resource Brokers or metaschedulers such as GRMS.

Since the eNANOS system supports both traditional jobs and multilevel parallel jobs, the resources supporting eNANOS can be seen as a normal resource

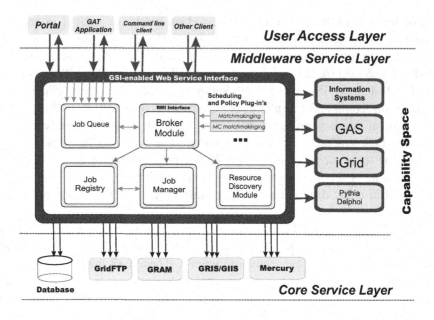

Figure 2.   General GRMS architecture.

or as a specific case for those jobs that require support from the local environment. The idea of integrating this execution environment into a Grid is to improve the behavior of the Grid in general, taking advantage of the complementary functionalities provided by eNANOS. The improvement is though in terms of improving the execution time of applications and the resource usage.

On the other hand, one of the important capabilities of the eNANOS System is the coordination between the different layers involved in a job execution and, in particular, the detailed information that is able to provide to the Grid level regarding the behavior of the applications in run time. The eNANOS offers some libraries and tools to obtain detailed information in run time about the progress of the applications and the performance as well.

As a Grid Resource Broker, GRMS performs the job scheduling and the resource management following some particular strategies. Hence, the GRMS system can consider the information offered by eNANOS regarding progress, performance and fine-grain monitoring to improve the scheduling strategies implemented into the scheduling engine of the GRMS.

Therefore, we have identified two different possible integration issues: using eNANOS as a new execution platform, and using eNANOS as a new information provider.

4.1   eNANOS as a new execution framework

Even though GRMS has been designed as an independent set of components for resource management processes, the core services used by GRMS are included into the Globus Infrastructure. As the eNANOS system is based on Globus, the integration of both components should be possible without changing the interface to the local resources.

In the eNANOS Execution Framework Globus is used as a middleware and a customized LoadLeveler jobmanager in local resources. Since the GRMS expects to find a Globus-based resource with a particular jobmanager for the queuing or fork system, the resources with eNANOS system installed should be presented as a new resource for the scheduling process. But we have to take into account certain particularities of the eNANOS-enabled systems, performing a special treatment for this kind of resources.

Since the main approach of the eNANOS system is the low level support for multilevel applications, the GRMS system can perform a special use of the eNANOS resources. In particular the most important consideration regarding this issue is the specification of parallel jobs.

The eNANOS system supports JSDL 1.0 for the specification of jobs. Moreover, in the eNANOS context is being implemented an extension of the JSDL 1.0 for multilevel parallel jobs [10]. In Figure 3 it is shown the XML schema of this extension for the JSDL.

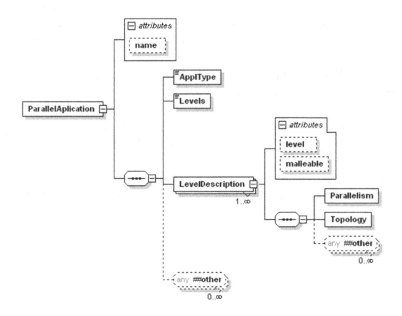

Figure 3.   JSDL 1.0 extension for parallel jobs schema.

The most important attributes for the local execution environment are:

- Application type. It is an enumeration type specifying the kind of application regarding its programming model (MPI, OpenMP, etc.)

- Number of MPI processes. It is just a positive integer value

- Number of OpenMP threads. It is just a positive integer value

- Malleability. It is a boolean that indicates if the application is malleable or not

- Topology. It is an enumeration type specifying the topology of the application. This value can be taken into account by the LRMS to decide the number of processes or threads that will be spawned for the application (specific, power of 2, etc.)

GRMS uses its own job description language (GJD). It is a XML-based language, which allows specifying a description of the job executable and also the job resource requirements. There are available several parameters in the GRMS Job Description, including the location of files, arguments, file arguments, executable, environment variables, standard input/output/error, checkpointing definition, name of hosts for the job execution, operating system, required LRMS, network parameters, system paths, minimum memory required and so on. Regarding the specification of the parallelism details of the applications, the GJD allows specifying the type of the application with the *<executable>* tag and the number of required processors with the *<cpucount>* tag. It only allows the threads and MPI programming models for parallel applications. The *<executable>* tag contains 'count' and 'type' attributes that denotes the number of executions of the executable and the way the job-manager submits a job respectively. For the 'type' attribute the following values are available: single (only 1 process or thread will be started), multiple (start count processes or threads), mpi (use the appropriate method to start the job compiled with a vendor-provided MPI library, the job is started with count nodes).

The description of a Grid job with the GJD is shown bellow. It is a MPI job with 4 processes, and it gets the configuration for submitting a NAS-BT from an input file.

```
 1  <grmsjob appid="appid">
 2    <simplejob>
 3      <executable type="mpi" count="4">
 4        <file name="exec-file" type="in">
 5          <url>file:////home/bench/nas-mz/exec-bt</url>
 6        </file>
 7        <arguments>
 8          <value>file.log</value>
 9          <file name="file.conf" type="in">
10            <url>gsiftp://pcmas.ac.upc.edu/~/ex/file.conf</url>
11          </file>
12        </arguments>
13      </executable>
14    </simplejob>
15  </grmsjob>
```

There are some attributes required by eNANOS not supported by the GRMS job description language. Thus, it is required to extend the specification of details about parallelism for applications in GRMS.

There are basically two different ways:

- Extending the GJD language

- Using a mechanism to specify more details with the current semantic

We have decided not extending the language used to describe jobs in the GRMS system. We have used some simple mechanism such as environment variables. We have chosen existing variable names from OpenMP for a good understanding and some other for other semantics. The complete list of considered environment variables is the following:

- OMP_NUM_THREADS. Indicates the number of OpenMP threads

- OMP_SCHEDULE. Indicates the scheduling policy to follow by the OpenMP runtime

- PAR_MALLEABLE. Indicates if the parallel application is malleable or not

- PAR_TOPOLOGY. Indicates the kind of topology followed by the application

These environment variables can be included externally to the GRMS system just by the job description file.

Another important issue to take into account regarding the definition of jobs is the identification of the jobs. Since this is a coordinated infrastructure and there are several layers involved in the architecture, the mapping of IDs into the different layers and the desciption of jobs is crucial.

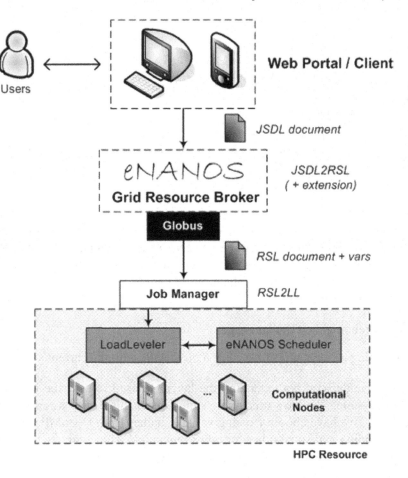

Figure 4.   Data flow between the main components of eNANOS.

Figure 4 shows the call procedure between the main eNANOS execution framework entities.

In our current execution environment, the eNANOS Grid Resource Broker receives a JSDL document from the Web Portal or from a client interface. Afterwards, the JSDL document is converted to RSL because the Grid broker is built on top of the Globus infrastructure.

Not all the information expressed in a JSDL document can be covered in an RSL document, then we use some environment variables as a simple mechanism to solve this problem. Finally, in the local resource the appropriate job manager transforms the RSL document to a LoadLeveler script.

An example of an obtained LoadLeveler script is shown below.

```
 1   #! /bin/sh
 2   #    Job command file created by GRAM/JobManager/loadleveler.pm
 3   # @ job_type      = parallel
 4   # @ initialdir    = /scratch/irodero/cpmd
 5   # @ input         = /dev/null
 6   # @ output        = cpmd.4.pwr4.out
 7   # @ error         = cpmd.4.pwr4.err
 8   # @ class         = short
 9   # @ restart       = yes
10   # @ total_tasks   = 2
11   # @ node          = 1
12   # @ environment = COPY_ALL;\
13   #    MP_EUILIB=ip;\
14   #    MP_EUIDEVICE=en0;\
15   #    PP_LIBRARY_PATH=/scratch_tmp/irodero/CPMD-3.9.1/PP_LIB;\
16   #    OMP_NUM_THREADS=16;\
17   #    PAR_TOPOLOGY=power2
18   #@ queue
19   #
20   /scratch/irodero/CPMD-3.9.1/cpmd.x
         /scratch/irodero/CPMD-3.9.1/inputs/small.inp
21   #
22   # End of job command file.
```

Since from both the Grid and the local environment it is required to know the mapping of a given job into the other layers (for example to ask for information to a local system), we need to include into the GRMS system another environment variable, but in this case it has to be assigned inside the GRMS system not by the user (because the Job ID is unknown before its submission).

- GRID_ID_ENV. Identification of the Grid job (given by the GRMS system).

4.2 eNANOS as a new information provider

In order to provide more details of job execution in the local environment (where eNANOS gives support for parallel applications) we have found two possible ways of integration as is shown in Figure 5:

- Provide an API for eNANOS functionalities that can be used directly from the GRMS system

- Using an Information system (such as Mercury) and adding a new plugin to eNANOS collect the information provided by eNANOS (information queried with general mechanisms)

The second solution should be better in terms of extensibility and generic, but for the first steps of integration is more complicated since there is no plugin implemented yet for eNANOS and the GRMS system has to be modified to support the new data in the scheduling engine.

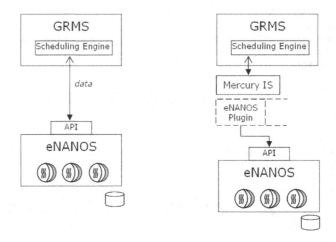

Figure 5.   Integration possibilities: by API (left) and by an IS (right).

Therefore, in this first step we have implemented an API for the eNANOS Execution Framework that allows the GRMS system to obtain information related to the application behavior in run time. As it is discussed in the previous section, the identification of jobs is very important to map the Grid jobs into the local execution platform when getting data. The API has been implemented in Java and consists of the following basic functionalities:

- **geteNANOSProgressInfo** (JOB_ID, REL/ABS)

- **geteNANOSPerformanceInfo** (JOB_ID, REL/ABS)

- **geteNANOSLocalInfo** (JOB_ID)

The schema of the information returned by the API methods includes several data from the local execution systems. Actually, when a job is in the RUNNING state, the XML includes a set of applications with their respective processes and threads. For each of these processes and threads there is also included information about performance metrics (such as MIPS or MFLOPS). This information is very important to know the behavior of the job since our project is targeted to parallel HPC applications, MPI and MPI+OpenMP as well.

This fine-grain information is provided by the NANOS Resource Manager (NANOS-RM) through its PS interface [11]. The NANOS-RM is the responsible of the CPU scheduling in the local system, so it is able to know the details of both the parallel applications and the CPU resources in real time. It provides for each application the number of processes (e.g. the number of MPI processes), the number of threads per process (e.g. the number of OpenMP threads), the status of these threads and the CPU where the threads are allocated in case of running threads.

The eNANOS execution environment also provides information about the progress and performance of the applications in run time. This information can be queried as an absolute value (for example 1500 MFLOPS) or as a relative one (value from 0 to 100 percent). Currently there are two different ways to generate this information: using a library to instrument the application or just using the library for performance developed on top of the progress indicators infrastructure. In the local system, the progress information is managed by a dedicated daemon which provides an API to access to the indicators information. Furthermore, the NANOS Scheduler also queries to the daemon API to collect this kind of information.

The XML schema of the data provided by the daemon through the client interfaces is shown in Figure 6.

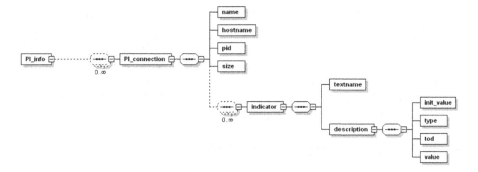

Figure 6. XML schema of the progress indicators data.

GRMS can use various scheduling strategies depending on its configuration and available environment. In most cases it uses multicriteria models for Grid scheduling (e.g.[4] [6]). Some of these models allow modifications of schedules in runtime based on dynamic information gathered from an environment. These methods can particularly take advantage of functionality provided by eNANOS since it allows getting information about performance of applications in runtime.

In particular, in [5] the dynamic rescheduling procedures implemented in GRMS are presented. They use checkpointing and migration mechanisms supported by GRMS. The scheduling model is also based on multicriteria methods. The complete description of the algorithm is available in the quoted paper. In a nutshell, GRMS reschedules automatically 'smaller' jobs if a 'large' job waiting in a GRMS queue cannot be executed due to lack of sufficient amount of resources (e.g. CPUs). By 'small' and 'large' jobs we mean here jobs that require small and large amount of resources respectively. A decision concerning which job should be migrated to which host is done based on multiple criteria.

We used in our experiment the following criteria for the evaluation of destination hosts: available memory, mean load during the last 1, 5 and 15 minutes,

CPU count, CPU speed. The following set of criteria was applied to evaluate checkpointing and migration costs: the number of hosts a job can migrate to (to minimize the risk of a failure), the size of a migrating job (memory allocated by this job), the job's current runtime (in order to migrate jobs that are not to finish soon).

Of course, the current runtime is not the best criterion for evaluation of migration costs of a given job. A job progress is much better metric for this. Taking advantage of this eNANOS functionality GRMS can better evaluate candidate jobs for migration and in this way improve efficiency of the whole schedule (for instance mean job completion time).

Another possibility of exploitation of eNANOS functionality for efficient dynamic rescheduling is use of information about job performance. If this performance is below a certain level (and progress is not advanced too much) then a better resource is found and a job is migrated to that resource (of course if checkpointing of this job is possible).

Ideally the information about a level of performance (or even better relative performance) below which a job should be rescheduled could be provided by end-users. They would have to specify it in a certain kind of agreement. Since currently such information cannot be passed in a GRMS job description we will consider these issues in the future.

5.   Conclusions and Future Work

In this paper we have presented the eNANOS Execution Framework as a target infrastructure to be integrated with Grid services such as a Resource Broker or metascheduler as in the case of GRMS. We have studied how to integrate these two components and which of the required changes are realistic. We also have studied how to describe accurately the parallel jobs in the Grid layer and how it influences the whole architecture (specially the lower layers). We have solved this problem with a very simple solution based on the use of environment variables. We have implemented an API to allow the GRMS system to obtain specific information from eNANOS. This API has been implemented in Java and provides the functionality to get information about the progress, performance and accurate description of them in a run time. Finally, we have discussed the possibilities for improving the scheduling strategies of the GRMS system using the functionality provided by the eNANOS system.

As future work we should include the implementation of new plugin for the Mercury information system to allow GRMS to get the information provided by eNANOS with more generic mechanisms. However, some changes in GRMS are needed. We also expect to implement new scheduling strategies and policies into the GRMS system and, finally, evaluate some real workloads on a testbed composed by resources of both PSNC and BSC institutions.

References

[1] CEPBA Tools Web Site. http://www.cepba.upc.edu/tools_i.htm

[2] Grid Resource Management System (GRMS). http://www.gridlab.org/grms

[3] Julita Corbalan, Alejandro Duran, Jesus Labarta. Dynamic Load Balancing of MPI+OpenMP applications. ICPP04, Montreal, Quebec, Canada. 2004.

[4] Kurowski K., Nabrzyski J., Oleksiak, A., Weglarz, J. Multicriteria Aspects of Grid Resource Management. In Grid Resource Management edited by J. Nabrzyski, J. Schopf, and J. Weglarz, Kluwer Academic Publishers, Boston/Dordrecht/London. 2003.

[5] Kurowski, K., Ludwiczak, B., Nabrzyski, J., Oleksiak, A., Pukacki, J. Improving Grid Level Throughput Using Job Migration and Rescheduling Techniques in GRMS. *Scientific Programming. IOS Press.* Amsterdam The Netherlands 12:4 (2004) 263-273

[6] Kurowski, K., Oleksiak, A., Nabrzyski, J., Kwiecień, A., Wojtkiewicz, M., Dyczkowski, M., Guim, F., Corbalan, J., Labarta, J.. Multi-criteria Grid Resource Management using Performance Prediction Techniques, In Proceeding of the CoreGrid Integration Workshop, Pisa, 2005.

[7] Cathy McCan, Raj Vaswani, John Zahorjan. A Dynamic Processor Allocation Policy for Multiprogrammed Shared-Memory Multiprocessors. ACM Transactions on Computer Systems. 1993.

[8] Ivan Rodero, Julita Corbalan, Rosa M. Badia and Jesus Labarta. eNANOS Grid Resource Broker. P.M.A. Sloot et al.(Eds.): EGC 2005, LNCS 3470, Amsterdam. February 2005.

[9] Ivan Rodero, Francesc Guim, Julita Corbalan and Jesus Labarta. eNANOS: Coordinated Scheduling in Grid Environments. Parallel Computing (ParCo) 2005, Malaga, Spain, September 2005.

[10] Ivan Rodero, Francesc Guim, Julita Corbalan and Jesus Labarta. How the JSDL can Exploit the Parallelism?. 6th IEEE International Symposium on Cluster Computing and the Grid (CCGrid2006), Singapore, 16-19 May 2006.

[11] Francesc Guim, Ivan Rodero, Julita Corbalan, Jesus Labarta, Ariel Oleksiak, Jarek Nabrzyski. Uniform job monitoring using the hpc-europa single point of access. International Workshop on Grid Testbeds, in conjunction with CCGrid2006, Singapore, 16-19 May 2006.

USER-TRANSPARENT SCHEDULING
FOR SOFTWARE COMPONENTS ON THE GRID

Cătălin L. Dumitrescu, Jan Dünnweber and Sergei Gorlatch
Mathematics and Computer Science Department
The University of Münster
CoreGRID Institute on Programming Models
CoreGRID Institute on Resource Management and Scheduling
duennweb@uni-muenster.de
dumitres@uni-muenster.de
gorlatch@uni-muenster.de

Dick H.J. Epema
Electrical Eng., Mathematics and Computer Science Department
Technical University of Delft
CoreGRID Institute on Resource Management and Scheduling
D.H.J.Epema@tudelft.nl

Abstract   Grid applications are increasingly being developed as workflows using well-structured, reusable components. We argue that components with well-defined semantics facilitate an efficient scheduling on the Grid. We have previously developed a user-transparent scheduling approach for Higher-Order Components (HOCs) – parallel implementations of typical programming patterns, accessible and customizable via Web services. Our approach combines three scheduling techniques: using cost functions for reducing communication overhead, reusability of schedules for similar workflows, and the aggregated submission of jobs. We analyze the user-transparent scheduling from four perspectives, namely: the easiness of integration within already existing Grid scheduling systems, the gains for individual users, the resource provider advantages, and the robustness with respect to execution failures. We perform our evaluation using the KOALA Grid scheduler extended to support our user-transparent scheduling, which we run on the DAS-2 system combining over 200 nodes at five sites in the Netherlands. The experimental results show an increase in throughput by more than 100%, a descreasing of the response time by 50%, and a failure reduction by 45% for the considered scenarios.

Keywords: User-Transparent Scheduling, Co-Allocation, Component Technology, Higher-Order Components

1.   Introduction

Grid technology provides a means for harnessing the computational and storage power of widely distributed collections of computers. Scheduling in a Grid environment is a complicated task and usually requires specific knowledge about the application being scheduled [3], in particular, the volume and the frequency of communication. Since the communication behavior of an arbitrary application cannot be foreseen during the setup of an application, it is typically the task of the application developer or the end user to provide information about the application's communication properties [5].

Grid applications are difficult to be developed from scratch: because of their complexity and scale, they increasingly rely on pre-packaged pieces of software which are called components, modules, templates, etc. in different approaches. In this paper we use Higher-Order Components (HOCs [16]) - reusable components that are customizable for particular applications using parameters which may be either data or code. HOCs include the required configuration to run on top of a standard Grid middleware [17] and can be remotely accessed via Web Services. Thereby, HOCs abstract over the technical features of Grid platforms and allow their users to concentrate on their applications. While providing more structure and reuse in the application development process, program components imply a change of focus for scheduling: it becomes mandatory to explore new solutions for mapping both single components and their compositions to available Grid resources.

We aim at user-transparent scheduling, i.e. techniques that free the end user from specifying application's communication behavior. Our approach to user-transparent scheduling makes use of: software components for building applications, scheduling cost-functions for lowering the communication costs, a reusable workflow technique for avoiding the need for a repeated scheduling when a workflow recurs, and an aggregated submission technique for avoiding multiple submissions of job to a single execution site. In this paper we present and analyze these techniques and their combined use for component-based Grid applications.

We use the KOALA system [21] as the basic scheduler for testing our user-transparent approach. KOALA supports co-allocation – the scheduling of parallel application on Grid resources. We enhance KOALA to schedule component-based applications using their specific communication properties.

The structure of this paper is as follows. First, we describe Higher-Order Components and the user-transparent scheduling approach; second, we introduce our integration and evaluation methodology; and third, we prove its advantages in the context of KOALA Grid scheduler and DAS-2, the Dutch Grid system, deployed at five sites in the Netherlands.

2. Context and Background

In this section, we describe the general context in which our approach to the user-transparent scheduling of component-based applications on Grids is developed. We first introduce the targeted environment of this work, and the concept of HOC – Higher-Order Component – for Grid application programming.

2.1 Environment Description

The main elements of the Grid environment considered in this work are as follows: (Figure 1 contains a high-level overview showing some of these elements):

- Worker Node: a resource for computing and storing data;
- Execution Site: a collection of nodes placed in a single administrative domain;
- Work unit (or job): a sequential code executed on a single node;
- Application: computation composed of work units;
- Resource Manager (RM): a specific software that allocates resources and monitors applications submitted by the users at a site level;
- Security Gate: a software that authenticates and authorizes user requests and invokes the RM whenever an application is submitted;
- Client: a computer used for submitting HOC-based applications to the Grid built out of several sites;
- HOC Service Node: a resource providing a Web service for accessing a HOC implementation;

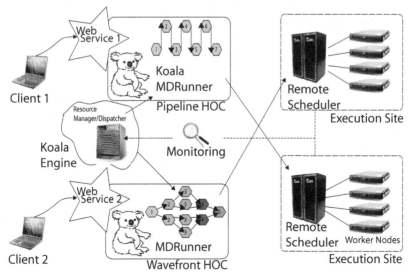

Figure 1. Grid Environment: High-Level Overview.

- Grid Resource Dispatcher: software that maps HOC applications onto a Grid, i. e. , it aggregates resources (nodes and sites) and reserves them for work unit execution.

In this environment, the HOC client submits a request for a specific HOC-based application by means of the HOC Web service. The HOC Web service generates a scheduling description of the application and passes it to the scheduler for running the application on the execution environment. Once the resource dispatcher aggregated the required amount of resources for the application, it returns a handle to the HOC Web service and steps aside from further interaction. Further, it is the task of the HOC Web service to actually submit the application to the Grid and to monitor its progress. In this manner, any HOC-based application can be scheduled over a Grid environment without the need of direct user interaction.

2.2   Higher-Order Components

HOCs are high-level programming constructs, pre-packaged with (parallel) implementations and the required middleware configuration files. Each HOC implements a generic pattern of parallel behavior with a specific communication structure. A HOC can be customized for a particular application by providing it with arguments which may be either data or application-specific code. HOCs were given their name (Higher-Order Components) because of their code parameters, in analogy with higher-order functions which accept functions as arguments. HOCs are made accessible to the Grid user via specialized Web services. Every HOC is by default configured to run on top of a specific middleware (Globus).

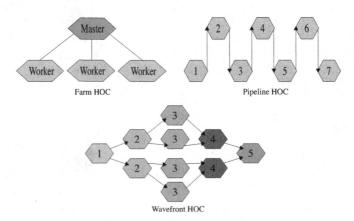

Figure 2.   Examples of Communication Structures in HOCs.

Currently three different HOCs are available: Farm-HOC [16], Pipeline-HOC [13] and Wavefront-HOC [14] (see Fig. 2). The Farm-HOC is used for running "embarrassingly parallel" applications without dependencies between tasks. All farm implementations have in common the existence of a *Master* process that partitions data; the parts are then processed in parallel using multiple *Worker* processes. In contrast, in the Pipeline-HOC, all inputs pass through each pipeline stage in the same order, while the parallelism is achieved by overlapping the processing of several input instances. The third component studied in the paper, the Wavefront-HOC, implies a set of computations advancing as a hyperplane in a multidimensional variable space.

2.3   User-Transparent Scheduling for HOCs

Applications using HOCs have well-defined requirements in terms of data distribution and communication schemata, i. e. , which data is sent, when, and to how many processors, is completely determined by the HOC type and does not depend on the particular application where that HOC is used. Many different applications can be built using the same HOCs or combinations of them, but our user-transparent scheduling of HOC-based applications works independently of application-specific code and data parameters.

The following techniques are combined together in our implementation:

- *Cost functions* take in account the different characteristics of the environment in which a HOC application is executed. Various costs functions are employed for achieving an adequate distribution of resources to the work units (the "where?" part of scheduling). In [8], we have identified bandwidth-aware cost function, which provides the highest communication time reduction for the most HOCs;

- *Reusability of schedules for similar workflows* avoids successive job submissions with similar communication patterns. Job submission operations are expensive in Grids [10]. In our approach, different applications using the same HOCs will be mapped onto the same resources;

- *Aggregated submission of work units* exploits the fact that in many cases work units receive similar parameters for execution (similarly to an MPI application). Our scheduling system will place multiple job execution requests to avoid the necessity for individual HOC work unit submissions.

While user-transparent scheduling of single HOCs is already a complex operation, compositions of HOCs also occur in practice and must be scheduled on the Grid. This can be the case, when scientific applications are divided into several subproblems of different sizes and complexities. We schedule applications that make use of multiple HOCs composed together by applying our submission technique recursively to each single HOC in the composition, processing the global HOC first, and then down to inner ones.

3. Implementation of the Scheduler

We describe in this section our approach for implementing user-transparent scheduling in general and the metrics used to evaluate the performance of our implementation in different scenarios.

3.1 Integration of Existing Systems

We have chosen a layered solution for supporting HOC scheduling, because it provides the advantage of easily incorporating already existing scheduling solutions, and because of its flexibility in addressing various classes of parallel applications. We were interested in a minimal integration effort while taking advantage of already existing infrastructures. Based on existing Grid schedulers (KOALA [21], Pegasus [6], GridBus [4]) or brokers (GRUBER [9]), we have chosen a three-layers scheduling architecture [7] represented in Figure 3, and consisting of:

1. *Translation layer* for mapping the user's selection of a component to an associated communication pattern and for using a description of this model in order to select and provide as input to the cost management. This layer is also responsible for identifying whenever the reusable technique could be invoked and reusable submissions can be performed;

2. *Mapping and observation layer* for tracking allocated resource status and work units' progress and for taking action whenever a failure occurs and additional resources are needed. Any already existing Grid scheduling infrastructure is incorporated by this layer in our approach;

3. *Resource management layer* for acquiring and aggregating adequate resources to fulfill user objectives (reservation). This layer implements the aggregated submission of work units as described before and it is usually represented by different supporting tools of a Grid scheduler (i.e, runners for KOALA or site-selectors for GRUBER).

3.2 Performance Evaluation of Scheduling

We make two assumptions about the Grid on which our scheduling architecture operates. First, providers are interested in better utilizations of their resources (i.e., throughput); second, consumers want to achieve better performance for their applications and to acquire as many resources as possible when their applications require a lot of computational power (e.g., short response times). We employ two metrics for quantifying the performance of our

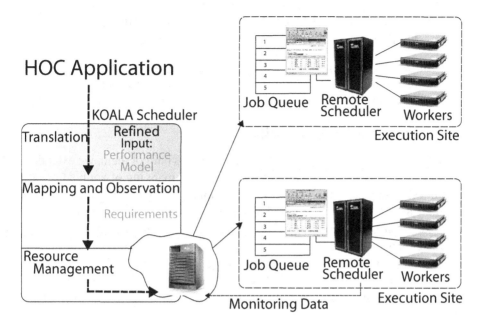

Figure 3. The Three-Layer, User-Transparent Scheduling Infrastructure.

user-transparent scheduling approach from both a user and a provider point of interest:

Metric-I. *Response Time* (RT):

$$RT = \sum_{i=1..N} RT_i/N \qquad (1)$$

with RT_i being the individual job time response and N being the number of jobs processed during the execution period [11];

Metric-II. *Throughput* is defined as the number of work units executed on the Grid in a pre-defined interval of time [11].

There are many cases in which a Grid resource or service may fail in a dynamic, heterogeneous, and large-scale environment. Failures may occur in a Grid at infrastructure, middleware, application, and user levels, and may be transient or permanent; for a review of research focusing on causes of failures in Grid we refer to [18]. Due to the heterogeneity of Grids and their sheer size, failures appear much more often than in traditional parallel and distributed environments [10, 19]. We employ a third performance metric, namely:

Metric-III. *Failure Rate* [18], defined as the ratio of completed jobs to the total amount of jobs submitted from a fixed set of jobs.

4.   KOALA-based User-Transparent Scheduling Evaluation

In this section, we report the results of our work to support user-transparent scheduling within the KOALA Grid scheduler and the experimental results for three HOC types on the Dutch Grid system, DAS-2 [15].

4.1   Integration Feasibility

For efficiently scheduling HOCs and applications built of them, we extended the KOALA scheduler with support for cost-based mapping of applications to resources, aggregated submission and reusable schedule identification. The standard KOALA version provided resource reservation and job co-allocation, basic job submission, tracking of job execution and re-submissions.

Our enhanced KOALA version adds the implementation of a specialized KOALA runner, the MDRunner, for handling HOC-based applications as explained in the following. Each HOC client starts such a MDRunner, while KOALA processes jobs as co-allocated jobs and performs adequate reservations.

In the resulting infrastructure, the responsibilities are distributed as follows:

- HOCs provide a high-level interface to the end user, allowing to compose applications in terms of patterns such as a wavefront or a pipeline;

- The MDRunner makes the scheduling of HOC applications transparent to the user. It automatically generates the scheduling requirements descriptions for instantiating a specific HOC pattern (Farm, Pipeline, Wavefront, etc); it also decides if aggregated submission or schedule reuse could be employed for the current application;

- The KOALA engine performs the resource acquisition and aggregation, by collecting information about resources, keeping track of application requirements and scheduling components to different Grid sites;

- The MDRunner and the KOALA engine share the functionalities of monitoring the application progress and the preservation of application-specific constraints, e. g. , time limits to be met.

The MDRunner implements six cost functions that optimize over different communication requirements [8]:

1 link count-aware: optimizes over the number of network connections a message has to pass;

2 bandwidth-aware: optimizes over the available bandwidth of a link;

3 latency-aware: optimizes over the latency of a link;

4 network utilization-aware: optimizes over the instantaneous network utilization at the submission time;

5 application communication-aware: optimizes over the communication pattern;

6 predicted variance-aware: optimizes over the predicted network bandwidth availability during the entire execution.

The gain in performance of each of these costs is analyzed in the following subsections.

4.2 Performance Results

We have performed 10 runs of each HOC type using synthetic applications that imitate the behavior of a real application in terms of communication patterns and computation requirements. We present our results for the three performance metrics as defined in the previous section. Each HOC-based application was composed of 15 to 20 work units and exchanged 20 messages with variable sizes between 1Mb to 10 Mb.

4.2.1   User Gains.   We focus first on the response time for the user, achieved by our scheduling approach. The results are provided in Table 1, with all the values being expressed as percentages of the response time achieved under the KOALA's default scheduling policy. As can be observed, our techniques support a reduction of the response time by 60% in average.

Table 1.   Average Response Time (%)

Cost Function	Synthetic HOC Workload Type		
	Farm $20\times30\times1M$	*Pipeline* $20\times30\times10M$	*Wavefront* $20\times30\times5M$
CF (Close-to-File)	51.89	70.09	73.20
Link	45.37	55.06	65.40
Bandwidth	40.93	53.67	60.95
Latency	48.47	48.89	68.75
Network	48.54	50.52	67.15
Application	42.72	56.53	58.83
Predicted	44.02	53.63	57.96

4.2.2   Resource Provider Satisfaction.   We show now the throughput performance when schedules are reused for HOC-based applications that exhibit the same workflow, i.e., they employ the same HOCs in identical order. Table 2 captures our results. We observe a high throughput improvement due to the schedule reuse: the reduction of the scheduling overhead allows to increase the total throughput by more than 100% in our test scenario, where synthetic HOC applications were submitted under a Poisson distribution. These applications involved 20 work units, 30 messages of sizes between 1 and 10 Mb (detailed in the Tables' headers) [8].

Table 2.   Throughput Gains (%)

Cost Function	Synthetic HOC Workload Type		
	Farm $20\times30\times1M$	*Pipeline* $20\times30\times10M$	*Wavefront* $20\times30\times5M$
CF	93.7	112.9	101.8
Link	100.7	116.3	161.0
Bandwidth	118.6	126.4	170.4
Latency	117.4	133.6	161.6
Network	106.3	134.8	170.2
Application	101.0	117.4	127.3
Predicted	118.2	123.6	194.0

4.2.3   Failure Analysis.   Now, we turn our attention to analyzing the success rate of HOC applications on DAS-2. We classify failures into two types [10]:

- job failure is defined as the incapacity to run a job at a certain site, error that results in the entire workflow failure;

- workflow failure is defined as the incapacity to either start or complete the workflow; this error is usually caused either due to a failure in submission or in the resource acquisition mechanism.

For this analysis, we experimented with over 20k work units (corresponding to $\approx$ 1k workflows). Our results are presented in Table 3. While, in average, the rate of failures dropped under user-transparent scheduling approach, the work unit execution failures increased due to the DAS-2 uSLA [12] for stopping jobs longer than 15 minutes and our approach for schedule reuse. Thus, a more careful approach should be devised for these scenarios in the future.

5.   Related Work

In the context of application-to-resource dynamic binding, the optimal mapping problem has been approached in different ways for various types of systems.

Table 3. Detailed Failures (%)

Failure Type	User-Transparent	Basic Scheduling
Remote environment failure	5	11
GridFTP failure	0	0
Work unit execution failure	4	2
Workflow submission timeout failure	1	5
Total job failures	9	13
Total workflow failures	10	18

For example, Aldinucci et al. [1] focus on the ASSIST coordination language - a language that allows to describe arbitrary graphs of modules which are connected by typed streams of data. A specialized compiler translates the graph of modules into a network of processes on the Grid, under pre-specified rules. The difference in our approach is that we avoid application migration, because this feature is costly in practice, and we use instead the schedule reuse technique.

In [2], the Performance Evaluation Process Algebra (PEPA) for expressing performance models is described. PEPA [2] is also used in [1] for the analysis of the static information about a structured parallel application, given by its flow graph. In our work, we combine the information given by the static structure of a parallel program with monitoring information gathered at runtime.

Furmento et al. [20] analyze two main policies when considering application performance for Grids: *Minimum Execution Time* and *Minimum Cost*. They also introduce three cost models (unit cost per unit time and processor). Based on these assumptions, they derive various prediction results about the performance of a specific application (linear equation solver). Their initial results demonstrated the importance of finding the effective utilization of Grid resources by high performance applications, as well as the importance of information associated with various components in the system. The experiments were conducted in a small computational setting composed of at most three systems that had between 1 and 16 processors, while no Grids were considered.

6.   Conclusions

In this paper we introduced the user-transparent scheduling approach for Higher-Order Components and analyzed it from four perspectives, namely: the easiness of integration within already existing Grid scheduling infrastructures, the gains for individual users, the resource provider satisfactions and the change in job failures. The motivations of this work are Grid applications that increasingly rely on workflows using well-structured, reusable components. Our approach combines several scheduling techniques, like cost-based technique for lowering the communication costs, reusable technique for avoiding the need for a repeated scheduling phase when a workflow recurs, and aggregated submission technique. We performed our evaluation by extending the KOALA Grid scheduler to support user-transparent scheduling, and by running the extended version on the DAS-2 testbed combining over 200 nodes at five sites in the Netherlands. Our experimental results show an increase in throughput with more than 100%, a lowering of the response time by 50%, and a failure reduction by 45% for the considered scenarios.

Acknowledgments

This research work is carried out under the FP6 Network of Excellence CoreGRID funded by the European Commission (Contract IST-2002-004265). We would like to thank the DAS-2 system team for kindly providing their resources for our experiments. We also thank Jürgen Vörding for his help on this paper.

References

[1] A. Benoit and M. Aldinucci. Towards the Automatic Mapping of ASSIST Applications for the Grid. In *Proceedings of CoreGRID Integration Workshop*, University of Pisa, Italy, Nov. 2005.

[2] A. Benoit, M. Cole, S. Gilmore, and J. Hillston. Evaluating the performance of pipeline-structured parallel programs with skeletons and process algebra. *PAPP Workshop*, 2005.

[3] A. I. D. Bucur and D. H. Epema. The influence of communication on the performance of co-allocation. In *Workshop on Job Scheduling and Parallel Processing*, pages 66–86, London, 2001. Springer.

[4] R. Buyya, D. Abramson, and J. Giddy. An economy driven resource management architecture for computational power grids. In *Parallel and Distributed Processing*, 2000.

[5] A. Dan, C. Dumitrescu, K. Ranganathan, and M. Ripeanu. A Layered Framework for Connecting Client Objectives and Resource Capabilities. *International Journal of Cooperative Communication Systems*, 2006.

[6] E. Deelman, J. Blythe, Y. Gil, C. Kesselman, G. Mehta, S. Patil, M.-H. Su, K. Vahi, and M. Livny. Pegasus : Mapping scientific workflows onto the grid. In *2nd EUROPEAN ACROSS GRIDS CONFERENCE*, Nicosia, Cyprus, 2004.

[7] C. Dumitrescu, D. H. Epema, J. Dünnweber, and S. Gorlatch. User Transparent Scheduling of Structured Parallel Applications in Grid Environments. In *HPC-GECO/CompFrame Workshop held in Conjunction with HPDC'06*, 2006.

[8] C. Dumitrescu, D. H. Epema, J. Dünnweber, and S. Gorlatch. Reusable Cost-based Scheduling of Grid Workflows Operating on Higher-Order Components. Technical Report TR-0044, CoreGRID - Network of Excellence, 2006.

[9] C. Dumitrescu and I. Foster. GRUBER: A Grid Resource Usage SLA BrokER. In *Proc. of 11th International Euro-Par Conference (Euro-Par'05), Portugal*, 2005.

[10] C. Dumitrescu, I. Raicu, and I. Foster. Experiences in running workloads over Grid3. In *Grid and Cooperative Computing (GCC)*, 2005.

[11] C. Dumitrescu, I. Raicu, and I. Foster. DI-GRUBER: A Distributed Approach for Resource Brokering. In *Proc. of SuperComputing Conference, Seattle, USA*, 2006.

[12] C. Dumitrescu, M. Wilde, and I. Foster. A Model for Usage Policy-based Resource Allocation in Grids. In *Policies for Distributed Systems and Networks, 2005. Sixth IEEE International Workshop on Policy*, pages 191 – 200, June 2005.

[13] J. Dünnweber, S. Gorlatch, A. Benoit, and M. Cole. Integrating MPI-Skeletons with Web services. In *Proceedings of the International Conference on Parallel Computing, Malaga, Spain*, September 2005.

[14] J. Dünnweber, S. Gorlatch, S. Campa, M. Danelutto, and M. Aldinucci. Using code parameters for component adaptations. In *CoreGRID Integration Workshop, Pisa, Italy*, November 2005.

[15] Dutch University Backbone. The distributed ASCI supercomputer 2 (DAS-2), 2006.

[16] S. Gorlatch and J. Dünnweber. From Grid Middleware to Grid Applications: Bridging the Gap with HOCs. In *Future Generation Grids*. Springer Verlag, 2005.

[17] M. Humphrey, G. Wasson, J. Gawor, J. Bester, S. Lang, I. Foster, S. Pickles, M. M. Keown, K. Jackson, J. Boverhof, M. Rodriguez, and S. Meder. State and events for Web services: A comparison of five WS-resource framework and WS-notification implementations. In *14th IEEE International Symposium on High Performance Distributed Computing (HPDC-14)*, 2005.

[18] A. Iosup, D. H. Epema, C. Franke, A. Papaspyrou, L. Schley, B. Song, and R. Yahyapour. On Grid performance evaluation using synthetic workloads. In *The 12th Workshop on Job Scheduling Strategies for Parallel Processing (JSSPP)*, Saint Malo, FR, June 2006.

[19] A. Iosup and D. H. Epema. GrenchMark: A framework for analyzing, testing, and comparing grids. In *6th IEEE/ACM Int'l Symposium on Cluster Computing and the Grid (CCGrid)*, 2006.

[20] A. Mayer, S. McGough, and N. Furmento. ICENI: Optimisation of component applications within a grid environment. In *Parallel Computing Amsterdam*, 2002.

[21] H. Mohamed and D. H. Epema. The design and implementation of the KOALA coallocating grid scheduler. In .-. LNCS 3470, editor, *Proceedings of the European Grid Conference, Amsterdam*, 2005.

PROBLEM SOLVING ENVIRONMENT FOR DISTRIBUTED INTERACTIVE APPLICATIONS

Katarzyna Rycerz and Marian Bubak
Institute of Computer Science, AGH, al. Mickiewicza 30, 30-059 Kraków, Poland
Academic Computer Centre – CYFRONET, Nawojki 11, 30-950 Kraków, Poland
kzajac@agh.edu.pl
bubak@agh.edu.pl

Peter Sloot
Faculty of Sciences, Section Computational Science, University of Amsterdam
Kruislaan 403, 1098 SJ Amsterdam, The Netherlands
sloot@science.uva.nl

Vladimir Getov
School of Computer Science University of Westminster
Watford Rd, Northwick Park Harrow HA1 3TP, U.K.
V.S.Getov@wmin.ac.uk

Abstract   Interactive Problem Solving Environments (PSEs) offer an integrated approach for constructing and running complex systems, such as distributed simulation systems. To achieve efficient execution of High Level Architecture (HLA)-based distributed interactive simulations on the Grid, we introduce a PSE called Grid HLA Management System (G-HLAM) for their management. This is done by introducing migration and monitoring mechanisms for such applications. In this paper we present how G-HLAM can be applied to the applications supporting surgeons with simulations of vascular reconstruction, using distributed federations on the Grid for the communication among simulation and visualization components.

Keywords: PSE, distributed interactive simulation, Grid computing, HLA, migration

1.   Introduction

Problem Solving Environments (PSEs) are integrated computational systems that allow scientists to define complex problems, find the required nearest components and resources available, and utilize them efficiently. PSEs offer an integrated approach for constructing and running complex systems, such as distributed simulation and decision support systems.

In this paper we focus on PSEs for running distributed interactive simulations on the Grid. This effort gives a potential opportunity for better and more convenient usage of distributed resources that are needed by such simulations, but were previously inaccessible and are now available through Grid.

There are solutions that may be used as underlying frameworks for such PSEs. One of them is the High Level Architecture (HLA) [11] which offers many features for developers of interactive and distributed applications. HLA enables merging geographically distributed parts (called *federates*) of simulations (called *federations*) into a coherent entity. It is explicitly designed as support for interactive distributed simulations, it provides various services required for that specific purpose, such as time management, useful for time-driven or event-driven interactive simulations. It also provides data distribution management and enables all application components to access the entire application data space in an efficient way. On the other hand, the HLA standard does not provide automatic setup of HLA distributed applications and there is no mechanism for migrating federates according to the dynamic changes of host loads or failures, which is essential for Grid applications. Therefore, there is a need for a PSE that would manage HLA-based collaborative environments on the Grid.

The Grid Services concept provides a good starting point for building the Grid HLA Management System (G-HLAM) for that purpose, as described in [23]. The concept of G-HLAM can be also ported to component platforms like CCA [4], H2O [14], ProActive [20] or Grid Component Model [10].

The paper is organized as follows: in Section 2 we present an overview of most important PSEs for distributed interactive simulations. For each of these environments, we analyse the advantages and disadvantages for adapting Grid solutions. In Section 3 we describe benefits of using HLA for our purposes and present G-HLAM system. In Section 4 experimental results are presented and we conclude in Section 5.

2.   PSEs for distributed interactive applications

This Section presents the overview of Problem Solving Environments which may be applied for interactive distributed applications.

2.1 Computational Steering Environment

The aim of the Computational Steering Environment (CSE) [6] is to provide scientific end users with an environment in which they can easily define interactive interfaces to ongoing simulations. The CSE architecture is implemented as a set of processes - called satellites - which implement standard visualization operations. The simulation is also seen by the system as a satellite. Satellites cooperate by sending and receiving data from a central data manager which, in turn, notifies all interested satellites about data mutations. The most predominant satellite is the interactive graphics editing tool called Parametrized Graphics Object (PGO) editor, which allows the end user to sketch out visualizations. A two-way binding between visualization and data is achieved by binding the sketch to data within the data manager. CSE uses the TCP/IP protocol as a communication layer between satellites. The main disadvantage of the CSE is its centralization, which hampers its scalability in Grid environments. However, the idea of a data manager and satellites can be somehow extended (e.g. by building hierarchical or distributed data sets).

2.2 CUMULVS

Collaborative User Migration, User Library for Visualization and Steering (CUMULVS) [13] allows the programmer to add interactive steering and visualization to an existing parallel or serial program (task). With CUMULVS, each of the collaborators can start up an independent view program that will connect to the running simulation program. Viewers allow scientists to browse through the various data fields being computed and observe the ongoing convergence toward a solution. CUMULVS also allows an application program to perform user-directed checkpointing and automated restarts of parallel programs using checkpointing, even across a heterogeneous cluster of machines. A single user library interface routine passes control to CUMULVS periodically, to transparently handle the viewer attachment / detachment protocols, the selection and extraction of data, and the updating of steering parameters. CUMULVS allows each front-end viewer to interactively select the granularity and extent of data that it desires to view. Currently, CUMULVS uses PVM [21] as its message passing substrate; it allows for pairs of anonymous tasks to communicate with each other without both tasks being started at the same time. MPI does not allow these dynamics, so porting CUMULVS ideas to MPI would not be easy.

2.3 Cactus Problem Solving Environment

Cactus [1] is an open-source problem solving environment designed for scientists and engineers. The name Cactus comes from the design of a central core, which connects to application modules - or thorns - through an extensible interface. Thorns can implement custom-developed scientific or engineering applications, such as the Einstein solvers, or other applications such as computational fluid dynamics. Cactus is an environment for a wide range of issues, here we concentrate on its support for parallel or distributed simulations and their visualisation. In Cactus, different thorns can be used to implement different parallel paradigms, such as PVM, Pthreads [17], OpenMP [19], CORBA [5], MPICH-G etc. Cactus can be compiled with as many driver thorns as required (subject to availability), with the one actually used chosen by the user at runtime through a parameter file. Cactus provides the ability to stream online data from a running simulation via TCP/IP socket communications. Multiple visualization clients can connect to a running Cactus executable via a socket from any remote machine on the Grid, then request arbitrary data from the running simulation and display simulation results in real time. This can be done in two ways: by an HTTP control interface or through socket connections. Cactus already provides support for Grid–enabled MPI – MPICH-G. Its main disadvantage is that the parallelization is limited to domain decomposition. However, because of the modular architecture of Cactus, it appears that adding extended functionality would be quite easy for application developers.

2.4   Discover

Discover [15] is a interactive and collaborative system that enables geographically distributed scientists and engineers to collaboratively monitor, and control high performance parallel/distributed applications using web-based portals. Discover provides a three-tier architecture composed of detachable thin clients at the front-end, a peer-to-peer network of servers in the middle, and the Distributed Interactive Object Substrate (DIOS++) at the back-end. An important part of Discover is a rule-based visualization system. Rules are decoupled from the system and can be externally injected to manage such visualization behavior at runtime, as autonomically selecting the appropriate visualization routines and methods and adjusting the extraction threshold. To allow rule-based management, DIOS++ provides autonomic objects that extend application computational objects with sensors to monitor the state of the objects. It also contains actuators to modify the state of the objects, access policies to control accesses to sensors and actuators and rule agents to enable rule-based autonomic self-management. Discover uses HTTP for connection with visualisation thin clients and CORBA for communication with application engines. Discover already possesses a distributed and scalable peer-to-peer type of architecture. However, it can still be extended to take advantage from Grid technology, which would enable it to be automatically set up and effectively run in a non-centrally controlled environment consisting of different administrative domains.

2.5 TENT

TENT [24] is a software integration and workflow management system that helps improve the building and management of process chains for complex simulations in distributed environments. TENT allows for online steering, and visualization of simulations. Wrappers are used to interface application modules (e.g. Computation Fluid Dynamics (CFD), Computation Structural Mechanics (CSM), visualisation or filters) with the system. The system consists of base components which include: modules for controlling workflows; factories for starting system and applications in the distributed environment; the name server as the central information service. There are also support components – additional services for special application scenarios not covered by the basic functionality. Examples include: a data server for storing data files, a monitoring and reporting component, and several special control components (e.g., for coupled simulations like the ones parallelized with MPI). The system is controlled by a user through a GUI. TENT uses CORBA for communication between parts of the system. TENT is already Grid–enabled: it supports MPICH-G2 simulations. The Globus Toolkit version 2 is used for resource selection, for starting applications, and for data transfer and security.

2.6 Interactive Simulation Systems Conductor

Interactive Simulation Systems Conductor (ISSConductor) [27] is an agent oriented component framework for Interactive Simulation Systems. The system introduces two kinds of agents: Module Agents that are specific for different modules of interactive application like simulation, visualization and interaction and Communication Agents that are used for communication between Module Agents and actual modules. Module Agent uses an extended finite state machine to model the run-time behavior of a component, and adopts first order logic to represent the interaction constraints between components and to implement them in the knowledge bases of agents. ISS-Conductor separates the basic computational functions of a component from its run-time behavior controls, and provides a high level interface for users to design interaction scenarios. The framework is very general and can be used for various interactive applications. ISS-Conductor is built on top of HLA described in the previous Section. Currently, ISS-Conductor is not Grid-enabled, however it can easily take advantage of the system presented in this paper, since it is built over the HLA standard.

2.7 Comparision of existing PSE's

In this Section we have presented environments that support interactive steering of simulations. For each of presented systems we described the

Table 1.   Main features of the interactive simulation and visualization environments

System	Type of simulation and its distribution	Protocol	Porting to the Grid issue
CSE	runtime steering – multiple visualizations for one simulation	TCP/IP	scalability issue
CUMULVS	runtime steering of parallel simulations (PVM)	PVM	porting to MPI issue
CACTUS	runtime steering of parallel or distributed simulations PVM, Pthreads, OpenMP, CORBA, MPICH-G	two possibilities: 1) HTTP 2) HDF5 format over TCP/IP	support for MPICH-G
Discover	parallel and distributed applications in general	HTTP, CORBA	scalable architecture that could be extended to allow automatic setup and effective run in non-centrally controlled Grid environment
TENT	parallel and distributed simulations	CORBA	TENT is already Grid enabled by using GTv2 and MPICH-G2 features [24]
ISS-Conductor	distributed simulations	HLA	no adaptation to changing environment, no automatic setup, no dynamic discovery

architecture and protocols used to connect simulations with visualizations. For each of the systems we also analyzed the possibilities of adapting it to the Grid environment. A summary of the features of the presented systems is show in Tab. 1. CSE, CUMULVS, Cactus, Discover and TENT focus more on support for steering simulations without much concern for advanced simulation composition from distributed components which often use different time management. ISS-Conductor is a high–level system built over HLA - a standard allowing for interoperability between different types of simulations. Basing on this analysis, we have chosen HLA as a base for distributed interactive simulations running on the Grid. It is a well recognized standard and offers all the necessary functionality for simulation developers. Its important feature is that the local time management mechanism of one simulation component (federate) is not visible to other federates. Hence, all forms of time management (time–driven, event–driven, parallel discrete event, real–time–driven) may be linked together. HLA also allows to build scalable simulation systems. It separates the communication infrastructure from the actual simulation. Additionally, it introduces a uniform way of describing events and objects being exchanged between federates. All of these features allow interoperability between various simulations. Although HLA originates from the defense technology, there is a growing interest from non-military areas like manufacturing, transportation and gaming industries. Therefore companies are currently working on more scalable and efficient implementations of the standard [22]. Recently, open source implementation was also released [18].

3. PSE for HLA-based simulations

3.1 Need for a Grid for HLA-based applications

Usually, parts of distributed simulations require different resources: quick access to database, computational power or specific VR hardware. It is quite unlikely to find those resources at one geographical site. Additionally, if more simulations need to be run concurrently, one site with computational power may not be sufficient. A similar problem arises when many visualisations (users) located in different places want to observe the same simulation. Therefore, the application modules usually have to be located in geographically different places and the Grid concept that facilitates access to computing resources may be a very promising approach here.

As stated above, HLA has advanced mechanisms supporting distributed simulations, so execution of HLA–based applications on the Grid should be natural extension of its usage. However, the HLA standard was developed assuming a certain quality of service in the underlying environment. Therefore, there is a need for adaptation of HLA–based applications to the dynamically changing Grid as well as for automatic setup, dynamic discovery and fault-tolerance mechanisms.

The Grid [7] is designed to coordinate resources that are not under central control. Additionally, the Web services [25] concept of abstract interfaces allows for modular design (OGSA, WSRF) [8]. However, the Grid environment is shared between many users and its conditions can change in an unpredictable way. Therefore, there is a need for a system that adapts HLA-based applications to a dynamically–changing environment and requires fault tolerance mechanisms such as migration of its distributed federates or their monitoring.

In addition, the Grid idea is to facilitate access to computing resources and make it more transparent to the user. Currently, setting up distributed applications based on HLA requires tedious setup and configuration. The HLA standard does not cover aspects of dynamic discovery of HLA federations. Therefore, there is a need for a mechanism that sets up an HLA–based application on geographically distributed system (i.e. the Grid) in a more convenient way. Subsequently, HLA federates should be able to find one another dynamically and transparently to the user. Additionally, HLA does not provide security mechanisms similar to the one provided by the Grid Security Infrastructure (GSI) [9].

3.2   Grid HLA Management System

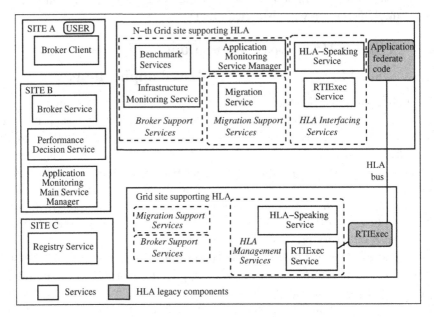

Figure 1.   Grid HLA Management System Architecture (G-HLAM consists of services which control the whole HLA application and the services that should be installed on each HLA-enabled Grid site.

The Grid HLA Management System (G-HLAM) supports efficient execution of HLA-based simulations on the Grid. The system is built on top of the Open Grid Services Infrastructure as presented in [26, 23, 12]. In the future we would like to use also lightweight Grid Component platform [2] for that purpose.

The architecture of G-HLAM system is shown in the Fig. 1. The group of main G-HLAM services consists of: a *Broker Service* which coordinates management of the simulation, a *Performance Decision Service* which decides when the performance of any of the federates is not satisfactory and therefore migration is required, and a *Registry Service* which stores information about the location of local services. On each Grid site, supporting HLA, there are local services for performing migration commands on behalf of the *Broker Service*, as well as for monitoring federates and benchmarking. *Application Monitoring Services* are based on the OCM-G monitoring system [3]. The *HLA-Speaking Service* is one of the local services interfacing federates with the G-HLAM system, using GRAM for submission of federates.

A more detailed description of the *HLA-Speaking Service*, together with the GridHLAController library, which actually interfaces the application code with the system, can be found in [12].

4. Application of G-HLAM to vascular reconctruction

In this section we present results of the experiment in which G-HLAM was applied as the prototype collaborative environment for vascular reconstruction. The prototype consists of two types of modules communicating with HLA: *simulation module* (MPI parallel simulation) and *visualization-receiver modules* (responsible for receiving data from the simulation). At each time step, the simulation calculates velocity vectors of simulated blood flow in 3D space and sends them to visualisations modules. In our experiment, we have measured the duration time of first 8 steps of the simulation that included actual calculations and sending time.

We show how migration improves performance from the point of view of the user – i.e. how sending output data from the simulation changes after migration if the partial simulation results are actually observed by someone. The experiment was performed on the DutchGrid DAS2 testbed infrastructure and at CYFRONET, Krakow, as shown in Tab. 2. We used GT v3.2 and HLA RTI 1.3v5. In the presented experiment one simulation was migrated. The num-

Table 2. Grid testbed infrastructure

Operating System	Red Hat Enterprise Linux Advanced Server, version 3		
Network	10 Gbps (DAS2) + 155 Mbps (DAS2-Cyfronet)		
Role	Name	CPU	RAM
Migration source	DAS2 Nikhef	Pentium III 1 GHz	1 GB
Migration destination	DAS2 Leiden	Pentium III 1 GHz	2 GB
visualizations	DAS2 Delft	Pentium III 2GHz	2 GB
	DAS2 Utrecht	Pentium III 1 GHz	1 GB
	DAS2 Vrije	Pentium III 1 GHz	2 GB
RTIexec	Cyf Krakow	Xeon 2.4 GHz	1 GB

ber of visualization-receivers was fixed and equal to 25. In this experiment we show how migration can improve the efficiency of simulation execution when its results are sent online to many users. The bandwidth available for testing was broad (10Gbps), so communication did not play an important role and calculations were the most time–consuming part of the execution. In order to create conditions in which migration would be useful, we increased the load of the Grid site where the simulation was executed (cluster in Amsterdam) by submitting non–related, computationally–intensive jobs. Next, we imitated a *Resource Broker* and migrated the simulation to another site which was not overloaded (cluster in Leiden). The actual migration was conducted by *Migration Service* using *HLA–Speaking Service*. The experiments were performed

Table 3.   Impact of migration on simulation performance within the collaborative environment

Number of simulation's step	Calculations plus sending from sim. to vis. time	Note
1	112	before migration
2	109	before migration
3	100	before migration
4	177	including migration
5	30	after migration
6	45	after migration
7	46	after migration
8	39	after migration

at night in order to avoid interference from other users. Tab. 3 shows duration times of interactive steps with a human in the loop (for the first 8 steps). At each step, the simulation calculates data and sends it to the 25 visualization-receivers modules using HLA. Tab. 3 shows that before migration the average time in a single step was around 107 sec and after migration around 40 sec (which is 2.6 times shorter). The time of the step when migration was performed was 1.6 longer then the average time before migration. The results show that it is better to spend some time on migration to another site, from where the response time is shorter. In our experiment, in each step, the simulation produces 52000 velocity vectors of simulated blood flow in 3D space.

5.   Summary and future work

In this paper we have presented the brief analysis of PSEs supporting the development, execution and/or steering of simulations. For each of these environments, we have analysed the advantages and disadvantages for adaptation of Grid solutions. According to our analysis, there was no solution that allowed to run HLA simulations, including legacy codes, on the Grid in efficient way as it can be achieved by the system we have developed – G-HLAM. In particular, we have shown that migration of badly performing parts of simulations to a better location reduces computation and communication time and effectively improves the overall performance.

The future work will concentrate mainly on using component architectures (like CCA [4], H2O [14], ProActive [20], GCM [10]), as they are a very promising approach due to such features as lightweight environments [2], dynamic behavior, scalability to suit various environmental requirements etc. Applying the advantages of these technologies to distributed interactive simulations will allow not only for technological migration of existing G-HLAM functionality, but also for it's extension to achieve reusability and interoperability of simulation models.

Acknowledgments

The authors would like to thank Piotr Nowakowski for useful remarks. This research is partly funded by the the Polish Foundation for Science (FNP), EU IST Project CoreGRID and the Polish State Committee for Scientific Research SPUB-M grant.

References

[1] G. Allen, W. Benger, T. Dramlitsch, T. Goodale, H. Hege, G. Lanfermann, A. Merzky, T. Radke, E. Seidel, and J. Shalf. Cactus Tools for Grid Applications. *Cluster Computing*, 4(3):179–188, 2001.

[2] R. M. Badia, O. Beckmann, M. Bubak, D. Caromel, V. Getov, S. Isaiadis, V. Lazarov, M. Malawski, S. Panagiotidi, and J. Thiyagalingam. Lightweight grid platform: Design methodology. In S. Gorlatch and M. Danelutt, editors, *Proceedings of the CoreGRID Workshop "Integrated Research in Grid Computing, November 28-30, 2005*, pages 126–134, Pisa, 2005. Technical Report TR-05-22.

[3] B. Baliś, M. Bubak, W. Funika, T. Szepieniec, R. Wismüller, and M. Radecki. Monitoring Grid Applications with Grid-enabled OMIS Monitor. In F. Riviera, M. Bubak, A. Tato, and R. Doallo, editors, *Proc. First European Across Grids Conference*, volume 2970 of *Lecture Notes in Computer Science*, pages 230–239. Springer, Feb. 2003. http://www.icsr.agh.edu.pl/ocmg.

[4] The Common Component Architecture Forum, 2004. http://www.cca-forum.org/.

[5] CORBA project home page. http://www.corba.org/.

[6] CSE project home page. http://www.cwi.nl/projects/cse/cse.html.

[7] I. Foster. What is the Grid? A three checkpoints list. *GridToday Daily News And Information For The Global Grid Community*, 1(6), July 2002.

[8] I. Foster, C. Kesselman, J. Nick, and S. Tuecke. The Physiology of the Grid: An Open Grid Services Architecture for Distributed Systems Integration. *Open Grid Service Infrastructure WG, Global Grid Forum*, June 2002.
http://www.globus.org/alliance/publications/papers.php.

[9] Globus project home page. http://www.globus.org/.

[10] GridComp project home page. http://gridcomp.ercim.org/.

[11] High Level Architecture specification. http://www.sisostds.org/stdsdev/hla/.

[12] K. Rycerz and M. Bubak and M. Malawski and P. M. A. Sloot. A grid service for management of multiple hla federate processes. In Roman Wyrzykowski and Jack Dongarra and Norbert Meyer, Jerzy Wasniewski, editor, *Parallel Processing and Applied Mathematics: 6th International Conference, PPAM 2005, Poznan, Poland, September 11-14, 2005, Revised Selected Papers*, volume 3911 of *Lecture Notes in Computer Science*, pages 699–706, Heidelberg, 2006. Springer-Verlag.

[13] J. Kohl and P. Papadopoulos. Cumulvs User's Guide Computational Steering And Interactive Visualization In Distributed Applications. http://www.virtc.com/Products/.

[14] D. Kurzyniec, T. Wrzosek, D. Drzewiecki, and V. S. Sunderam. Towards Self-Organizing Distributed Computing Frameworks: The H2O Approach. *Parallel Processing Letters*, 13(2):273–290, 2003.

[15] H. Liu, L. Jiang, M. Parashar, and D. Silver. Rule-based Visualization in the Discover Computational Steering Collaboratory. *Future Generation Computer Systems*, 21(1): 53–59, January 2005.

[16] MPICH-G home page. http://www.niu3.edu/mpi.

[17] B. Nichols, D. Buttlar, and J. Farrell. *Pthreads Programming A POSIX Standard for Better Multiprocessing*. O'Reilly, 1996.

[18] Open HLA Project home page. http://sourceforge.net/projects/ohla.

[19] OpenMP project home page. http://www.openmp.org/.

[20] ProActive project homepage. http://www-sop.inria.fr/oasis/ProActive/.

[21] Parallel Virtual Machine home page. http://www.csm.ornl.gov/pvm/pvm_home.html.

[22] RTI Verification Status Board. https://www.dmso.mil/public/transition/hla/rti/statusboard.

[23] K. Rycerz, M. Bubak, M. Malawski, and P. M. A. Sloot. A Framework for HLA-Based Interactive Simulations on the Grid. *SIMULATION*, 81(1):67–76, 2005.

[24] A. Schreiber, T. Metsch, and H.-P. Kersken. A Problem Solving Environment for Multidisciplinary Coupled Simulations in Computational Grids. *Future Generation Computer Systems*, 21(6):942–952, June 2005.

[25] Web Services. http://www.w3.org/2002/ws/.

[26] K. Zając, M. Bubak, M. Malawski, and P. M. A. Sloot. Towards a Grid Management System for HLA-Based Interactive Simulations. In S. J. Turner and S. J. E. Taylor, editor, *Proceedings Seventh IEEE International Symposium on Distributed Simulation and Real Time Applications (DS-RT 2003)*, pages 4–11, Delft, The Netherlands, October 2003. IEEE Computer Society.

[27] Z. Zhao, G. D. van Albada, A. Tirado-Ramos, K. Zając, and P. M. A. Sloot. ISS-Studio: a Prototype for a User-friendly Tool for Designing Interactive Experiments in Problem Solving Environments. In P. M. A. Sloot, D. Abrahamson, A. V. Bogdanov, J. J. Dongarra, A. Y. Zomaya, and Y. E. Gorbachev, editors, *Computational Science - ICCS 2003, Melbourne, Australia and St. Petersburg, Russia, Proceedings Part I*, volume 2657 of *Lecture Notes in Computer Science*, pages 679–688. Springer Verlag, June 2003.

FAULT-TOLERANT DATA SHARING FOR HIGH-LEVEL GRID PROGRAMMING: A HIERARCHICAL STORAGE ARCHITECTURE

Marco Aldinucci, Marco Danelutto
Computer Science Department, University of Pisa
Largo Bruno Pontecorvo 3, 56127 Pisa, Italy
aldinuc@di.unipi.it

Gabriel Antoniu, Mathieu Jan
INRIA Rennes
Campus de Beaulieu, 35042 Rennes, France
gabriel.antoniu@irisa.fr, mathieu.jan@irisa.fr

Abstract   Enabling high-level programming models on grids is today a major challenge. A way to achieve this goal relies on the use of environments able to transparently and automatically provide adequate support for low-level, grid-specific issues (fault-tolerance, scalability, etc.). This paper discusses the above approach when applied to grid data management. As a case study, we propose a 2-tier software architecture that supports transparent, fault-tolerant, grid-level data sharing in the ASSIST programming environment (University of Pisa), based on the JuxMem grid data sharing service (INRIA Rennes).

Keywords: Grid, shared memory, High-level programming, memory hierarchy, P2P.

1.   Introduction

Grid computing has emerged as an attempt to provide users with the illusion of an infinitely powerful, easy-to-use computer, which can solve very complex problems. This very appealing illusion is to be provided (1) by relying on the aggregated power of standard (so, inexpensive), geographically distributed resources owned by multiple organizations; (2) by hiding as much as possible the complexity of the distributed infrastructure to users. However, the current status in most software grid infrastructures available today is rather far away from this vision. When designing programs able to run on such large-scale platforms, programmers often need to explicitly take into account resource heterogeneity, as well as the unreliability of the distributed infrastructure. In this context, the grid community converges towards a consensus about the need for a high-level programming model, whereas most of the grid-specific efforts are moved away from programmers to grid tools and run-time systems. This direction is currently pursued by several research initiatives and programming environments, such as ASSIST [17], eSkel [9], GrADS [14], ProActive [8], Ibis [16], Higher Order Components [11], etc., along the lines of CoreGRID's "invisible grid" approach to next generation grid programming models.

In this work, we explore the applicability of the above approach to data management for high-level grid programming. We consider three main aspects that need to be automatically handled by the data storage infrastructure: data access transparency, data persistence and storage fault-tolerance.

Transparent access to data across the grid.   One of the major goals of the grid concept is to provide an easy access the underlying resources, in a *transparent* way. The user should not need to be aware of the localization of the resources allocated to the application submitted. When applied to the management of the data used and produced by applications, this principle means that the grid infrastructure should automatically handle data storage and data transfer among clients, computing servers and storage servers as needed. However, most projects currently still rely on the *explicit data access model*, where clients have to move data to computing servers. In this context, grid-enabled file transfer tools have been proposed, such as GridFTP [5], DiskRouter [12], etc. In order to achieve a real virtualization of the management of large-scale distributed data, a step forward has been made by proposing a *transparent data access model*, as a part of the concept of *grid data-sharing service*, illustrated by the JUXMEM software experimental platform [6].

Persistent storage of data on the grid.   Since grid applications typically handle large masses of data, data transfer among sites can be costly, in terms of both latency and bandwidth. Therefore, the data-sharing service has to provide persistent data storage. Data produced by one computation can be made available to some other computation through direct access via globally shared data identifiers, by avoiding repeated transfers of large volumes of data between the different components of the grid.

Fault-tolerant storage of grid data. Data storage on the grid must cope with events such as storage resources joining and leaving, or unexpectedly failing. Replication techniques and failure detection mechanisms are thus necessary, in order to enhance data availability despite disconnections and failures. Such mechanisms need to be coupled with checkpoint/restart techniques for application components with data replication mechanisms. This way, in reaction to faults, checkpointed application components could be migrated to available resources and restarted, as long as the application status and the application data remain available thanks to fault-tolerant storage.

While the above properties are desirable in general for grid data sharing, in this paper we restrict our discussion to the more specific case of applications based on the ASSIST [3] programming environment, developed at the University of Pisa. ASSIST provides a programming model that enables transparent data sharing among distributed execution entities. However, its dedicated storage component (called ad-HOC [4]) does not enforce data persistence and is not tolerant to node failures. Such features are exhibited by the JUXMEM [6] grid data-sharing service developed at INRIA Rennes, which enables transparent access to grid-scale storage, based on P2P techniques. The goal of this paper is to study how ASSIST and JUXMEM could be integrated, in order to better support a high-level grid programming approach.

2. Analysis: using JUXMEM to enable grid-level, fault-tolerant storage in ASSIST

This section describes ASSIST's main features, then briefly introduces the data sharing facilities available with ad-HOC and JUXMEM (which exhibit complementary features); it finally proposes an integrated architecture which takes advantage of this complementarity.

2.1 Data sharing in ASSIST

The ASSIST programming model. ASSIST applications are described by means of a coordination language, which can express arbitrary graphs of software *modules*, interconnected by typed streams of data. Modules can be either sequential or parallel. A sequential module wraps a sequential function. A parallel module *(parmod)* can be used to describe the parallel execution of a number of sequential activities that run as *Virtual Processes* (VPs) on items coming from input streams. Each stream realizes a one-way, one-to-many asynchronous channel between sequential or parallel modules. VPs can be organized according to programmer-defined topologies (array, etc.). The AS-SIST compiler implements VPs according to the underlying middleware. It selects an appropriate granularity by mapping a subset of a *parmod*'s VPs to the basic execution entity, e.g. a POSIX process/thread, a Globus Grid Service, or a Web Service. The full support for the forthcoming CoreGRID Grid Component Model (GCM) is currently under investigation [10, 2].

Data sharing in ASSIST.   The ASSIST programming model enables data sharing both within VPs of the same module and between different modules by means of two different methods, respectively:

Attributes, which are global, typed variables of the module. Attributes are owned either by the module itself or by VPs; in particular arrays ownership can be partitioned among VPs according to user-defined rules.

References, which are global pointers in a shared memory space that is logically external to all application modules, thus can be accessed across different modules. ASSIST provides the programmer with an API to allocate, read, and write data structures in the shared space.

Note that, in both cases, ASSIST does not implement a built-in DSM to enable memory sharing; it rather provides hooks to attach ASSIST run-time support to an external DSM. This allows to test different solutions for data sharing, since the DSM can be replaced with almost no impact on the core code of the compiler and of its run-time support. Currently, ASSIST comes with a DSM built on top of a set of cooperating ad-HOC memory servers [4].

These variables adhere to the *transparent data access model*: programmers should neither care about data placement nor data splitting and distribution. These tasks are transparently and efficiently carried out by ad-HOC. However, in order to enforce fault-tolerance (and irrespectively of the checkpointing technique), ASSIST run-time needs to rely on permanent and robust data storage.

2.2   Existing building blocks: ad-HOC and JuxMem

Cluster-level sharing: ad-HOC.   ad-HOC (Adaptive Distributed Herd of Object Caches), is a distributed *object* repository [4] developed at University of Pisa. It provides the programming environment designer with building blocks to set up client-server and service-oriented infrastructures for data storage management. Clients may access data in servers through different protocols, which are implemented on client-side within a *proxy* library.

A set of cooperating ad-HOC servers implements a permanent storage facility, i.e. a repository for arbitrary length, contiguous segments of data, namely *objects* since each data chuck is wrapped and stored and in an object homed in one of the servers [4]. Objects can be grouped in ordered *collections* of objects, which can be spread across different servers. Both objects and their collections are identified by *keys* with fixed length. In particular, the key of a collection specifies to which *spread-group* the collection belongs. Such a group specifies how adjacent objects in the collection are mapped across the set of servers. Both classes of shared objects described in the previous section (attributes and references) are implemented in ASSIST via ad-HOC object collections and can thus be stored in a distributed way. The ad-HOC API enables to get/put/remove an object, and to create/destroy a key for a collection of objects. Each ad-HOC manages an *object storage* area for server home objects and a write-back *cache* for objects with a remote home. Basic ad-HOC operations do not natively ensure data coherence of cached objects. Nevertheless, server operations can be extended via the special operation execute that enables application proxies to put a serialized C++ object[1] in a server and invoke its *run* method to issue a consistent access (e.g. lock/unlock, coherent put, etc).

The extremely simple ad-HOC API is mainly aimed to implementation efficiency, which relies on non-blocking I/O. On each port, an ad-HOC can efficiently serve many clients, each of which supports thousands of concurrent connections while squeezing a close to ideal bandwidth even for fine-grained data accesses [4]. A set of ad-HOCs can efficiently cooperate across multi-tier networks and clusters with private address ranges, even when they are protected by firewalls. However, ad-HOC does not implement any form of fault-tolerance or automatic data replication: in the case a server permanently leaves the community implementing the data storage, some of the stored data will be lost. This problem is particularly severe if data structures are spread across all servers, since losing a single server may induce the corruption of the whole dataset.

Grid-level sharing: JuxMem. The JUXMEM [6] grid *data sharing service* developed at INRIA Rennes transparently manages data localization and persistence in dynamic, large-scale, distributed environments. The *data sharing service* concept is based on a hybrid approach inspired by Distributed Shared Memory (DSM) systems (for transparent and consistent data sharing) and peer-to-peer (P2P) systems (for scalability and volatility tolerance). The data sharing service can also transparently replicate data to ensure its persistence in case of failures. The consistency of the various replicas is then implemented through adequate fault-tolerant consistency protocols [7]. This approach will serve as a basis to the architecture proposed in this paper.

The JUXMEM API provides the users with classical functions for allocating (juxmem_malloc) and mapping/unmapping memory blocks (juxmem_mmap, etc.) When allocating a memory block, the client can choose to replicate data to enhance fault-tolerance, and then has to specify: (1) on how many clusters the data should be replicated; (2) on how many providers in each cluster the

---

[1]Object data is serialized at run-time and send to the server, while code must be provided (in advance) to the server as dynamically linkable library.

data should be replicated; (3) the consistency protocol that should be used to manage this data. This results into the instantiation of a set of data replicas (associated to a group of nodes), called *data group*. The allocation operation returns a global data ID. This ID can be used by other nodes in order to identify existing data. It is JUXMEM's responsibility to localize the data and perform the necessary data transfers based on this ID. This is how JUXMEM provides a transparent access to data. To obtain read and/or write access on a data, a process that uses JUXMEM should acquire the lock associated to the data through either juxmem_acquire or juxmem_acquire_read. This permits to apply consistency guarantees according to the consistency protocol specified by the user at the allocation time of the data. Note that juxmem_acquire_read allows multiple readers to simultaneously access the same data.

The general architecture of JUXMEM mirrors a federation of distributed clusters and is therefore *hierarchical*. The goal is to accurately map the physical network topology, in order to efficiently use the underlying high performance networks available on grid infrastructures. Consequently, the architecture of JUXMEM relies on node sets to express the hierarchical nature of the targeted testbed. They are called *cluster groups* and correspond to physical clusters. These groups are included in a wider group, the *juxmem group*, which gathers all the nodes running the data-sharing service. Any cluster group consists of *provider* nodes which supply memory for data storage. Any node may use the service to allocate, read or write data as *clients*, in a peer-to-peer approach. This architecture has been implemented using the JXTA [1] generic P2P platform.

Table 1.   Properties for cluster-level and grid-level sharing.

	Cluster sharing (ad-HOC)	Grid sharing (JuxMem)
Throughput	High	Medium/High
Latency	Low	High
Fault-tolerance	No	Yes
Protocols for data consistency	No	Yes

ad-HOC and JuxMem: a quick comparison at hand.   Due to different design goals, ad-HOC distributed storage server and of the JUXMEM data-sharing service exhibit different features (as summarized in Table 1).

ad-HOC provides transparent and permanent access to distributed data. It enables the distribution and the parallel access to collections of objects (e.g. arrays). It is robust w.r.t. node additions and removal, which should be driven by a proper node agreement protocol to guarantee data safety. It does not checkpoint/replicate data, thus is not fault-tolerant. Data accesses exhibit low

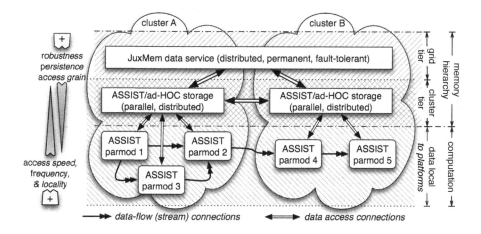

Figure 1. Target architecture illustrating the interaction of ad-HOC and JuxMem.

latency, high-bandwidth, high-concurrency and scalability. It is mainly targeted to *cluster-level* sharing. It is developed in C++.

JUXMEM provides transparent and permanent access to distributed data. It is fully fault-tolerant w.r.t. node additions and fail-stop by means of data consistent replication. Data accesses exhibit a higher latency, medium to high-bandwidth, and scalability. It relies on the JXTA generic P2P framework. It is targeted to *grid-level* sharing. It is developed in C and Java.

3. Proposal: an integrated 2-tier architecture

Memory hierarchy is an effective way to enhance data management efficiency while respecting data access transparency. We propose a 2-tier memory hierarchy which trades off storage performance vs. robustness: it enables ASSIST modules to rely on a fault-tolerant grid storage while still exploiting low-latency/high-bandwidth data accesses, which are typical of a fast, cluster-level DSM. The big picture is sketched in Fig. 1: the two levels of hierarchy are called *grid tier* and *cluster tier*. The hierarchy is connected to an additional tier where computation is figured out (at the bottom on the figure). This third level (represented at the bottom) also includes data storage that is local to platforms[2]. The top two tiers of the memory hierarchy are specified as follows:

The grid tier enables data sharing across multiple *parmods* running on *different* clusters. It is implemented via JUXMEM. Accesses to data stored

---

[2]Register file level in classic memory hierarchies.

in JUXMEM are assumed to be *less frequent, coarse-grained, with less performance constraints.*

The cluster tier enables data sharing among multiple parallel codes (VPs, *parmods*) within a single cluster. It is implemented via an ad-HOC-based storage component. Accesses to data stored in ad-HOC are assumed to be *frequent, fine-grained, with high-performance constraints.*

In the following, we define why and when the data stored at the cluster level should be copied/stored at the grid level and vice-versa. The answers come directly from the analysis of hierarchy goals.

Sharing across multiple clusters.   A natural interaction between the two levels of the hierarchy will take place whenever data produced and stored on a cluster (at the ad-HOC level) has to be made available on another cluster (multi-site deployment). At the programming level this may be triggered by passing a reference across the clusters via streams. Notice that this functionality can also be implemented at ad-HOC level by "horizontally" connecting ad-HOC storage components of different clusters. However, the hierarchical solution has some advantages: (1) data can be shared also among different applications thanks to persistence of grid level; (2) ASSIST does not need any more to handle the co-allocation of resources (possibly via job schedulers) for all *parmods* distributed on different clusters, since JUXMEM can serve as temporary storage; (3) data shared at this level can be considered safe w.r.t. node and networks faults (as this aspect is handled by the JUXMEM-based grid-level).

The first point allows the user to use command scripts implementing a functionality similar to UNIX pipes in grid distributed fashion, while sharing data among the different processes through JUXMEM. The second point addresses a very hot topic in grid middleware design: multi-site co-allocation. Let us suppose as an example that modules mapped on cluster A (see Fig. 1) start well before modules on cluster B. Data coming on stream from parmod 2 can be transiently buffered on grid storage up to the moment parmod 4 starts. This scenario can be extended to all cases in which data dependencies among clusters can be described by a Direct Acyclic Graph (co-allocation is not logically needed). The third point is discussed in details in the next paragraph.

Fault tolerant data storage/checkpointing.   Since the ad-HOC provides efficient access latency, it can be used as a cache for intra-cluster data sharing. Since it is not fault-tolerant, the ad-HOC can periodically save application data to JUXMEM. This feature could also be used for application checkpointing in general, as the computation status can be saved together with the data. Checkpointing is driven by ASSIST run-time support, which stores checkpoint information on the cluster tier, and then triggers a flush of "dirty" objects to the grid tier. Basically the cluster tier is used as a write-back cache. In the same way, this information could also be used to migrate *parmods* from one cluster to another. In such a case, ad-HOC data can be saved to JUXMEM on the initial cluster and then read from JUXMEM after migration on the second cluster.

Locality. The use of a memory hierarchy adequately supports clustered locality. Grids are generally structured as federations of clusters, where each cluster is pretty homogeneous and exhibits high-bandwidth/low-latency connectivity due to the spatial proximity and to the reduced security constraints, but also to the use of high-performance System Area Networks, such as Myrinet or Infiniband. High-level parallel languages and their run-time environments aim at enhancing clustered locality (1) by providing programmers with language paradigms (constructs, skeletons, design patters, etc.) leading to known and regular interaction patterns among concurrent activities; (2) by statically and/or dynamically mapping/enforcing clustered locality of a groups of activities demanding frequent interactions. A few examples are: the iterated halo-swap paradigm and the block data distribution [9], the Divide&Conquer paradigm supported by dynamical load balance based on hierarchical work-stealing [15]. Component technology and related design methodologies further enforce clustered locality by encouraging application designer to aggregate related activities within a (possibly compound) component. As result, most of the shared memory accesses have a limited scope in terms of accessing entities, and those entities are preferably mapped and deployed on the same cluster, thereby improving the local-to-remote access ratio.

4.   ASSIST and fault-tolerance: a sample scenario

The simplest scenario showing how to exploit the benefits of the integrated 2-tier architecture leverages the fault tolerant data storage/checkpointing features described above. In this scenario, parmods are considered in insulation. The goal is to protect them against a site fail-stop (due either to node crashes or to connectivity failures). The nature of the parmod construct suggests that there exist a quite strong relationship among the parallel activities within it, whereas activities in different parmods definitely exhibit a weaker relationship. A parmod is therefore usually deployed within a single site. The parmod status, which is normally stored in the ad-HOC tier, can periodically be snapshotted and saved into the JUXMEM tier. As we shall see in the next section, this can be done by leveraging already existing mechanisms that enforce the generation of a coherent snapshot of the status. The snapshot can be enriched with all the information needed to restart (in some other site) the parmod from the snapshot that can retrieved from a JUXMEM-managed backup copy living on a still alive site. Other parmods can detect the site crash through a broken stream event; among those, a leader elected via JUXMEM tier support, can restart a new copy of the parmod by instanciating the snapshotted status. If

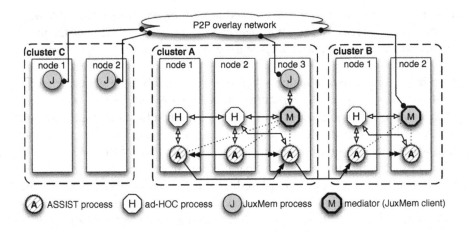

Figure 2.   Implementation of proposed architecture using ad-HOC and JUXMEM (the application is sketched in Fig. 1). Dashed lines represent synchronizations inducing mediator actions.

necessary, the parmods directly connected with the restored one should update their status before proceeding.

5.   Design and Implementation

A prototypal implementation has recently been completed and is currently being tested. It will mainly be used to analyze the hierarchy's efficiency and limitations in order to refine the design phase. The current implementation relies on a set of external *mediator* processes that are started with ad-HOC servers by the ASSIST launcher. The mediator can take into account remote commands (through a TCP port), which trigger data copying from the cluster tier to the grid tier and vice-versa. Available commands include copying a set of ad-HOC objects (which can be spread across the nodes of the distributed ad-HOC server) to new or to existing JUXMEM memory areas, and vice-versa. In both cases, the data exchanged between the two tiers flow through the mediator. In one case, it reads a series of data objects from ad-HOC, collapses them in a single data chunk, and writes it into JUXMEM; in the other case, it fetches a data chunk from JUXMEM, splits and spreads it to ad-HOC servers of the cluster. Such an interaction is represented in Fig. 5, where J processes act as JUXMEM storage providers and M processes (representing the mediators) act as JUXMEM clients. Mediators and providers can be hosted on the same node, on different nodes in the same cluster or on different clusters.

These tasks leverage existing features of the ASSIST compiler. Since the compiler can produce dynamically adaptable code, it already identifies within *parmod* so-called *reconf-safe* points and instruments it with the required agreement protocols for coordinated checkpointing. In these points, the compiler can ensure a coherent and known state of application processes and the shared memory. This information can be dumped, as it can serve to restart the whole application or *a proper subset* of it from last *reconf-safe* point. This technique has been successfully used to enable dynamic migration of VPs and *parmods* [10].

Fault-tolerant storage. The proposed architecture can transparently be used to provide fault-tolerant storage for ASSIST by using the primary-backup approach, where the cluster tier behaves as a primary replica and the grid tier as backup. In particular, *attributes* can be safely stored in *reconf-safe* points. In these points ASSIST run-time triggers an update of backup copies via the mediator process. A similar technique is used for *references*. However since these are managed directly by programmers in the user code, the triggering is achieved by extending the API with a `safe_write` operation (alternatively, the `write` operation can be transparently turned into a `safe_write` operation).

Checkpoint/rollback. A fault-tolerant storage is necessary but not sufficient to make ASSIST fault-tolerant. However, a *parmod* can easily be made fault-tolerant by triggering a checkpoint of its data *and status* into JUXMEM. Starting from one of these checkpoints, a whole *parmod* can be rolled back by using already existing primitives for dynamic adaptation (see [10] for details).

Ensuring fault-tolerance of a complete ASSIST application is slightly more complex. This requires to equally taking into account the global status of streams established among *parmods*. Classic techniques based on message logging could than be used, while relying on the proposed memory hierarchy as a stable storage. This point is under investigation.

5.1 Preliminary Experiments

The main goal of preliminary experiments conducted on the 2-tier architecture aims to assess and quantify the behaviour of the two tiers, independently considered, on the same running environment. At this end we run a set of read/write benchmarks between the mediator and the two tiers on a cluster composed of Intel Xeon5150@2.66GHz 8GBytes RAM nodes wired via a GigaEthernet. Benchmarks consist in the writing or reading of 1000 objects of a given size. Tested configurations and results of write throughput benchmark are shown in Fig. 3 for the ad-HOC tier, and Fig. 4 for the JUXMEM tier. Each tier is tested for its own peculiar features, i.e. objects distribution onto a set of parallel servers for ad-HOC; and objects replication onto a set of memory providers for JUXMEM. Both sets of tests include the extreme case of a single server (no distribution, no replication) where the two tiers behave identically. Tests show that the two tiers achieve a very good throughput.

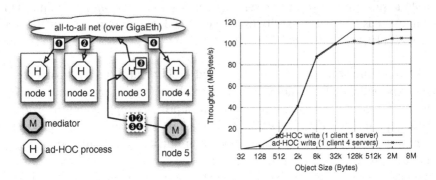

Figure 3.   Preliminary results: the tested architecture and the mediator throughput on ad-HOC side. In the first experiment objects are stored on a single ad-HOC server, in the second objects are distributed onto 4 ad-HOC servers.

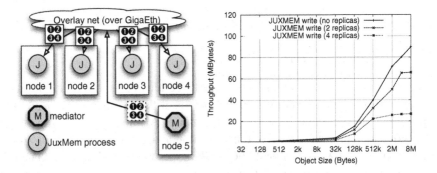

Figure 4.   Preliminary results: the tested architecture and the mediator throughput on JUXMEM side. In the first experiment objects are stored on a single JUXMEM provider, in the second and the third objects are replicated across 2 and 4 JUXMEM providers, respectively.

As mentioned above, the ad-HOC does not include any protocol to manage consistent data replication, thus it implements a lighter data access protocol with respect to JUXMEM. This enables ad-HOC to achieve the same throughput of JUXMEM for a smaller object size. Read throughput benchmarks, which are not reported in the paper, gives almost identical figures. Notably, the ad-HOC exploits a slightly better throughput when objects are not distributed (single server case). This is due to the single connection between the mediator and the ad-HOC servers. The bottleneck can be removed by connecting the mediator with more than one ad-HOC server [4].

Differently from ad-HOC, JUXMEM can transparently and consistently manage object replication: this enables the definition of a permanent, fault-tolerant tier. Obviously, consistent data replication has a cost. As shown in Fig. 4, this cost linearly depends from the number of replicas in the case of write operation. On the contrary, read operations exhibit a throughput similar to write with no replicas independently of the number of replicas.

Overall, the preliminary experiments confirm the complementarity of the two tiers, which deliver their optimal data throughput at different object size. Experimental results enable to reason about the size increase and frequency reduction the mediator should perform between the two tiers. These values do not depends only from platforms and networks speed, but also from distribution and replication degree chosen for the two tiers, respectively.

6. Conclusion

This paper addresses the problem of how to support of high-level grid programming by means of a software infrastructure that automatically and transparently handles low-level, grid-specific issues, such as multi-site resource distribution, fault-tolerance, etc. It proposes a hierarchical grid data storage architecture whose goal is to provide the ASSIST grid programming environment with grid-scale, fault-tolerant data-sharing facilities, as provided by the JUXMEM grid data-sharing service. This work is a specific integration effort between existing researches carried out by two partners within the Institute on Programming Model (WP3) of the CoreGRID NoE. We mainly focus on architecture design, however a prototypal implementation has recently been completed and preliminary experiments are under way. The work in progress concerns the assessment of the performance of memory accesses between the two tiers of the hierarchy.

Long-term aims. Many approaches to data management on grid aim to optimize the access to very large, quite localized, mostly read-only scientific data [13]. However, in many real applications, data is inherently distributed across application components. We believe that a mature programming model for the grid should provide designers with an abstract view of the data, and a high-level API to access it. Due to the hierarchical nature of typical grid platforms, any implementation of data management system will benefit from a clear understanding of qualitative and quantitative aspects governing a distributed memory hierarchy on the grid. These aspects may be used to enhance and automatize the distributed management of data in development tools for the grid. The proposed architecture appears flexible enough to investigate the benefits and overheads of hierarchical data management, and the extent to which data can be transparently moved (horizontally and vertically) across the tiers of the hierarchy.

Acknowledgments.   We are grateful to Massimo Torquati and Daniele Buono who contributed to software development and experimentation. This work has been partially supported by the FP6 Network of Excellence Core-GRID funded by the European Commission (Contract IST-2002-004265), and by the Region of Brittany (France).

References

[1] The JXTA (juxtapose) project. http://www.jxta.org.

[2] M. Aldinucci, C. Bertolli, S. Campa, M. Coppola, M. Vanneschi, L. Veraldi, and C. Zoccolo. Self-configuring and self-optimizing grid components in the GCM model and their ASSIST implementation. In *Proc of. HPC-GECO/Compframe (held in conjunction with HPDC-15)*, IEEE, pages 45–52, Paris, France, June 2006.

[3] M. Aldinucci, M. Coppola, M. Danelutto, M. Vanneschi, and C. Zoccolo. ASSIST as a research framework for high-performance grid programming environments. In J. C. Cunha and O. F. Rana, editors, *Grid Computing: Software environments and Tools*, chapter 10, pages 230–256. Springer, Jan. 2006.

[4] M. Aldinucci and M. Torquati. Accelerating apache farms through ad-HOC distributed scalable object repository. In M. Danelutto, M. Vanneschi, and D. Laforenza, editors, *Proc. of 10th Intl. Euro-Par 2004 Parallel Processing*, volume 3149 of *LNCS*, pages 596–605. Springer, Aug. 2004.

[5] B. Allcock, J. Bester, J. Bresnahan, A. L. Chervenak, C. Kesselman, S. Meder, V. Nefedova, D. Quesnel, S. Tuecke, and I. Foster. Secure, Efficient Data Transport and Replica Management for High-Performance Data-Intensive Computing. In *Proc. of the 18th IEEE Symposium on Mass Storage Systems (MSS 2001), Large Scale Storage in the Web*, page 13, Washington, DC, USA, 2001. IEEE Computer Society.

[6] G. Antoniu, L. Bougé, and M. Jan. JuxMem: An adaptive supportive platform for data sharing on the grid. *Scalable Computing: Practice and Experience*, 6(3):45–55, Sept. 2005.

[7] G. Antoniu, J.-F. Deverge, and S. Monnet. How to bring together fault tolerance and data consistency to enable grid data sharing. *Concurrency and Computation: Practice and Experience*, 2006. To appear.

[8] F. Baude, D. Caromel, and M. Morel. On hierarchical, parallel and distributed components for grid programming. In V. Getov and T. Kielmann, editors, *Proc. of the Intl. Workshop on Component Models and Systems for Grid Applications*, CoreGRID series, pages 97–108, Saint-Malo, France, Jan. 2005. Springer Verlag.

[9] M. Cole. Bringing skeletons out of the closet: A pragmatic manifesto for skeletal parallel programming. *Parallel Computing*, 30(3):389–406, 2004.

[10] CoreGRID NoE deliverable series, Institute on Programming Model. *Deliverable D.PM.02 – Proposals for a Grid Component Model*, Nov. 2005.

[11] J. Dünnweber and S. Gorlatch. HOC-SA: A grid service architecture for higher-order components. In *IEEE International Conference on Services Computing, Shanghai, China*, pages 288–294. IEEE Computer Society Press, Sept. 2004.

[12] G. Kola and M. Livny. Diskrouter: A Flexible Infrastructure for High Performance Large Scale Data Transfers. Technical Report CS-TR-2003-1484, University of Wisconsin-Madison Computer Sciences Department, Madison, WI, USA, 2003.

[13] E. Laure, H. Stockinger, and K. Stockinger. Performance engineering in data Grids. *Concurrency & Computation: Practice & Experience*, 17(2–4):171–191, 2005.

[14] S. Vadhiyar and J. Dongarra. Self adaptability in grid computing. *Concurrency & Computation: Practice & Experience*, 17(2–4):235–257, 2005.

[15] R. V. van Nieuwpoort, T. Kielmann, and H. E. Bal. Efficient load balancing for wide-area divide-and-conquer applications. In *PPoPP '01: Proc. of the 8th ACM SIGPLAN symposium on Principles and practices of parallel programming*, pages 34–43, New York, NY, USA, 2001. ACM Press.

[16] R. V. van Nieuwpoort, J. Maassen, G. Wrzesinska, R. Hofman, C. Jacobs, T. Kielmann, and H. E. Bal. Ibis: a flexible and efficient Java-based grid programming environment. *Concurrency & Computation: Practice & Experience*, 17(7-8):1079–1107, 2005.

[17] M. Vanneschi. The programming model of ASSIST, an environment for parallel and distributed portable applications. *Parallel Computing*, 28(12):1709–1732, Dec. 2002.

PAL: EXPLOITING JAVA ANNOTATIONS FOR PARALLELISM*

Marco Danelutto*, Marcelo Pasin*,•, Marco Vanneschi*
*Dept. Computer Science – Univ. of Pisa – Italy & CoreGRID Programming Model Institute
• EIA/FR – Fribourg – Switzerland
marcod@di.unipi.it, marcelopasin@gmail.com, vannesch@di.unipi.it

Patrizio Dazzi°,*, Domenico Laforenza*, Luigi Presti°
°IMT (Lucca Institute for Advanced Studies) – Lucca – Italy
*ISTI/CNR – Pisa – Italy & CoreGRID Programming Model Institute
patrizio.dazzi@isti.cnr.it, domenico.laforenza@isti.cnr.it, luigi.presti@imtlucca.it

Abstract   We discuss how Java annotations can be used to provide the meta information needed to automatically transform plain Java programs into suitable parallel code that can be run on workstation clusters, networks and grids. Programmers are only required to decorate the methods that will eventually be executed in parallel with standard Java 1.5 annotations. Then these annotations are automatically processed and parallel byte code is derived. When the annotated program is started, it automatically retrieves the information about the executing platform and evaluates the information specified inside the annotations to transform the byte-code into a semantically equivalent multithreaded or multitask version, depending on the target architecture features. The results returned by the annotated methods, when invoked, are futures with a wait-by-necessity semantics.

A PAL (*Parallel Abstraction Layer*) prototype exploiting the annotation based parallelizing approach has been implemented in Java. PAL targets JJPF, an existing, skeleton based, JAVA/JINI programming environment, as Parallel Framework. The experiments made with the prototype are encouraging: the design of parallel applications has been greatly simplified and the performances obtained are the same of an application directly written in JJPF.

Keywords: Asynchronous method invocation, wait-by-necessity, annotations, skeletons, grids.

---

*This work has been partially supported by Italian national FIRB project no. RBNE01KNFP GRID.it and by the FP6 Network of Excellence CoreGRID funded by the European Commission (Contract IST-2002-004265).

1.   Introduction

Grid computing [18] enables the use a (very) large number of networked processing resources equipped with suitable middleware to provide powerful platforms that can be used to support high performance computing, pervasive (global, ubiquitous) computing as well as to provide advanced "knowledge utility" environments [17]. Developing parallel/distributed applications targeting the grid is in general more complex than developing similar applications for traditional parallel architectures and workstation clusters. Besides being in charge of the whole parallel application structure as well as of all the relative communication, synchronization, mapping and scheduling structure, the programmer must also take into account that grid processing resources are often heterogeneous and that the availability of both the computing and the interconnection resources may vary in time. As the programmers usually write applications directly interacting with the middleware, the whole process is cumbersome and error prone. In the last years, several efforts have been spent to face this problem, and several approaches have been conceived to design high-level programming languages/environments that can automate most of the tasks required to implement working and efficient grid applications. Some approaches aim at providing programmers with different programming environments implementing as much as possible the "invisible grid" concept advocated by the EC Next Generation Grid Expert Group [22, 17]. As an example the Grid Component Model (*GCM*) currently being developed within the CoreGRID Institute on Programming model [10, 25] will eventually provide the grid programmers a component based programming model where all the details and issues related to the usage of the grid as the target architecture will be dealt with in the compiler and run time tools. Other approaches offer a lower abstraction level but allow more programming freedom and guarantee a higher level of personalization. In other words, programmers can customize their applications and deal with some aspects related to the parallelism as, for example, parallelism degree and the parallel program structure (farm, pipeline, ...). The approaches belonging to this category force the programmer to structure the parallel application he wants to implement adequately. Typically, such approaches allow the application "business logic" to be separated from the activities required to coordinate and to synchronize parallel processes [15, 3]. On the other side, several environments have been proposed to use more classical, low level programming paradigms on the grid. Several implementation of MPI [2] have been ported on top of different grid middleware [20] as well as several implementations of different kinds of RPC have been designed [26, 19, 27]. However, all these approaches, while leaving the programmer a higher freedom of structuring the parallel applications in an arbitrary way, require the programmers explicitly deal with all the awkward details mentioned above.

In this work, we introduce Parallel Abstraction Layer (PAL) as a bridge between a currently popular programming model and the typical current parallel computer architectures, such as clusters and the grid. To avoid the problems typically present in a fully automated parallel approach [13, 4], PAL leaves to programmer the responsibility to choose which parts of code have to be computed in parallel through the insertion of non-functional requirements in the source program code. Using the information provided by programmers PAL transforms the program code into a parallel one which structure depends on the specified non-functional requirements.

A prototype of PAL has been implemented using Java. It allows to autonomically transforming the byte-code of an annotated method in a multithreaded byte-code version, suitable for multiprocessor computers and in a parallel byte-code version using the JJPF (a Java/Jini Parallel Framework, [11]) parallel programming environment, targeting both clusters/networks of workstations and grids. The initial tests have shown for both versions encouraging results.

2. Parallel Abstraction Layer (PAL)

We fully subscribe the opinion "*...people know the application domain and can better decompose the problem, compilers can better manage data dependence and synchronization*" [21]. Our approach to parallel grid programming relies on programmer knowledge to "structure" the parallel schema of application and then to the compiler/run time tool ability to efficiently implement the parallel schema conceived by the programmer. The general idea is outlined in Figure 1.

This is much in the sense of what's being advocated in the algorithmic skeletons approach [9]. Actually, here we propose a general-purpose mechanism that does not require complex application structuring by the programmer. In

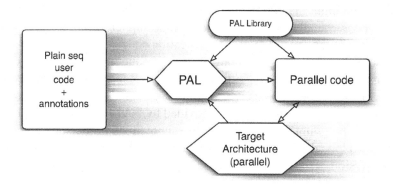

Figure 1. PAL approach overview.

```
public class Mandelbrot{
    public void paint(GraphicsContext gcont) {
        // computing image size
        ...
        Vector<PFFuture<Vector<Vector<Integer>>>> man =
            new Vector<PFFuture<Vector<Vector<Integer>>>>(numOfLines);

        for(int i=0;i<numOfLines;i++)
            man.add(createLines(...);
        ...
    }

    @Parallel(parDegree=16)
    public PFFuture<Vector<Vector<Integer>>> createLines (params ...){

        Vector<Vector<Integer>> v = new Vector<Vector<Integer>>();

        // compute points ...
        for (int i = 0; i<cls; i++) {
            ...
            v.add(point);
        }
        return new PFFuture<Vector<Vector<Integer>>>(v);
    }
}

public class Main {
    ...
    public static void main(String[] args) {
        Class [] toBeTransformed = new Class[2];
        toBeTransformed[0] = Main.class;
        toBeTransformed[1] = Mandelbrot.class;
        PAL.transform(toBeTransformed,args);
        Mandelbrot mBrot = new Mandelbrot();
        BufferedImage bi = new BufferedImage(2400,1600,TYPE_INT_BGR);
        mBrot.paint(GraphicsEnvironment.getLocalGraphicsEnvironment().createGraphics(bi));

    }
}
```

Figure 2.   Sample code using PAL.

fact the programmer is only required to insert, in the source code, some hints that will be eventually exploited in the runtime support to implement efficient parallel/distributed execution of the application code.

These hints may consist of non-functional requirements. As an example, performance contracts (SLA, Efficiency, Price, Reliability, Resource constraints, Software, tools, standards, parallelism degree etc.) can be specified through the annotation mechanisms provided by both Java and .NET [1].

Once the programmer has inserted the annotations in the source code, the run time exploits the information conveyed in the annotations to implement a parallel version of the program running on top of the target parallel/distributed architecture.

The programmers are required to give some kind of "parallel structure" to the code directly at the source code level, as it happens in the algorithmic skeleton case. However, the approach discussed in this work presents at least three additional advantages.

- First, annotations can be ignored and the semantics of the original sequential code is preserved. This means that the programmer application code can be run through a classical compiler/interpreter suite and debugged using normal debugging tools.

- Second, annotations are processed at load time, typically exploiting reflection properties of the hosting language. As a consequence, while handling annotations, a bunch of knowledge can be exploited which is not available at compile time (kind of machines at hand, kind of interconnection network, etc.) and this can lead to more efficient parallel implementations of the user application.

- Third, the knowledge concerning the kind of target architecture can be exploited leading to radically diverse implementation of the very same user code. As an example, if the run time can figure out that the target architecture where the program is running happens to be a grid, it can transform the code in such a way very coarse grain parallelism is exploited. On the other hand, in case the run time figures out that user asked to execute the code on a SMP target, a more efficient, possibly finer grain, multithreaded version of the code can be produced as the result of the annotation handling.

In order to experiment the feasibility of the proposed approach, we considered the languages that natively support code annotations. Both Java and .NET frameworks provide an annotation mechanism. They also provide an intermediate language (IL) [32], portable among different computer architecture (compile once – run everywhere), and holding some information typically only available at source code level (e.g. code annotations) that can be used in the runtime for optimization purposes.

The optimization we propose consists in the automatic restructuring of the application in order to exploit the application parallelism with respect to programmer's annotations (non-functional application requirements). The transformation process is done at load time, that is at the time we have all the information we need to optimize the restructuring process with respect to the available parallel tools and underlying resources. The code transformation works at IL level thus it does not need that the application source code is sent on target architecture. Furthermore, IL transformation introduces in general fewer overheads than the source code transformations followed by re-compilation.

More in detail, we designed a *Parallel Abstraction Layer* (PAL) filling the gap between the traditional and the parallel programming metaphor. PAL is a generative [24] metaprogramming engine, which gathers, at load time, all information on available parallel tools and computational resources. Then, it analyzes the IL code looking for programmer annotations (non-functional requirements) directly transforms the sequential IL code to the parallel code, satisfying in the meanwhile the performance contracts supplied by the programmers through the annotations in the source code. The structure of the new IL code depends on the selected parallel framework and on the presence and/or value of some non-functional requirements.

PAL exploits the parallelism by asynchronously executing parts of the original code. The parts to be executed asynchronously are individuated by the user annotations. In particular, we used Java and therefore the more natural choice was to individuate method calls as the parts to be asynchronously executed. PAL translates the IL codes of the "parallel" part by structuring them as needed by the parallel tools/libraries available on the target architecture. Asynchronous execution of method code is based on the concept of *future* [7–8]. When a method is called asynchronously it immediately returns a future, that is a stub "empty" object. The caller can then go on with its own computations and use the future object just when the method call return value is actually needed. If in the meanwhile the return value has already been computed, the call to reify the future succeeds immediately, otherwise it blocks until the actual return value is computed and then returns it.

PAL programmers must simply put a `@Parallel` annotation (possibly enriched with some other non-functional requirements, such as the required parallelism degree, as an example) on the line right before method declaration to mark that method as a candidate for asynchronous execution. This allows keeping applications similar to normal sequential applications, actually. Programmers may simply run the application through standard Java tools to verify it is functionally correct. The PAL approach also avoids the proliferation of source files and classes, as it works transforming IL code, but raises several problems related to data sharing management. As an example, methods annotated with a `@Parallel` cannot access class fields: they may only access their own parameters and the local method variables. This is due to the impossibility to intercept all the accesses to the class fields, actually. Then PAL autonomically performs at load time activities aimed at achieving the asynchronous and parallel execution of the PAL-annotated methods and at managing any consistency related problems, without any further programmer intervention.

3.   A PAL prototype

We have implemented a PAL prototype in Java 1.5, as Java provides a manageable intermediate language (Java byte-code [31]) and natively supports code annotations, since version 1.5. Furthermore, it owns all the properties needed by our approach (type safety, security, etc.). The prototype works taking the program byte-code as input and transforming it in a parallel or multithreaded byte-code (see Fig. 2). In order to do this it uses ASM [5]: a Java byte-code manipulation framework.

The current prototype accepts only one kind of attribute to the @Parallel annotation: a parDegree denoting the number of processing elements to be used for the method execution. PAL uses such information to make a choice between the multithreaded and distributed version. This choice is driven by the number of processors/cores available on the host machine: if the machine owns a sufficient number of processors the annotated byte-code directly compiled from user code is transformed in a semantically equivalent multithreaded version. Otherwise PAL chooses to transform the compiled byte-code in a semantically equivalent parallel version that uses several networked machines to execute the program.

Concerning this second case, PAL only produces parallel code compliant with the JJPF framework [11–12], at the moment. JJPF is a framework, based on Jini Technology, designed to provide programmers with an environment supporting the execution of skeleton based parallel applications, providing fault-tolerance and load balancing. PAL basically transforms code in such a way the user code relative to methods to be computed asynchronously is embedded into some code suitable to be run on the remote JJPF servers displaced onto the processing elements. Conversely, the main code invoking the @Parallel methods is used to implement the "client" code, i.e. the application the user runs on its own local machine. This application eventually will interact with the remote JJPF servers according to proper JJPF mechanisms and protocols. Method call parameters, the input data for the code to be executed asynchronously, are packaged in a "task". When a server receives a task to be computed, it removes its server-descriptor from the processing elements available for JJPF. When the task computation is completed the server re-inserts its descriptor from the available ones. In other words, when a annotated method is called an empty future is immediately returned, a "task" is generated and it is inserted into the JJPF queue; eventually it is sent to one of the available processing element, which remove itself from the available resources, computes the task and returns the result that JJPF finally put inside the proper future. This implementation schema looks like very close to a classical master/slave implementation.

We could have used any other parallel programming framework as the PAL target. As an example, we could have used Globus toolkit. However, JJPF was more compact and required a slightly more compact amount of code to be targeted, with respect to the Globus or other grid middleware frameworks. As the principles driving the generation of the parallel code are the same both using JJPF and other grid middleware frameworks, we preferred JJPF to be able to implement a proof-of-concept prototype in a short time.

Current PAL prototype therefore accepts plain Java programs with methods annotated as @Parallel and generates either multithreaded parallel code or parallel code suitable for the execution on a network of workstations running Java/JINI and JJPF. It has some limitations, however. In particular, the only parameter passing semantics available for annotated methods is the *deep-copy* one, and the current prototype does not allows to access the class fields from inside the annotated methods.

In order to enable the PAL features, the programmer has only to add a few lines of code. Figure 2 shows an example of PAL prototype usage, namely a program computing the Mandelbrot set. The Mandelbrot class uses a @Parallel annotation to state that all the createLines calls should be computed in parallel, with a parallelism degree equal to 16. Observe that, due to some Java limitations (see below), the programmer must specify PFFuture as return type, and consequently return an object of this type. PFFuture is a template defined by the PAL framework. It represents a container needed to enable the future mechanism. The type specified as argument is the original method return type. Initially, we tried to have to a more transparent mechanism for the future implementation, without any explicit Future declaration. It consisted in the load-time substitution of the return type with a PAL-type inheriting from the original one. In our idea, the PAL-type would have filtered any original type dereferentiation following the *wait-by-necessity* [6] semantics. Unfortunately, we had to face two Java limitations that limit the current prototype to the current solution. These limitations regard the impossibility to extend some widely used Java BCL classes (String, Integer,...) because they are declared final, and the impossibility to intercept all class field accesses.

In the Main class, the user just asks to transform the Main and the Mandelbrot classes with PAL, that is, to process the relevant PAL annotations and to produce an executable IL which exploits parallelism according to the features (hw and sw) of the target architecture where the Main itself is being run.

4.   Experimental results

To validate our approach we ran some experiments with the current prototype. We run tests were covering both cases: multithreaded and parallel transformations. In the former case, we used, as test bed, a hyper-threading bi-processors workstation (Intel Xeon 2Ghz, Linux kernel 2.6). In the latter case, instead, we used a blade cluster (24 machines single PentiumIII-800Mhz processor with multiple Fast Ethernet network, Linux kernel 2.4). For both cases, our test application was a fractal image generator, which computes sections of the Mandelbrot set. We picked up Mandelbrot as it is a very popular benchmark for embarrassingly parallel computation. PAL addresses exactly these kinds of computations, as it only allows executing remotely methods not

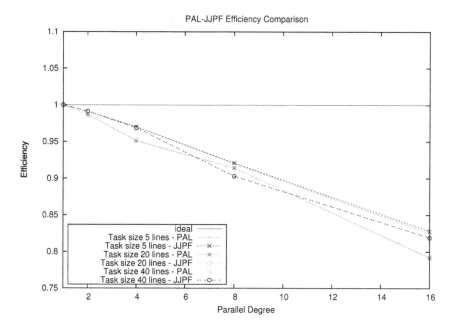

Figure 3. Mandelbrot computation: efficiency comparison with different image resolution, processing element number and task computational weight.

accessing shared (static) variables nor having any kind of side effects. On the one hand, this obviously represent a limitation, as PAL cannot compete, as an example, with other approaches supporting plain loop parallelization. On the other hand, a huge amount of embarrassingly parallel applications are executed on clusters, workstation networks and grids. Most of times, the implementation of these applications requires a significant programming effort, despite being "easy" embarrassingly parallel, far more consistent than the effort required to execute the same kind of application exploiting PAL.

To study in more detail the behavior of the transformed version in several contexts, we ran the fractal generator setting different combinations of resolution (600x400, 1200x800, 2400x1600) and task computational weights, starting from 1 up to 40 lines at time. Clearly when the task size (number of lines to compute) increases, the total number of tasks decreases. The transformed multithreaded version has been executed only with `parDegree` value equals to 1 or 2 (we used a bi-processor test bed). Nevertheless, the multithreaded experiments achieved promising results, as the registered efficiency with parallel degree 2 is about 1, for all the combination (resolution and compute lines). Since in a multicore solution we have a lower communication impact than in a COW or grid solution, we can point out that this performance should be easily maintained with symmetric multiprocessors with even larger (multicore) processing elements.

When the very same source code is used on a distributed workstation network with JJPF we achieved performances definitely close to the ones we achieved with hand written JJPF code (see Fig. 3), instead. The Figure shows the result of the experiments with an image resolution of 2400x1600 (other results obtained using different image resolutions are comparable) when a different number of processing elements are used (i.e. when different values were passed to the @Parallel(parDegree=...) annotation).

These results demonstrate that PAL performance strictly depends on the parallel tool targeted by the PAL IL transformation techniques. Actually, the overhead introduced by PAL is negligible. Nevertheless, an overhead exists because PAL offers to programmers a general metaphor that is not specialized with respect to the parallel tool used at runtime.

5.   Related work

PAL offers a simple yet expressive technique for parallel programming. Exploiting "runtime compilation" it adapts the executable code to different architectures, such as shared memory multiprocessors and networked multicomputers. It does not introduce a new or different paradigm, while exploiting parallelism at the method call level. We found in the literature a certain number of systems with similar ideas. However, although different experiments exist in the so-called concurrent object-oriented languages scenario (COOLs) [29], we decided to discuss only those actually very similar to PAL.

In [23] the authors propose a Java version of OpenMP giving to the programmers the possibility to specify some PRAGMAs inside comments to source code. These pragmas are eventually used by a specific java HPC compiler to transform the original program in a different one exploiting parallelism, for instance through loop-parallelization. There are three important differences between this approach and the ours one: first of all PAL works at method level making method invocations asynchronous, while the work presented by Klemm et al. mainly works at the loop-parallelization level. Another very important difference is related to the moment in which the transformation is made: this approach works at compile time starting from source-code, while PAL directly transforms the byte-code at load and run time. As a consequence, PAL may optimize its transformation choices exploiting the knowledge available on the features of the computing resources of the target execution platform. Eventually, PAL uses *java Annotations* to enrich the source code, instead the Java version of OpenMP uses the source code comments. The former approach exploits Java basic features, in particular annotations, which type and syntax are checked by compiler, with the limitation that annotations cannot be placed everywhere in the source code. the latter solution instead is more "artificial" but it is not limited to classes, methods and class fields (as the *java Annotations*) and it can be also applied to pure Java code blocks.

If we limit the discussion to the approaches that transform a sequential object-oriented program into a concurrent one by replacing method invocations with asynchronous calls, (where parallelism can be easily extracted from sequential code without modification, without changing the sequential semantics and the wait for return values can be postponed to the next usage, eventually using future objects) the number of approaches similar to PAL is small. However, some other approaches share single points/features with our PAL approach.

Java made popular the remote method invocation (RMI) for interaction between objects in disjoint memories. The same properties that apply for parallelizing sequential local calls apply for remote ones, with the advantage that remote calls do not rely on shared memory. Parallelizing RMIs scales much better than local calls, as the number of local processors does not limit the number of parallel tasks. This led to many implementations of asynchronous RMIs. ProActive is a popular object oriented distributed programming environment supporting asynchronous RMIs [16]. It offers a primitive class that should be extended to create remote callable active objects, as well as a runtime system to remotely instantiate this type of objects. Any call to an active object is done asynchronously, and values are returned using future objects. Compilation is completely standard, but instantiation must be done supplying the new object location. All active objects must descend from the primitive active object class, so existing code must be completely encapsulated to become active, as there is no multiple inheritance in Java. Although concurrency is available through asynchronous calls, scalable parallelism is obtained creating several distributed objects, instead of calling several concurrent methods, which is not always a natural way of structuring the parallelism.

Some other systems, at different levels, offer asynchronous remote method calls, like JavaParty [30] and Ibis [33]. They provide a lower level of abstraction with respect to PAL, being more concerned with the performance of RMI and efficient implementation of asynchronous mechanisms. Usually they offer a good replacement for the original RMI system, either simplifying object declaration or speeding up the communication. Both rely on specific compilers to generate code, although Ibis generate standard JVM byte-code that could therefore be executed on any standard JVM.

6. Conclusion and future work

We propose a new technique for high level parallel programming based on the introduction of a *Parallel Abstraction Layer* (PAL). PAL doesn't introduce a new parallel programming model, but actually exploits the programmer knowledge provided through annotations to restructure the application once the available target parallel framework is known. The restructuring process is driven by the analysis of the non-functional requirements introduced with code annotations. This process is executed at load time directly at intermediate language level. This allows obtaining and to exploit at the right time all the information needed to parallelize the applications with respect to the parallel tools available on the target execution environment and to the user supplied non-functional requirements. A load time transformation allows hiding most of parallelization issues.

We developed a PAL Java prototype and we used it to perform some experiments. The results are very encouraging and show that the overhead introduced by PAL is negligible, while keeping the programmer effort to parallelize the code negligible. Nevertheless, the current prototype has some limitations. The non-functional requirements are limited to the possibility to indicate the parallelism degree, the parameter passing semantic to PAL-annotated method is limited to deep-copy and the class fields are not accessible from PAL-annotated methods. Eventually, the programmer has to include an explicit dereferentiation of objects returned by PAL-annotated methods.

We are currently investigating other possibilities, in order to complete the PAL design. In particular, we are considering to support distributed field access from inside PAL-annotated methods as well as to provide a larger choice of parameter passing semantics in PAL-annotated method, which is fundamental to provide a larger programming freedom. In the near future we also want to increment the set of available non-functional requirements that can be specified inside @Parallel annotation, and to add PAL the ability to generate code for different parallel frameworks, including plain Globus grids. Last but not least, we're interested to merge the PAL experience with similar research performed at our Dept. by other people in the .NET (Mono [28]) framework [14].

References

[1] Java specification requests 175: A metadata facility for the java programming language. http://www.jcp.org, September 2004.

[2] Mpi: A message-passing interface strandard. http://www.mpi-forum.org, 1994.

[3] M. Aldinucci, M. Danelutto, and M. Vanneschi. Autonomic QoS in ASSIST Grid-aware components. In *Euromicro PDP 2006: Parallel Distributed and network-based Processing*. IEEE, February 2006. Montbéliard, France.

[4] G. S. Almasi and A. Gottlieb. *Highly parallel computing*. Benjamin-Cummings Publishing Co., Inc., Redwood City, CA, USA, 1989.

[5] C. T. Bruneton E, Lenglet R. Asm: a code manipulation tool to implement adaptable systems, grenoble, france. Adaptable and Extensible Component Systems, Nov. 2002.

[6] D. Caromel. Service, asynchrony, and wait-by-necessity. *Journal of Object-Oriented Programming*, Nov/Dec 1989.

[7] D. Caromel and L. Henrio. *A Theory of Distributed Object*. Springer-Verlag, 2005.

[8] D. Caromel, L. Henrio, and B. Serpette. Asynchronous and deterministic objects, 2004.

[9] M. Cole. Bringing Skeletons out of the Closet: A Pragmatic Manifesto for Skeletal Parallel Programming. *Parallel Computing*, Volume 30, Number 3, pages 389–406, 2004.

[10] Programming model Institute home page, 2006. http://www.coregrid.net/mambo/content/ category/3/13/261/.

[11] M. Danelutto and P. Dazzi. A java/jini framework supporting stream parallel computations. In *Proc. of Intl. PARCO 2005: Parallel Computing*, September 2005.

[12] P. Dazzi. Jjpf: a parallel programming framework based on jini. Master's thesis, University of Pisa, July 2004. *JJPF: uno strumento per calcolo parallelo con JINI*.

[13] N. DiPasquale, T. Way, and V. Gehlot. Comparative survey of approaches to automatic parallelization. In *MASPLAS'05*, April 2005.

[14] C. Dittamo. Annotation based techniques for the parallelization of sequential programs (in Italian), July 2006. Graduation thesis, Dept. Computer Science, Univ. of Pisa.

[15] J. Dünnweber and S. Gorlatch. Component-based Grid Programming using the HOC-Service Architecture. In I. H. Fujita, editor, *New Trends in Software Methodologies, Tools and Techniques*, Frontiers in Artificial Intelligence and Applications. IOS Press, 2005. ISBN 1-58603-556-8.

[16] D. C. et al. Proactive. http://proactive.objectweb.org, 1999.

[17] K. J. et al. Future for European Grids: GRIDs and Service Oriented Knowledge Utilities, January 2006. Third report of the Next Generation Grids expert group, available at http://cordis.europa.eu/ ist/ grids/ pub-report.htm.

[18] I. Foster and C. Kesselman. *The Grid: Blueprint for a New Computing Infrastructure*. Morgan Kauffman, 1999.

[19] GGF RPC WG home page, 2006. https://forge.gridforum.org/projects/gridrpc-wg/.

[20] MPICH-G2 home page, 2006. http://www3.niu.edu/mpi/.

[21] A. S. Grimshaw. The mentat computation model data-driven support for object-oriented parallel processing. Technical report, Dept. Comp. Science, Univ. Virginia, 28 1993.

[22] E. N. G. G. E. Group. Next Generation Grids 2 Requirements and Options for European Grids Research 2005-2010 and Beyond, July 2004. ftp://ftp.cordis.europa.eu/ pub/ ist/ docs/ ngg2_eg_final.pdf.

[23] M. Klemm, R. Veldema, M. Bezold, and M. Philippsen. A proposal for openmp for java. In *Proceedings of the International Workshop on OpenMP*, June 2006.

[24] Krzysztof Czarnecki and Ulrich W. Eisenecker. *Generative Programming - Methods, Tools, and Applications*. Addison–Wesley, June 2000.

[25] L. Henrio et al. . Proposals for a Grid Component Model. Technical Report D.PM.02, CoreGRID, December 2005.

[26] Y. Nakajima, M. Sato, T. Boku, D. Takahashi, and H. Goto. Performance Evaluation of OmniRPC in a Grid Environment. In *Proc. of SAINT2004, Workshop on High Performance Grid Computing and Networking*, pages 658–664, January 2004.

[27] Ninf: A Global Computing Infrastructure, 2006. http://ninf.apgrid.org/.

[28] Novell. Mono project. http://www.mono-project.com/, 2005.

[29] M. Philippsen. A survey of concurrent object-oriented languages. *Concurrency: Practice and Experience*, Volume 12, Number 10, pages 917–980, 2000.

[30] M. Philippsen and M. Zenger. JavaParty – transparent remote objects in Java. *Concurrency: Practice and Experience*, Volume 9, Number 11, pages 1225–1242, Nov. 1997.

[31] F. Y. Tim Lindholm. *The Java Virtual Machine Specification*. Sun Microsystems Press, second edition edition, 2004.

[32] S. Tse. Typed intermediate languages. Technical report, Dept. Comp. Science, University of Pennsylvania, 2004.

[33] R. V. van Nieuwpoort, J. Maassen, G. Wrzesinska, R. Hofman, C. Jacobs, T. Kielmann, and H. E. Bal. Ibis: a flexible and efficient java-based grid programming environment. *Concurrency and Computation: Practice & Experience*, Volume 17, Number 7-8, pages 1079–1107, 2005.

A NEW APPROACH ON NETWORK RESOURCES MANAGEMENT IN GRIDS*

Ranieri Baraglia, Domenico Laforenza, Renato Ferrini,
Nicola Tonellotto
Information Science and Technologies Institute, CNR, 56126 Pisa, Italy
ranieri.baraglia@isti.cnr.it, domenico.laforenza@isti.cnr.it, renato.ferrini@isti.cnr.it,
nicola.tonellotto@isti.cnr.it

Davide Adami[†], Stefano Giordano
Department of Information Engineering, University of Pisa, 56100 Pisa, Italy
[†] *CNIT Research Unit, Dept of Information Engineering, University of Pisa*
davide.adami@cnit.it, s.giordano@iet.unipi.it

Ramin Yahyapour
Robotics Research Institute, University of Dortmund, 44221 Dortmund, Germany
ramin.yahyapour@udo.edu

Abstract   Currently, Grid applications are usually developed for a network offering only a best effort packet delivery service. Nevertheless, High Performance Computing applications with Quality of Service requirements stress the capabilities of the interconnecting network of the target Grid infrastructure. Therefore, the application runtime environment must interact, through a Grid Resource Broker, with a Network Resource Manager to obtain information about the network and to reserve network resources among the computational resources that will host the execution of the applications.

   The paper presents the design and the development of a Grid Network-Aware Resource Broker. It enhances the features of a Grid Resource Broker with the capabilities provided by a Network Resource Manager. The innovative contribution of the presented integration is the possibility to design and implement new mapping/scheduling mechanisms to take into account both network and computational resources. Finally, we will show how to exploit the new features offered by the Grid Network-Aware Resource Broker in scheduling parallel applications with QoS requirements.

Keywords: Grid Computing, High-level Programming Environment, Resource Management, Quality of Service, MPLS, DiffServ

*This work has been supported by: the Italian MIUR FIRB Grid.it project, No. RBNE01KNFP, on High-performance Grid platforms and tools, and the European CoreGRID NoE (contract no. IST-2002-004265).

1.   Introduction

The Grid is a promising infrastructure that can allow scientists and engineers to access a distributed heterogeneous computing environment in a secure and uniform way. Currently, research is focused on the abstraction of the underlying physical resources and their cooperation. Meanwhile, to guarantee high-level programming capabilities, software interoperability and reuse, as well as the ability to follow the evolution of the underlying technologies, new application Programming Environments are required. The complete unawareness of users and programmers of the Grid management leads to the concept of the *Invisible Grid*, a virtual "supercomputer" whose resources can be allocated to the applications "automatically".

To enforce this vision, a layered approach is needed. The programmer develops applications exploiting high-level interfaces exposed by the Grid Programming Environment. Then applications are compiled and linked with an Application Manager that must take care of interactions with the Grid middleware. The middleware provides several services including functionalities that directly interact with the management of physical resources. This management is related to dynamic resource allocations for the given application needs at launch time and during runtime. By exploiting structured approaches to parallel programming (i.e. skeleton libraries and programming languages [1, 3, 4, 2]) and component-based technologies, it is possible to recursively build parallel applications comprising a large number of interacting modules. Using a structured model to develop Grid applications makes possible to specify the computational and network requirements that the run-time target platform must satisfy. This information can be obtained from a smaller set of user-defined QoS requirements. Before starting the execution, the Resource Management System must exploit this data to discover adequate computational and network resources, reserving and configuring them if necessary. This process must be carried out orchestrating the interactions between several Grid Middleware Services.

Up to now, several efforts have been carried out to coordinate the interaction between computational and storage resources only. However, also the network places a central role in the execution of complex tightly coupled applications, involving both the transfer of big amount of data and the interaction between different application modules. Both computational and network resources are shared between several users, generally with local administrative policies, and without guarantees about the features of the connections. Scientific applications usually rely on the availability of appropriate computational capabilities, where appropriate means that each operation must be executed according to a service performance contract. When an application consists of several interconnected modules, every single module must satisfy some performance requirements to obtain the desired user-dependent QoS. The interconnection mechanism between application modules may sustain the communications between them. When the information exchange between these application modules may affect the overall performance, network connections with guaranteed Quality of Service (QoS) are necessary to satisfy the application performance constraints.

In this work, we focus on the integration between computational and network resources managers to enforce QoS on the execution of parallel applications. In Sect. 2 and 3 we present, respectively, the design and the implementation of a Grid Resource Broker and a Network Resource Manager. Sect. 4 proposes an approach to the problem of orchestrating the interaction between computational and network resources exploiting our managers implementations. In Sect. 5 we show some results in the management of parallel applications with QoS requirements, and in Sect. 6 we draw our conlusions and outline future research directions.

2. Grid Resource Broker

A large class of HPC applications can be modelled through Task Interaction Graphs (TIGs) [9]. A weighted Task Interaction Grap may be adopted to model a parallel application. The nodes represent computations and are characterised by a computational bandwidth (MFlop/s). The edges represent data communications and are characterised by a transmission bandwidth. Such bandwidths can be obtained either by static program analysis or by executing the code on a reference system. During the execution of the application, the nodes and the edges continuously receive, elaborate and send data, with different bandwidths. Suitable resources must be selected and managed to provide a certain level of performance to the application, i.e. to support the minimum bandwidth requirements of the nodes and edges.

The Grid Execution Agent (GEA) [11] has been designed and implemented to act as the Grid Resource Broker of the *Grid.it* Project [13]. Currently, it implements several components to manage Globus based Grids as well as collections of resources accessible through SSH. It partially exploits the CoG Kits [10] and only manages computational resources, providing the following features: management of security mechanisms, resource discovery, resource selection and mapping, data staging, execution of the modules of the application.

The input of the brokering process is a description of the application; this description is coded in an XML format, called Application Level Description Language, which identifies the processes constituting the application with associated resource requirements. Moreover, this document includes the TIG of the application with the bandwidth requirements.

This description is parsed and checked and an internal representation of the application is built. The next step is the formulation of a query for the resources independent of the specific Information Services (which will be queried). A query can contain simple resource requirements as well as specific requirements on the aggregate characteristics of a set of resources. When the query has been created, the resources search procedure starts, interacting directly with different Grid middlewares. The current implementation of GEA permits to interact in parallel with custom Information Services, Globus Monitoring and Discovery Services and the Network Weather Service.

At the end of the resource discovery phase, a Grid Virtual Representation is built. This representation encapsulates a logical view of the Grid resources fulfilling the submitted query. During the mapping phase, an allocation of the application processes to the resources is calculated. This problem is complex, so some heuristics must be used. We introduced some constraints to simplify the problem: every single resource contributes with its full computational power to the execution of the application, and the inbound/outbound bandwidth of the resource sustains the application traffic. In this way, it is possible to identify the resources able to support the required computations, then we are able to derive the QoS that the network interconnecting several resources must provide. After the mapping phase, there is the actual execution of the application. The first step in this phase is to build an abstract representation of the tasks to be performed: stage in, activation, (possibly coallocated) execution and stage out. These tasks are organized in an abstract workflow exploiting the information provided by the application description. The information derived in the mapping phase is used to translate the workflow in a concrete representation of the tasks. This representation contains every detail needed to automatically enact the workflow and start the execution of the application.

3.   Network Resource Manager and Information Services

The cooperation of the network infrastructure and the Application Manager requires the design and the development of a new Grid Middleware Service, called Network Resource Manager (NRM), which can be invoked by the Application Manager through the Resource Management functionality. In this framework, the NRM has an interface to request a pre-defined network service and may include several modules to optimize the utilization of network resources. A Network Information System (NIS) is also necessary to collect information about the network status and to control service agreements. Since these components are essential to achieve a Grid network-aware environment, our approach is based on a centralized architecture where a new entity, the Grid Network Resource Broker (GNRB), provides both NRM and Network Information System (NIS) functionalities (see Fig. 1).

The GNRB architecture consists of a Network Resource Management System (NRMS) and a Network Configuration Management System (NCMS).

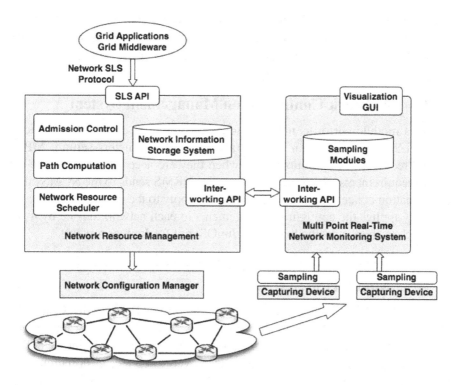

Figure 1.   GNRB architecture and Multi-Point Real-Time Network Measurement System.

3.1   Network Resource Management System

The NRMS performs policy and admission control, path computation and network resource scheduling functions as described in [7]. When a network service request is delivered to the GNRB, the Policy and Admission Control module checks if the user is allowed to ask for the service. Then, the compliance of the request with the Service Level Agreement (SLA) established between the Network Provider and the Virtual Organization is verified. The next operation is performed by the Path Computation Element (PCE), which determines if the new incoming service request may be accepted, must be rejected or reclassified. The PCE executes a path computation algorithm (e.g. Shortest Path First with Multiple Constraints algorithm) over a graph, representing the network topology, whose edges are weighted according to the required performance metrics. The structure of the graph and the weights assigned to each edge are determined through information stored in the Network Information Storage System (NISS). The main modules of the NISS are the *data collection module*, which allows asynchronous exchanges of information between the NISS and the Multi-Point Real-Time Network Measurement Systems, and the *data organization modules,* where status information is organized hierarchically, in compliance with the entity.characteristic.subcharacteristic representation [6]. The network information storage database contains statistics concerning the status of the network at path, link and node levels.

3.2   Network Configuration Management System

This module performs network nodes configuration (i.e. Label Switched Path, LSP, set up and tear down, traffic control parameters setting, MPLS-based recovery configuration, etc.) when they are necessary to meet the network requirements of grid applications. The NRMS sends to the NCMS all the information concerning the configuration to apply to the network devices. The NCMS applies the configuration statements to each network device by using, for each of them, specific tools (e.g. JunOScript for Juniper routers).

3.3   GNRB and Multi-Point Real-Time Network Monitoring System

The GNRB interfaces through the Inter-Working APIs with the Multi-Point Real-Time Network Monitoring System, which allows to monitor the network status and the available network resources. Different Multi-Point Real-Time Monitoring Systems modules may be deployed to collect information about the network, such as physical and logical (i.e. MPLS, IP) topologies, performance metrics (e.g. link utilization, throughput, end-to-end delay, jitter, etc.), performance of recovery mechanisms, etc [12].

Network status data, both static and dynamic, has to be reported to the GNRB through an Inter-Working API. Subsequently, network performance parameters must be evaluated and stored into the NISS database in a preliminary phase when the network infrastructure is set up. The knowledge of the physical and IP configuration information enables the topology discovery and requires a protocol to exchange information with network devices. Moreover, to deliver real-time metrics reports to the GNRB, ad-hoc measurement systems have to be deployed. For example, a network bandwidth probe might rely upon SNMP-enabled network devices, such as routers and switches.

At the end, network performance may be evaluated through experiments in the real network scenario and simulations carried out to achieve the bounds of the network performance metrics.

4.   Network-aware Grid Resource Broker

Concerning Grid network services use cases, two areas have been identified [5]: (i) Path-Oriented, including a number of network services which aims at the usage of different types of network connectivity; (ii) Knowledge-Based, including all the network services concerning the collection and usage of network performance information.

When the network architecture is also considered, Grid network services must be mapped into Service Level Specifications (SLSs), which may consist of expected throughput, drop probability, latency, constraints on the ingress and egress points at which the service is provided, traffic profiles, disposition of traffic submitted in excess of the specified profile, and marking and shaping services provided.

In our implementation, the Grid Resource Broker and the Network Resource Manager are implemented through the GEA and the GNRB, respectively. In the GNRB architecture, the network services that the Grid Resource Broker can request are the following:

- **Network Topology**, with information about network performance metrics (link available bandwidth, link delay, etc.) In this case, the GEA may choose the computational resources taking also into account the network status. Anyway, the network only provides a Best Effort service without any performance guarantees.

- **Weighted Topology**: i.e. the best network paths calculated according to a predefined network metric, which assure the connectivity among the Grid application nodes. In particular, when the GNRB receives a weighted topology discovery query, the NRMS retrieves the information on the network resources status from the NIS database, and determines the paths satisfying the query through the execution of the path computation algorithm.

- **QoS Support**: i.e. a set of network paths among the Grid application nodes, satisfying specific QoS constraints (Peak Rate and Burst Size, Mean Rate and Burst Size, Maximum Latency, Mean Latency) for the whole execution time of the application. Therefore, it can be necessary to reserve on-demand network resources to satisfy the application requirements or to reject the request if there are not enough available resources.

In our architecture, the SLS Signalling Protocol is used by the GNRB and the Application Manager to exchange query/response messages formatted by using XML-based schemes. Fig. 2 shows an example of two QoS Support service requests, for EF (Peak Rate and Burst Size) and AF (Average rate and Burst Size) services, respectively.

In the GEA architecture, several assumptions about the computational resources have been done. The GEA mainly targets the execution of HPC applications. These applications are commonly executed on computing resources that are part of a Grid composed by several scientific research labs (HPC

```
<requestedMapping>                      <requestedMapping>
  <id>1</id>                              <id>2</id>
  <service>EF</service>                   <service>AF</service>
  <componentPath>                         <componentPath>
    <srcLan entryRouter="10.0.0.1">         <srcLan entryRouter="10.0.0.1">
      100.2.255.23/19                         192.168.1.0/24
    </srcLan>                               </srcLan>
    <dstLan entryRouter="10.0.0.2">         <dstLan entryRouter="10.0.0.2">
      255.243.23.11/31                        10.0.0.1/16
    </dstLan>                               </dstLan>
    <requestedBandwidth>                    <requestedBandwidth>
      <peak>10</peak>                         <mean>100</mean>
      <burst>10</burst>                       <burst>10</burst>
    </requestedBandwidth>                   </requestedBandwidth>
  </componentPath>                        </componentPath>
</requestedMapping>                      </requestedMapping>
```

Figure 2.   Example of two QoS Support service requests.

Grids). In this scenario, it is possible to make some assumptions about computational resources and Local Area Networks. Usually, the shared resources are clusters of computers or computers connected either to switched LANs that can be seen as clusters. While the computing resources of a cluster are (almost) homogeneous, the clusters are heterogeneous. The computing resources of a cluster share a dedicated Local Area Network. We assume that the selected computing resources in a cluster contribute with their full computational power to the execution of an application, and the LAN bandwidth is fairly distributed between the computing resources and the background traffic does not exist. With these assumptions, it is clear that potential bottlenecks are the links between the LANs relative to each cluster participating in the execution. The interconnection link share the same backbone network used by normal users of the scientific labs. Then, the Network Resource Manager must enforce LSPs between the Edge Label Switching Routers (E-LSRs) of the backbone. The scheduling process performed by the Grid Resource Broker is depicted in Fig. 3.

The scheduling process starts with the description of the application. The description includes the weighted TIG of the application, where the vertex and edge weights represent respectively computational and communication bandwidths, as well as architectural constraints such as target CPUs, minimum memory/hard disk requirements, available libraries, operating systems. Next, application nodes are clustered in order to minimize the scattering of the nodes on several LANs. Then the GEA will start to query the Grid Information Service to collect information about the available resources and select resources able to fulfil the requirements of the single nodes of the application. While resources are discovered, their static topology is build in a dendrogram. It is a tree graph wherer the single resources are the leaves, and resources in the same LAN/cluster, share the same parent node. All such parent nodes can be seen as representatives of the LAN/cluster, and may be grouped again in MANs and WANs.

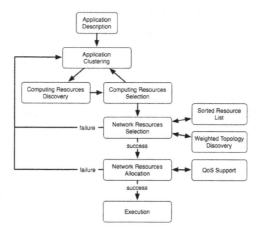

Figure 3.   Scheduling Process.

Resource discovery, selection and application clustering phases can be iterated several times to find a solution. At the end of the application clustering phase, we are able to find several mappings of the application nodes to available computing resources. Then, resources are grouped in LANs and the cumulative bandwidth requirements between LANs can be arranged in new graphs, one for each solution. Through the NISS, the E-LSRs interconnecting the LANs are identified, and an XML query is submitted to the NRM. This query includes the list of solutions found with inter-LAN bandwidth requirements, i.e. mean bandwidth, peak bandwidth and burst size. The GNRB will check the status of network resources and, if possible, select one of the solutions listed in the query. Next, the GEA requests the allocation and reservation of the required LSPs between the LANs returned from the GNRB and, if this phase is successful, starts the execution of the application, which will run over the backbone with guarantees of network services.

5.   Experimental Evaluation

In this section we will show how it is possible to apply the proposed scheduling strategy proposed. In particular, a real application will be clustered and mapped on the resource of the *Grid.it* testbed. The details of the scheduling algorithm are outside the scope of this paper. Basically, the algorithm tries to schedule the nodes of the application on the Grid resources trying to guarantee a QoS level to the whole application. When many scheduling solutions are available, the one which mimimizes the intra-LAN communication is selected.

The testbed used to evaluate the algorithm is a Grid composed by 23 heterogeneous computational resources (7 workstations and 2 clusters), distributed in three LANs connected through 1Gb/s optical links. Fig. 4 shows the structure and the node/edge bandwidths of a rendering application, structured according to the pipeline of farms programming paradigm, used in the experimental evaluation. The first sequential stage requests the rendering of a sequence of scenes. The second one is a data-parallel module composed by an emitter, a collector and five workers that render each scene (exploiting the PovRay rendering engine). The third stage collects images rendered by the second one, and builds Groups Of Pictures (GOPs) that are sent to the fourth stage performing DivX compression in a data-parallel module composed by two workers. The last stage collects DivX compressed pieces and stores them in an AVI output file. Computational and transmission values have been collected through a short profiling execution of the application on a reference architecture.

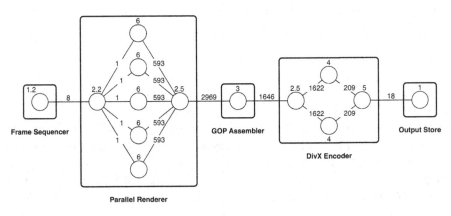

Figure 4.   A parallel renderer/encoder used during the tests.

A critical point of the scheduling algorithm is the clustering mechanism used to aggregate the application nodes. Several heuristics can be used; in these tests we used the one presented in [8]. By tuning the clustering parameters, it is possible to obtain several clustering solutions. During the scheduling phases, the resources to execute the modules of the applications are selected. Such selection is based on a two-levels best fit list scheduling. We first selected the best LAN to host a subset of modules (i.e. a cluster), and then the modules are scheduled on such LAN. The resulting inter-LAN communication values are influenced by two effects:

1 a single cluster may be too "large" to be scheduled on a single LAN, and it must be split across several LANs. It happens with few and big clusters, and this effect worsen the final inter-LAN communication value;

2 several clusters may be scheduled on the same LAN, if there are available resources, improving the final inter-LAN communication value.

	MCR	LAN ISTI	LAN CNIT	LAN IET	Average Affinity	Inter LAN Comm. (clustering)	Inter LAN Comm. (scheduling)
	50	14	0	0	13.35		0.00%
3 clusters	100	14	0	0	5.63	0.12%	0.00%
	150	8	1	5	4.32		20.81%
	50	14	0	0	13.93		0.00%
5 clusters	100	14	0	0	6.72	3.98%	0.00%
	150	6	1	7	4.48		24.48%
	50	14	0	0	14.75		0.00%
10 clusters	100	14	0	0	7.00	30.27%	0.00%
	150	9	1	4	4.82		26.04%

Figure 5.   Inter-LAN communications with different cluster sizes and QoS requirements.

In Fig. 5 we can see that increasing the number of clusters causes an increment in the inter-LAN communications (more clusters, more edges on the cuts). This is a kind of optimality parameter for the results of the scheduling phase. In fact, let us consider the clustering result as the best one for the application. If the scheduling phase is able to schedule every single cluster completely onto a single LAN, eventually we cannot obtain an inter-LAN communication value worse than the previous one. In the case of three clusters, the scheduling algorithm is forced to split the big cluster in several LANs, while in the case of ten clusters, the heuristics is able to completely allocate the largest cluster on a LAN and to allocate several small clusters on the same LANs.

6.   Conclusion

The paper presents a new architecture for a Grid Resource Broker. This architecture addresses the issues related to the performance of HPC applications taking into account advanced network infrastructure offering QoS support and Traffic Engineering capabilities.

In particular the proposed implementation allows to automatically prepare and launch Grid applications, taking care of all the details needed to interface the middleware such as resource discovery and selection, data staging, interaction with local resource managers. To this purpose a new network entity has been introduced: the Grid Network Resource Broker allows to request information about the network status and, if necessary, can reserve network resources to satisfy the QoS requirements of applications. Finally, a new mapping/scheduling mechanism exploiting these features has been discussed.

References

[1] C. Pèrèz, T. Priol, and A. Ribes, "A Parallel Corba Component Model for Numerical Code Coupling," in *Int. J. of High Performance Computing Applications*, vol. 17, no. 4, pp. 417–429, 2003.

[2] M. Dìaz, B. Rubio, E. Soler, and J. M. Troya, "SBASCO: Skeleton-based scientific components," in *Proc. 12th Euromicro Conference on Parallel, Distributed, and Network-Based Processing (PDP'04)*, A Coruña, Spain, Feb. 2004.

[3] H. Kuchen, "A Skeleton Library," in *Proc. 8th Euro-Par Conference*, London, UK, Aug. 2002.

[4] M. Vanneschi, "The programming model of ASSIST, an environment for parallel and distributed portable applications," in *Par. Comp.*, vol. 28, no. 12, pp. 1709–1732, Dec. 2002.

[5] T. Ferrari, (ed). "Grid Network Services Use Cases, Version 2.10.". *Grid High Performance Networking Research Group*, July 7, 2006.

[6] B. Lowekamp, B. Tierney, L. Cottrell, R. Hughes-Jones, T. Kielmann, M. Swany. "A Hierarchy of Network Performance Characteristics for Grid Application and Services," in *Grid Forum Document, GFD-R.023, Global Grid Forum*, May 24, 2004.

[7] D. Adami, N. Parlotti, S. Giordano, M. Repeti. "Design and development of a GNRB for the coordinated use of network resources in a high performance grid environment", in *Distributed Cooperative Laboratories*, pp.295 – 307, Springer-Verlag, 2005.

[8] E. Demaine and N. Immorlica. "Correlation Clustering with Partial Information", in *Proceedings of the 6th International Workshop on Approximation Algorithms for Combinatorial Optimization Problems*, Berlin, Germany, 2003.

[9] Sinnen, O. and L. Sousa, "A Classification of Graph Theoretic Models for Parallel Computing". Technical report, Instituto Superior Tecnico, Technical University of Lisbon, Portugal, 1999.

[10] G. von Laszewski, I. Foster, J. Gawor, and P. Lane. "A java commodity grid kit", in *Concurrency and Computation: Practice and Experience*, 13(8-9):643–662, 2001.

[11] R. Baraglia, M. Danelutto, T. Fagni, D. Laforenza, S. Orlando, A. Paccosi, N. Tonellotto, M. Vanneschi, and C. Zoccolo. "HPC application execution on Grids", in V. Getov, D. Laforenza, and A Reinefeld, editors, *Future Generation Grids*. Springer-Verlag Core-GRID Series, 2005.

[12] L. Valcarenghi, L. Foschini, F. Paolucci, F. Cugini, P. Castoldi. "Topology Discovery Services for Monitoring the Global Grid", in *IEEE Communications Magazione*, 44(3):110–117, 2006.

[13] Grid.it: Enabling Platforms for High-Performance Computational Grids Oriented to Scalable Virtual Organizations. http://grid.it/.

COMPONENTISING
A SCIENTIFIC APPLICATION
FOR THE GRID*

Nikos Parlavantzas, Vladimir Getov
Harrow School of Computer Science,
University of Westminster, HA1 3TP, U.K.
{N.Parlavantzas, V.S.Getov}@westminster.ac.uk

Matthieu Morel, Francoise Baude, Fabrice Huet, Denis Caromel
INRIA Sophia Antipolis,
2004, route des Lucioles, BP 93, France
FirstName.LastName@inria.fr

Abstract   Building and evolving grid applications is complex. A promising approach
to managing this complexity is component-based development, currently attracting growing interest in the grid community. Evaluating the effectiveness
of component-based development requires real-world experience. To this end,
this paper presents a case study in reengineering a high performance numerical solver to become a component-based grid application. The adopted component model is an extension of the generic Fractal model that specifically targets
grid environments. The paper provides qualitative and quantitative evidence that
componentisation has improved the modifiability and reusability of the application without significantly affecting performance.

Keywords: Grid component model, component-based development, scientific applications,
componentisation

---

*This work was carried out for the COREGRID IST project No 004265 funded by the European Commis-
sion

1. Introduction

As grid technologies are becoming widely available, managing the complexity of building and evolving grid applications is becoming increasingly important. A promising approach to addressing this concern is component-based development, which is currently attracting growing interest in the grid community. This is evidenced by the emergence of component models explicitly targeting the Grid, such as CCA (Common Component Architecture) [9], and GCM (Grid Gomponent Model) [10], currently under development within the CoreGRID European project. Perceived benefits of component-based development include reduced costs through reusing off-the-self components and increased adaptability through adding, removing, or replacing components. In evaluating the actual usefulness of component-based methods and models, real-word experience with building grid applications is invaluable.

This work presents our experience with applying component-based development to the domain of high performance scientific applications running on the Grid. Specifically, we describe how a numerical solver, originally implemented as distributed object application, was reengineered into a component-based grid application. The reengineering effort was based on a general componentisation process and a grid-enabled component model. The model extends the generic Fractal component model [7], similarly to the GCM, and it is implemented on top of the ProActive middleware [17]. We show that componentisation has increased the modifiability of the application without any significant negative effects on performance.

The rest of this paper is structured as follows. Section 2 provides background on the numerical application, called Jem3D, and section 3 presents our approach to reengineering this application. Section 4 then describes our componentisation experience and the resulting system. Section 5 provides some performance results, and section 6 discusses related work. Finally, section 7 concludes the paper.

2. Background on Jem3D

This section provides background on Jem3D, the application at the focus of this paper, and the ProActive library, the distributed object platform used by Jem3D.

2.1 The ProActive library

The ProActive library is a Java middleware for parallel, distributed, and concurrent programming [17]. The programming model relies on remotely accessible *active objects* communicating through asynchronous method calls with transparent futures. Two key features of ProActive are its support for typed group communication and descriptor-based deployment. *Group communication* enables triggering method calls on a group of active objects with compatible type, dynamically generating a group of results. This feature simplifies the implementation and enhances the efficiency of applications that contain similar activities running in parallel. *Descriptor-based deployment* enables deploying distributed applications anywhere without having to modify the source code. This is achieved by eliminating from the source code infrastructure details such as machine names and creation protocols and specifying them separately in XML descriptor files.

2.2   Jem3D overview

Jem3D is a numerical solver for the 3D Maxwell's equations modelling the time domain propagation of electromagnetic waves [4]. It relies on a finite volume approximation method operating on unstructured tetrahedral meshes. The complexity of the calculation is controlled by setting the *mesh size*; i.e., the triplet (m1 × m2 × m3) that specifies the number of points on the x, y, and z axes used for building the tetrahedral mesh. Parallelisation relies on dividing the computational domain into subdomains; the domain division is controlled by another triplet (d1 × d2 × d3) that determines the number of subdomains on each axis.

Figure 1 shows the runtime structure of Jem3D assuming a 2 × 2 × 1 domain division. The main elements of the architecture are outlined next. *Subdomains* correspond to partitions of the 3D computational domain; they perform electromagnetic computations and communicate with their closest neighbours in the 3D grid. Moreover, they send partial solutions with a predefined frequency to the main collector. The *main collector* is responsible for monitoring and steering the computation by interacting with the subdomains. The monitoring and steering functionality is used by one or more *steering agents*, dynamically registered with the main collector. The application includes a command-line agent and a graphical agent with visualisation capabilities. Steering agents communicate with each other to ensure that only a single agent at a time has the right to control the computation. Finally, the *launcher* is responsible for obtaining the input data, creating the main collector and the subdomains, setting up the necessary connections between them, initialising them with the necessary information, and starting the computation. Communication between the entities relies on the asynchronous remote invocation and group communication mechanisms provided by ProActive.

The original Jem3D application suffers from limited modifiability and limited reusability of its parts. This can be largely attributed to two factors. First, the application lacks reliable architectural documentation, which is essential for understanding and evolving complex software systems. Jem3D has

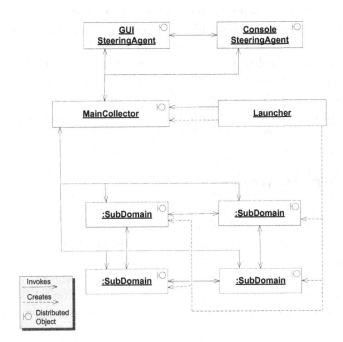

Figure 1.   Jem3D Architecture.

been subjected to successive changes by multiple people without corresponding updates to the architectural information. Second, the application parts are tightly coupled together. Indeed, as in most object-oriented applications, the code includes hard-wired dependencies to classes, which limits the reusability of classes, increases the impact of changes, and inhibits run-time variability. For example, changing the subdomain implementation requires updating the source code of both the main collector and the launcher and rebuilding the whole application. As another example, although the Jem3D parallelisation follows a typical *geometric decomposition pattern* [15], no part of the application can be reused in other contexts where this pattern is applicable. To address such modifiability and reusability limitations, Jem3D was re-engineered into a component-based system.

3.   Approach

Our approach to addressing the modifiability and reusability limitations of Jem3D has two ingredients: a general, architecture-based componentisation process, and the Fractal/ProActive component model. These ingredients are discussed in turn next.

3.1 Componentisation process

The purpose of the componentisation process is to transform an object-based system to a component-based system. This process assumes that the target component platform allows connecting components via provided and required interfaces, and that it minimally supports (or, it can be extended to support) the same communication styles as the object platform (e.g., remote method invocation, streams, events). The main activities and artefacts defined by the process are shown in Figure 2. Note that the activities typically proceed iteratively. For example, the activity "Restructure Original System" may start when an initial component architecture is designed, and it may be revisited when an updated architecture is available. The activities are outlined next.

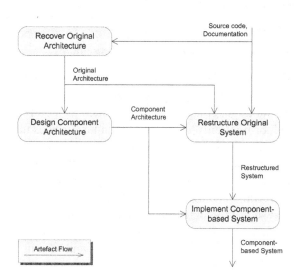

Figure 2. Componentisation process.

Recover Original Architecture   This activity uses as input the source code, documentation, build files, and any other artefacts of the original system. It involves analysing the source system, extracting architecturally significant information, and documenting different views of the original architecture. The documentation must minimally include a run-time view describing executing entities (e.g., distributed objects, objects, processes), communication paths, and interactions over those paths (e.g., sequences of remote method invocations).

Design Component Architecture   This activity produces the target component architecture using as input the original architecture. The activity can be divided into four steps:

- *Define initial architecture.* The executing entities of the original architecture are used as candidate components to form an initial component architecture.

- *Refine component selection.* Candidate components are decomposed into smaller components or integrated into larger components, and their relationships and interactions are updated accordingly. These changes are driven by modifiability and performance concerns. Decomposition is typically used to increase the reusability of components and the flexibility of the architecture, whereas integration is used to reduce performance overheads.

- *Specify component interfaces.* By analysing and organising the interactions between each component and its environment, this step identifies provided and required interfaces. Multiple interfaces for each component are defined in order to reduce dependencies.

- *Refine architecture using available component model features.* The component architecture is adapted to exploit all the available features provided by the target component model, such as hierarchical composition in Fractal, or implicitly-accessed, container services in CCM.

Restructure Original System   This activity restructures the original code to make it match closely the component architecture, without yet using the component platform. Specifically, the activity implements an interface-based version of the system in which entities communicate as much as possible via explicitly identified provided/required interfaces. The motivation is to validate a large part of the architecture at an earlier time, and to simplify the migration to the target platform. The activity can be divided into the following steps:

- *Align code with component architecture.* This step ensures that the code includes classes which correspond to all intended components, and that these classes implement all interfaces provided by their corresponding components.

- *Add dependency injection mechanism.* Supporting configurable connections requires a uniform mechanism for injecting references to required interfaces into objects. Such mechanisms are provided by most component models, and are manifested as standard methods for accepting and managing interface references. This step ensures that all classes corresponding to intended components support an injection mechanism, thus making their dependencies explicit and externally modifiable.

- *Use injection mechanism.* This step modifies the classes so that they invoke collaborating classes only through injected references. Moreover, the step modifies any "injector" code that supplies a class with references to required objects to use the uniform injection mechanism.

Implement Component-based system   This activity uses as inputs the component architecture and the restructured, interface-based version. It typically involves small changes for repackaging classes as components that execute on the target platform. It may also involve changes for exploiting features of the component model that were unavailable in the original object platform.

3.2   Fractal/ProActive component model

The second ingredient of our approach is Fractal/ProActive, which serves as the target component platform in the componentisation process. Fractal/ProActive is a parallel and distributed component model that aims at building grid applications [5]. It conforms to the generic Fractal model [7] and extends it with a number of features that support grid programming. Fractal/ProActive is implemented on top of the ProActive library [17]. Fractal and the Fractal/ProActive-defined extensions are examined in turn next.

Fractal components are runtime entities that communicate exclusively through interfaces of two types: *client interfaces* that emit operation invocations and *server interfaces* that accept them. Interfaces are connected through communication paths, called *bindings*. Fractal distinguishes *primitive* components from *composite* components formed by hierarchically assembling other components (called sub-components). Hierarchical composition is a key Fractal feature that facilitates understanding and developing component systems. Another important Fractal feature is its support for extensible reflective facilities. Each component is associated with an extensible set of *controllers* that enable inspecting and reconfiguring its internal features (e.g., modifying its set of sub-components). Finally, Fractal includes an architecture description language (ADL) for specifying configurations comprising components, their composition relationships, and their bindings.

The Fractal/ProActive model extends Fractal in the following ways. Primitive components are specialised to obtain the properties of remotely accessible active objects. Composite components can contain multiple active objects and can be distributed over different machines. Component communication relies on asynchronous method invocations. A multicast communication style is also supported, analogous to the group communication mechanism in ProActive. Specifically, the component model defines a specialisation of Fractal interfaces, called *multicast interfaces*, that enable treating a set of invocations as a single invocation. As with standard interfaces, multicast interfaces can have a client or server type. Finally, the model supports configurable component deployment based on the ProActive deployment descriptors.

4.   Componentising Jem3D

Jem3D was componentised using the approach presented previously. Most of the effort was spent on the architecture recovery activity because of the undocumented and degraded structure of the system. The run-time view of the original architecture was described using UML object diagrams—such as the one in Figure 1—and UML interaction diagrams. During the component architecture design, the launcher entity (an executing Java program) was decomposed into a *subdomain factory* component and an *activator* component; the former is assigned the responsibilities for creating, initialising, and connecting the subdomains, and the latter the responsibilities for obtaining the input data, passing them to the factory, and starting the computation. The reason for the decomposition was to make the factory reusable beyond Jem3D. A later iteration of the activity grouped the factory and the subdomains into a composite *domain* component, exploiting the hierarchical composition feature of Fractal/ProActive. Implementing the interface-based version served to increase confidence in the new component architecture and drastically simplified the final component-based implementation. The component-based implementation involved wrapping classes to form Fractal components and replacing a large part of the injector logic with Fractal ADL descriptions, as seen next.

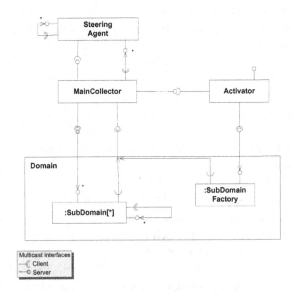

Figure 3.   Component-based Jem3D structure.

Figure 3 shows the static structure of the resulting component-based Jem3D using a UML component diagram (multicast interfaces are represented as stereotyped UML interfaces with special notation). The runtime configuration consists of multiple subdomains, logically arranged in a 3D mesh, with each subdomain connected to its neighbours via multicast interfaces. The runtime configuration also includes a dynamically varying number of steering agents. The main collector is connected to the current set of agents via a multicast interface. A multicast interface is also used to connect each agent to all other agents. The initial configuration of Jem3D is described using the Fractal ADL, as seen in Figure 4 (pseudocode is used for brevity). Note that the ADL is not used to express the configuration of subdomains, which depends on the dynamically-determined domain division. Since allowable configurations follow a fixed, canonical structure in the form of a 3D mesh, a parameterised description would be useful for automatically generating subdomain configurations. However, the Fractal ADL includes currently no variability mechanisms for expressing such descriptions. The ADL does include a simple parameterisation mechanism, which is used to configure the factory with the required subdomain implementation.

```
Component ConsoleSteeringAgent
          definition = SteeringAgentImpl
Component MainCollector
          definition = MainCollectorImpl
Component Activator
          definition = ActivatorImpl
Component Domain
          Interface ...// interfaces omitted
          Component SubDomainFactory
                    definition = FactoryImpl (SubDomainImpl)
          // bindings within composite (interfaces names omitted)
          Binding This to SubDomainFactory
          Binding SubDomainFactory to This
// bindings among top-level components (interface names omitted)
Binding ConsoleSteeringAgent to MainCollector
Binding MainCollector to ConsoleSteeringAgent
Binding Activator to MainCollector
Binding Activator to Domain
Binding MainCollector to Domain
Binding Domain to MainCollector
```

Figure 4.   Initial configuration in the ADL.

Evaluation   We now examine whether the new, component-based Jem3D addresses the modifiability and reusability limitations of the original system. Owning to the componentisation process, the new system has gained reliable architectural documentation, which facilitates understanding and evolving the system. Moreover, an important part of the architecture—i.e., the initial component configuration—is captured in the ADL. As a result, the component platform can automatically enforce architectural structure on implementation, which helps reduce future architectural erosion. The use of provided and required interfaces as specified by the component model minimizes inflexible, hard-wired dependencies and allows flexible configuration after development time. Considering the scenario of changing the subdomain implementation, this can now be achieved simply by replacing a name in the ADL description (i.e., the SubDomainImpl name in Figure 4). Moreover, the domain component now serves as a reusable unit of functionality that supports the geometric decomposition pattern. Specifically, the component accepts as input the subdomain implementation and the domain division and embodies the logic to create and manage the runtime subdomain configuration.

5.   Performance results

To assess the impact of componentisation on performance, we conducted experiments with the aim to compare execution times of the object-based and the component-based Jem3D versions. The experiments were performed on Grid'5000, a French experimental grid platform currently featuring 2000 processors distributed over 9 geographical sites [8]. The sites host locally administered clusters connected through 1Gb/s links. Each experiment involved running the two Jem3D versions for a given mesh size on the same number of processors allocated on up to 3 clusters of Grid'5000. Table 1 shows the mesh size and total number of processors used for each experiment.

Table 1.   Jem3D experiments.

Experiment	Mesh size	Number of Processors
1	$41\times41\times41$	20
2	$81\times81\times81$	70
3	$201\times201\times201$	130
4	$201\times201\times201$	138
5	$201\times201\times201$	258
6	$241\times241\times241$	258
7	$241\times241\times241$	308

Figure 5 shows the execution times for each experiment. We distinguish two kinds of execution time: (1) initialisation time, the time spent after deployment of the ProActive runtime and before the start of the calculation, and (2) computation time, the time spent performing the calculation. One can observe that execution times for the two versions are similar. As regards initialisation times, this result was unexpected as the component-based version creates a larger number of entities (e.g., the domain and factory components). Moreover, creating components is more costly than creating distributed objects due to the need to maintain extra meta-information. Initialisation times are similar probably because Fractal/ProActive incorporates optimisations absent from the ProActive library. Computation times are similar because the costs of subdomain communications are similar. This can be attributed to that the cost of remote object invocation outweighs any small overhead incurred by the component model. The domain component does impose an overhead on communications between the main collector and subdomains, but such infrequent communications have little impact on the calculation time. In summary, the results provide evidence that componentisation has no adverse impact on the performance of the Jem3D application.

Component based vs Object based

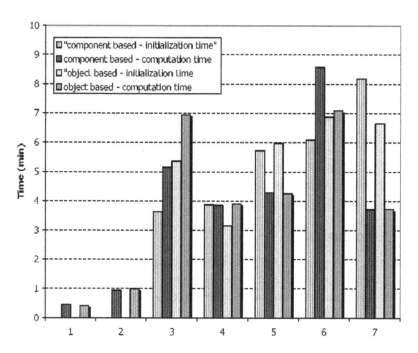

Figure 5. Comparison of execution times.

6. Related work

Regarding the application of components to grid computing, most related work to ours is that associated to the CCA (Common Component Architecture) [9]. CCA is a component model for high-performance scientific computing that has been applied to a wide range of application domains [6]. CCA components are dynamically connected through *provides* and *uses* ports. The main difference with Fractal is that CCA lacks hierarchical composition as a first-class part of the model. Ccaffeine [2] is an implementation of CCA that supports parallel computing. Ccaffeine-based components interact within a given process using CCA ports; parallel instances of Ccaffeine-based components interact across different processes using a separate programming model, typically MPI. XCAT3 [12] is another CCA implementation that supports components distributed over different address spaces and accessible as collections of grid services compliant to OGSI (Open Grid Services Infrastructure). [16] discusses assembling simulation software for partial differential equations from CCA/Ccaffeine components, which encapsulate existing numerical libraries. A simple process for converting such libraries to CCA components is presented in [3]; the process involves first grouping provided and used library functions to provides and uses ports, and then deciding how ports are associated to components. Such work deals with wrapping existing software packages as components rather than decomposing monolithic packages, which is the focus of our paper.

Several researchers have reported experiences with componentising large software systems. [13] describes the componentisation of operating system software for MPSoC (multi-processor system on chip) platforms. Componentisation relies on a lightweight Fractal implementation that targets embedded systems software. Other case studies have concentrated on componentising programmable controller software [14] and real-time telecommunication software [1]. Although such work does not address grid programming, it provides further evidence of the positive effects of componentisation on software modifiability.

7. Conclusion

This paper has presented a case study in reengineering a scientific application into a component-based, grid-enabled application built on Proactive/Fractal. The transformation from an object-based to a component-based system has followed a general, architecture-based componentisation process. The paper has provided qualitative evidence that componentisation using Fractal/ProActive is beneficial to the modifiability and reusability of the application. The paper has also provided quantitative evidence that componentisation has no adverse effect on performance.

There are three main directions for future work. First, we plan to apply the componentisation process and the Fractal/ProActive component platform to other applications in diverse domains. Such work will enable a more complete assessment of their usefulness and usability, and generate further suggestions for improvement. Second, we plan to provide tool support for the componentisation process. Specifically, we envision that the recovery, restructuring, and implementation activities will be largely automated using existing reverse engineering and program transformation tools. The architecture design activity will be supported by tools that employ clustering techniques, metrics, and heuristics, such as in [11]. Finally, we plan to add support for dynamic reconfiguration in the component-based Jem3D application in order to accommodate variations in the availability of underlying resources. Supporting reconfiguration will involve the introduction of manager components that build on the reconfiguration primitives already provided by the component model (e.g., connect or disconnect components), without requiring any change to existing code.

References

[1] H. Algestam, M. Offesson, L. Lundberg, "Using Components to Increase Maintainability in a Large Telecommunication System," Ninth Asia-Pacific Software Engineering Conference (APSEC'02), 2002, p. 65.

[2] B.A. Allan, R.C. Armstrong, A.P. Wolfe, J. Ray, D.E. Bernholdt, and J.A. Kohl, "The CCA core specifications in a distributed memory SPMD framework," *Concurrency Comput. Pract. Exp.*, no. 5, 2002, vol. 14, pp. 323-345.

[3] B.A. Allan, S. Lefantzi, J.Ray, "ODEPACK++: Refactoring the LSODE Fortran Library for Use in the CCA High Performance Component Software Architecture," Ninth International Workshop on High-Level Parallel Programming Models and Supportive Environments (HIPS'04), 2004, pp. 109-119.

[4] L. Baduel, F. Baude, D. Caromel, C. Delbe, S. Kasmi, N. Gama, and S. Lanteri. "A Parallel Object-Oriented Application for 3D Electromagnetism", 18th International Parallel and Distributed Processing Symposium, IEEE Computer Society, Santa Fe, New Mexico, USA, April 2004.

[5] F. Baude, D. Caromel, and M. Morel. "From distributed objects to hierarchical grid components", In International Symposium on Distributed Objects and Applications (DOA), Springer, Catania, Italy, volume 2888 of LNCS, 2003, pages 1226 – 1242.

[6] D.E. Bernholdt, B.A. Allan, R. Armstrong, F. Bertrand, K. Chiu, et al., "A Component Architecture for High Performance Scientific Computing", ACTS Collection special issue, *Intl. J. High-Perf. Computing Applications,* 20 (2006)

[7] E. Bruneton, T. Coupaye, and J. B. Stefani, "Recursive and dynamic software composition with sharing", In Proceedings of the Seventh International Workshop on Component-Oriented Programming (WCOP2002), 2002.

[8] F. Cappello, F. Desprez, M. Dayde, E. Jeannot, et al, "Grid'5000: A Large Scale, Reconfigurable, Controlable and Monitorable Grid Platform", 6th IEEE/ACM International Workshop on Grid Computing, Grid'2005, Seattle, Washington, USA, November 13-14, 2005.

[9] CCA Forum Home Page, The Common Component Architecture Forum, 2004. http://www.cca-forum.org.

[10] Grid Component Model (GCM) Proposal, CoreGRID Deliverable, D.PM.002, Nov. 2005.

[11] S.D. Kim, S.H. Chang, "A Systematic Method to Identify Software Components", 11th Asia-Pacific Software Engineering Conference (APSEC'04), 2004, pp. 538-545.

[12] S. Krishnan and D. Gannon. "XCAT3: A Framework for CCA Components as OGSA Services", 9th Intl Workshop on High-Level Parallel Programming Models and Supportive Environments,IEEE Computer Society Press, 2004.

[13] O. Layaida, A.E. Özcan, and J.B. Stefani. "A Component-based Approach for MPSoC SW Design: Experience with OS Customization for H.264 Decoding", 3rd Workshop on

Embedded Systems for Real-Time Multimedia under CODES+ISSS, New York, USA, 2005.

[14] F. Lüders, I. Crnkovic, P. Runeson, "Adopting a Component-Based Software Architecture for an Industrial Control System – A Case Study, Component-Based Software Development for Embedded Systems", Springer, LNCS 3778, ISBN: 3-540-30644-7, 2005, p 232-248

[15] B.L. Massingill, T.G. Mattson, and B.A. Sanders. "Patterns for parallel application programs", In Proceedings of the Sixth Pattern Languages of Programs Workshop (PLoP99), 1999

[16] B. Norris, S. Balay, S. Benson, L. Freitag, P. Hovland, L. McInnes and B. Smith, "Parallel components for PDEs and optimization: some issues and experiences", *Parallel Computing*, Volume 28, Issue 12, December 2002, pp 1811-1831.

[17] ProActive web site, http://www.inria.fr/oasis/ProActive/

A PEER-TO-PEER FRAMEWORK FOR RESOURCE DISCOVERY IN LARGE-SCALE GRIDS

Domenico Talia, Paolo Trunfio, and Jingdi Zeng*
DEIS, University of Calabria
Via Pietro Bucci 41C, 87036 Rende (CS), Italy
talia@deis.unical.it
trunfio@deis.unical.it
zeng@si.deis.unical.it

Mikael Högqvist
Konrad-Zuse-Zentrum für Informationstechnik Berlin
Takustrasse 7, D-14195 Berlin-Dahlem, Germany
hoegqvist@zib.de

Abstract   As Grids enlarge their boundaries and users, some of their functions should be decentralized to avoid bottlenecks and guarantee scalability. A way to provide Grid scalability is to adopt *Peer-to-Peer* (*P2P*) models to implement non hierarchical decentralized Grid services and systems. A core Grid functionality that can be effectively redesigned using the P2P approach is *resource discovery*. This paper proposes a P2P resource discovery architecture aiming to manage various Grid resources and complex queries. Its goal is two-fold: to address discovery of multiple resources, and to support discovery of dynamic resources and arbitrary queries in Grids. The architecture includes a scalable technique for locating dynamic resources in large-scale Grids. Simulation results are provided to demonstrate the efficiency of the proposed technique.

Keywords: Grid computing, Peer-to-Peer, Resource discovery, Distributed Hash Tables.

---

*Currently with DeVry University, New Jersey, USA.

1.   Introduction

In Grid environments, applications are composed of dispersed hardware and software resources that need to be located and remotely accessed. Efficient and effective resource discovery is then critical. Peer-to-Peer (P2P) techniques have been recently exploited to achieve this goal.

A large amount of work on P2P resource discovery has been done, including both unstructured and structured systems. Early unstructured P2P systems, such as Gnutella [1], use the *flooding technique* to broadcast the resource requests in the network. The flooding technique does not rely on a specific network topology and supports queries in arbitrary forms. Several approaches [2–4], moreover, have been proposed to solve two intrinsic drawbacks of the flooding technique, i.e., the potentially massive amount of messages, and the possibility that an existing resource may not be located. In structured P2P networks, Distributed Hash Tables (DHTs) are widely used. *DHT-based systems* [5–7] arrange $< key, value >$ pairs in multiple locations across the network. A query message is forwarded towards the node that is responsible for the key in a limited number of hops. The result is guaranteed, if such a key exists in the system. As compared to unstructured systems, however, DHT-based approaches need intensive maintenance on hash table updates.

Taking into account the characteristics of Grids, several P2P resource discovery techniques have been adapted to such environments. For instance, DHT-based P2P resource discovery systems have been extended to support range value and multi-attribute queries [8–12]. Two major differences between P2P systems and Grids, however, determine their different approaches towards resource discovery. First, P2P systems are typically designed to share files among peers. Differently, Grids deal with a set of different resources, ranging from files to computing resources. Second, the dynamism of P2P systems comes from both nodes and resources. Peers join and leave at any time, and thus do the resources shared among them. In Grid environments, nodes connect to the network in a relatively more stable manner. The dynamism of Grids mainly comes from the fast-changing statuses of resources. For example, the storage space and CPU load can change continuously over time.

Highlighting the variety and dynamism of Grid resources, this paper proposes a DHT-based resource discovery architecture for Grids. The rest of the paper is organized as follows. Section 2 introduces existing Grid resource discovery systems that relate to our work. Section 3 discusses characteristics of Grid resources and related query requirements. Section 4 unfolds the picture of the proposed architecture, and studies the performance of its dynamic resource discovery strategy through simulations. Section 5 concludes the paper.

2.   Related work

Several systems exploiting DHT-based P2P approaches for resource discovery in Grids have been proposed [8–12]. Two important issues addressed by these systems are multi-attribute resource discovery and range queries.

Multi-attribute resource discovery refers to the problem of locating resources that are described by a set of attributes or characteristics (e.g., OS version, CPU speed, etc.). To resolve a multi-attribute query, the most used approach is to decompose the query in a set of sub-queries (one per attribute), and then to perform a single-attribute search for each sub-query. The retrieved results are then intersected at the querying node to find the final set of resources that satisfies the original query [8–10].

Range queries look for resources specified by a range of attribute values (e.g., a CPU with speed in the range from 2.2 GHz to 3.6 GHz). These queries are not supported by standard DHT-based systems such as Chord [5], CAN [6], and Pastry [7], because those systems make use of hash functions that do not preserve the locality of values. To support range queries, a typical approach is to use locality preserving hashing functions, which retain the order of numerical values in DHTs [8–9].

MAAN [8] provides support for multi-attribute range queries by exploiting the Chord protocol [5]. Each node in MAAN is part of a Chord overlay. The values of the resources are mapped to the Chord key space using a locality preserving hash function and having one different registration for each resource attribute. Each registration is composed by a pair $< attribute-value, resource-info >$. Each node is responsible of maintaining the information of the registered keys that fall into the key space sector it supervises.

The resolution of multi-attribute range queries is implemented in two different ways. The first one follows the general approach described above: if a query is composed of M sub-queries, each sub-query is resolved separately in the proper attribute space. The results are then collected and intersected at the query originator node. The complexity of this approach is $O(\sum_{i=1}^{M}(logN + N \times s_i))$, where M is the number of sub-queries, N is the number of peers, and s_i is the selectivity of sub-query i, defined as the ratio of the query range width to the size of the whole identifier space.

The second method is defined as a single-attribute dominated routing. Let X be the set of resources that satisfies query Q. X should satisfy all the sub-queries of Q, then $X = \bigcap_{1 \leq i \leq M} X_i$, where X_i is the set that satisfies the sub-query on attribute a_i. MAAN uses Chord to find a single set of candidate resources X_k for attribute a_k. X_k is a superset of X, so all the solutions for query Q are contained in X_k. Since all the resources store a $< attribute-value, resource-info >$ pair, it is possible to exploit the resource-info field to find the X_k's resources that match all the other sub-queries. This method has a complexity of $O(logN + N \times S_{min})$, where S_{min} is the minimum selectivity for all attributes.

Andrzejak and Xu [9] propose an extension of CAN [6] to support range queries in a Grid information system. For each attribute of a generic Grid resource either a standard DHT or the proposed CAN extension is used depending on its type. In particular, attributes which have a limited number of values are handled by standard DHT systems, while for "continuous" types of attributes the extended CAN system is adopted. To locate resources specified by several attributes, the information infrastructure queries for each attribute present in the query the appropriate DHT and then concatenates the results in a database-like "join" operation.

A subset of the Grid servers participates as nodes in a CAN-based P2P-network and store the pairs $< attribute\text{-}value, resource\text{-}ID >$. Each one of them is responsible for a given subinterval of the attribute values. Such a server is called an *Interval Keeper* (*IK*) and the corresponding subinterval its *interval*. Each server in the Grid reports its current attribute value to an IK with the appropriate interval. The authors propose different strategies for propagating range-query requests and to minimize the communication overhead during the attribute updates.

Another example of DHT-based system is XenoSearch [10], which exploits and extends the Pastry framework [7]. XenoSearch allows multi-dimensional search by using a separate Pastry ring for each attribute. A peer registers itself separately in each ring. Range queries for a single attribute are possible thanks to the fact that the information is conceptually stored in a tree where the leaves are the peer nodes. The tree internal nodes are called *Aggregation Points* (*AP*). Each AP summarizes the range of values of the nodes below it in the tree. An AP is distinguished by a key in the same key space as the attributes. The key of an AP is a prefix of the keys of its child nodes. By knowing the key of an AP, it is possible to determine the range of values of the leaf-nodes of that AP. An AP key is mapped into the Pastry ring and the closest peer in the key space is in charge for maintaining the information related to that AP.

As before, multi-attribute queries are resolved by decomposing each query in a set of sub-queries, and resolving all the sub-queries in parallel. The client that originated the query is given a set of possibly matching peers. The client has to further query the nodes to know the real server's resource state. This is necessary because the information in the system is refreshed only periodically.

In order to efficiently support multi-attribute queries, the systems described above arrange attribute values on multiple DHTs, one per attribute. Some other systems [11–12] adopt a single DHT for all attributes, using specific strategies to map multiple values into a single key space. Both multi-DHT and single-DHT approaches have proved effective, but multi-DHT architectures are easier to implement and provide multi-attribute search capabilities in a simple way.

The system proposed in this paper uses multiple DHTs to manage attributes of multiple resources. This provides a straightforward architecture, and leaves space for potential extensions.

Two works that are strictly related to our framework are the Gnutella-based *dynamic querying* protocol [13], and the algorithm for broadcast over DHTs proposed in [14].

Dynamic querying [13] is a strategy used to reduce the number of messages generated by flooding. In dynamic querying, the peer that initiates a search controls the query propagation by sending it only to a subset of its neighbors and with a small Time-to-Live (TTL). If this first attempt does not produce the expected number of results, the originating peer proceeds iteratively by sending the query to a different set of neighbors with increased TTL. For relatively popular contents this strategy significantly reduces the number of messages without increasing the response time.

Broadcast in DHT-based P2P networks [14] adds a broadcast service to a class of DHT systems that have logarithmic performance bounds. In a network of N nodes, the node that starts the broadcast reaches all other nodes in the network with exactly $N - 1$ messages (that is, no redundant messages are generated), with $logN$ steps.

The approach for dynamic resource discovery proposed in this paper is inspired by both the dynamic query strategy and the broadcast approach mentioned above. It uses a DHT for broadcasting queries to all nodes without redundant messages, and adopts a similar "incremental" approach of dynamic query. This approach reduces the number of exchanged messages and response time, which ensures scalability in large-scale Grids.

3. Resources and query types

In Grids, *resources* belong to different *resource classes*. A *resource class* is a "model" for representing resources of the same type. Each resource class is defined by a set of attributes which specify its characteristics. A *resource* is an "instance" of a resource class. Each resource has a specific value for each attribute defined by the corresponding resource class. Resources are univocally identified by URLs.

An example of resource class is "computing resource" that defines the common characteristics of computing resources. These characteristics are described by attributes such as "OS name", "CPU speed", and "Free memory". An instance of the "computing resource" class has a specific value for each attribute, for example, "OS name = Linux", "CPU speed = 1000MHz", and "Free memory = 1024MB". Table 1 lists some examples of Grid resources classes. A more complete list of resource classes can be found in [15].

Table 1.   Examples of Grid resource classes.

Resource class	Description
Computing resource	Computing capabilities provided by computers, clusters of computers, etc.
Storage resource	Storage space such as disks, external memory, etc.
Network resource	Network connections that ensures collaboration between Grid resources.
Device resource	Specific devices such as instruments, sensors, etc.
Software resource	Operating systems, software packages, Web services, etc.
Data resource	Various kinds of data stored in file systems or databases.

Resource classes can be broadly classified into *intra-node* and *inter-node* resources. "Computing resource" is an example of intra-node resource class. An example of inter-node resource class is "network connection" (see Table 1), which defines network resource characteristics. Figure 1 shows a simple Grid including four nodes and three resource classes. As examples of intra-node resources, $NodeA$ includes two instances of resource class a and one instance of resource class b. The figure also shows two inter-node resources: one between $NodeA$ and $NodeD$, and the other between $NodeB$ and $NodeD$.

The attributes of each resource class are either *static* or *dynamic*. *Static* attributes refer to resource characteristics that do not change frequently, such as "OS name" and "CPU speed" of a computing resource. *Dynamic* attributes are associated to fast changing characteristics, such as "CPU load" and "Free memory".

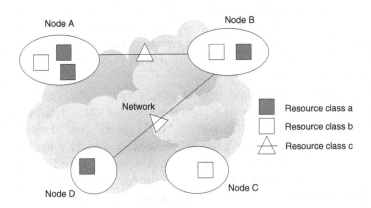

Figure 1.   Inter-node and intra-nodes resources.

The goal of resource discovery in Grids is to locate resources that satisfy a given set of requirements on their attribute values. Three types of queries apply to each attribute involved in resource discovery:

- *Exact match query*, where attribute values of numeric, boolean, or string types are searched.

- *Range query*, where a range of numeric or string values is searched.

- *Arbitrary query*, where for instance partial phrase match or semantic search is carried out.

A *multi-attribute* query is composed of a set of sub-queries on single attributes. Each sub-query fits in one of the three types as listed above, and the involved attributes are either static or dynamic.

Complex Grid applications involve multiple resources. Thus, *multi-resource* queries are often needed. For instance, one can be interested in discovering two computing resources and one storage resource; these resources may not be geographically close to each other. A multi-resource query, in fact, involves a set of sub-queries on individual resources, where each sub-query can be a multi-attribute query.

Taking into consideration both characteristics and query requirements of Grid resources, the P2P search techniques exploited in our framework are listed in Table 2.

Table 2.   P2P search techniques for different types of resources and queries.

	Static Grid resources	Dynamic Grid resources
Exact queries	Structured	Unstructured
Range queries	Structured	Unstructured
Arbitrary queries	Unstructured	Unstructured

As shown in the table, structured search is used only for exact and range queries on static Grid resources. This is because DHT-based structured systems are not effective for dynamic resources and arbitrary queries. In fact, DHT-based P2P systems were not originally designed for queries of arbitrary expression forms. Moreover, fast-changing resources, such as CPU load, require frequent updates on DHTs, and thus cause prohibitive maintenance costs. On the other hand, unstructured approaches are used for both dynamic Grid resources and arbitrary queries on static resources. This is because unstructured systems generally do not require table updates and maintenance. However, the huge amount of messages generated by flooding-based unstructured systems requires the use of appropriate strategies to ensure scalability in large networks.

4.   System architecture

The framework aims to provide a generic architecture that leverages existing techniques to fulfill various resource discovery needs in Grid environments. In order to exploit diverse resource discovery techniques, the DHT-based architecture described in Figure 2 is proposed.

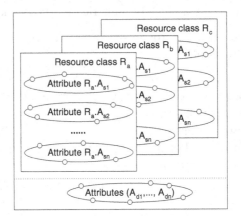

Figure 2.   System architecture.

The system is composed of a set of *virtual planes*, one for each resource class. Within the virtual plane of resource class R_a, for example, static attributes $R_a.A_{s1}$, ..., $R_a.A_{sn}$ are associated to their DHTs, respectively. Exact or range queries on *static* attributes are carried out using the DHTs corresponding to these attributes.

An additional "general purpose" DHT is dedicated to queries on dynamic attributes and to arbitrary queries on static attributes. This DHT is different from the DHTs in the virtual planes. The DHTs in the virtual plane are standard DHTs, in which both nodes and resource identifiers are mapped to the same ring. In general purpose DHT, only node identifiers are mapped to the ring, while resources are not mapped to it. In other words, there are not pointers to resources in the general purpose ring.

The general purpose DHT is used to broadcast queries to all Grid nodes whose identifiers are mapped to the ring. All Grid nodes reached by a query are in charge of processing it against the local resources, and sending the response to the node that initiated the query. The mechanisms used for broadcasting a query on this ring are described in Section 4.3.

4.1   Local components

Figure 3 shows the software modules inside each Grid node. With multiple virtual planes defined in the system, each node participates in all DHTs of these virtual planes. Therefore, multiple finger tables corresponding to each DHT co-exist in each node, as illustrated in Figure 3. For example, finger tables $FT(R_a.A_1)$, $FT(R_a.A_2)$,..., and $FT(R_a.A_n)$ correspond to DHTs of attributes $R_a.A_{s1}...R_a.A_{sn}$ in Figure 2.

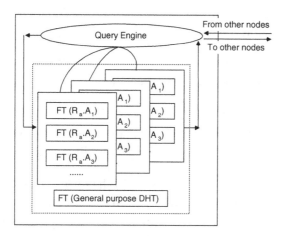

Figure 3.   Software modules inside each Grid node. FTs are finger tables associated to the used DHTs.

The finger table of the general purpose DHT, that is, *FT(General purpose DHT)*, is used to reach individual nodes and locate dynamic attributes $A_{d1},...,A_{dn}$. A query engine processes resource discovery requests and associates them to different query instances and thus DHTs. The results are then generated at the node where related queries are initiated.

4.2   Static attribute discovery

A number of systems that support multi-attribute range query have been proposed. As discussed in Section 2, they either use one DHT for all attributes, or arrange attribute values on multiple DHTs. While both single-DHT and multi-DHT approaches have proved effective, we adopt the multi-DHT strategy because of its simplicity and extension potentials.

Assume there are p classes of resources, each of which has q types of attributes. Although one node does not necessarily have all attributes, it is included in all DHTs, and the values of its blank entries are left as null. The number of finger tables that a node maintains is $p \times q$.

While existing approaches support resource discovery on single or multiple attributes of one resource class, the architecture proposed in this paper manages multiple resources. One way to do this is to hash the string of "resource class + attribute" into a *DHT ID*; this ID is used to identify the corresponding finger table inside a node.

4.3   Dynamic attribute discovery

As mentioned in Section 2, our approach for dynamic resource discovery exploits both the dynamic query [13] and the broadcast over DHT [14] strategies. The general purpose DHT and associated finger tables, as illustrated in Figures 2 and 3, are used only to index Grid nodes, without keeping pointers to Grid resource attributes. Queries are then processed by the local query engine of each node.

4.3.1   To reach all nodes.   To reach all nodes without redundant messages, the broadcast strategy is based on a DHT [14]. Taking a fully populated Chord ring with $N = 2^M$ nodes and a M-bit identifier space as an example. Each Chord node k has a finger table, with fingers pointing to nodes $k + 2^{i-1}$, where $i = 1, ..., M$. Each of these M nodes, in turn, has its fingers pointing to another M nodes. Each node forwards the query to all nodes in its finger table, and in turn, these nodes do the same with nodes in their finger tables. In this way, all nodes are reached in M steps. Since multiple fingers may point to the same node, a strategy is used to avoid redundant messages. Each message contains a "limit" argument, which is used to restrict the forwarding space of a receiving node. The "limit" argument of a message for the node pointed by finger i is finger $i + 1$.

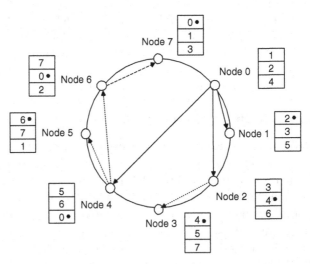

Figure 4.   An example of broadcast.

Figure 4 gives an example of an eight-node three-bit identifier Chord ring. The limit of broadcast is marked with a black dot. Three steps of communication between nodes are demonstrated with solid, dotted, and dashed lines. Obviously, node 0 reaches all other nodes via $N - 1$ messages within M steps.

The same procedure applies to Chord ring with $N < 2^M$ (i.e., not fully populated networks). In this case, the number of distinct fingers of each node is $logN$ on the average.

4.3.2 Incremental resource discovery.

The broadcast over DHT presented above adopts a "parallel" approach. That is, the node that initiates the discovery tasks sends the query message to all its fingers in parallel.

Although no redundant messages are generated in the network, its $N - 1$ messages can be prohibitive in large-scale Grids. Referred to as "incremental", our approach uses a mixed parallel and sequential query message forwarding.

A "parallel degree" D is introduced to adjust the range of parallel message forwarding, and thus curb the number of exchanged messages. Given a node that initiates the query, it forwards the query message in parallel to nodes pointed by its first distinct D fingers. If there is a positive response, the search terminates; otherwise, this node forwards the query message to the node pointed by its $D + 1$ finger. This procedure applies to nodes pointed by the rest of fingers, sequentially, until a positive response returns.

When $D = M$, our incremental approach turns into the parallel one; when $D = 1$, the incremental approach becomes a sequential one, where nodes pointed by all fingers are visited one after another.

The number of generated messages by the incremental approach is obviously less than or equal to that of the parallel one. The response time of incremental approach, however, may be prolonged owing to its sequential query message forwarding. We argue that this does not necessarily hold true. In large-scale Grids, multiple query requests at one node can be prominent, which adds extra delay to response time. Under this circumstance, the incremental approach shall benefit from its reduced number of messages that shortens this extra delay.

4.3.3 Performance evaluation.

A discrete-event simulator has been implemented to evaluate the performance of the incremental approach in comparison with the parallel approach. Two performance parameters have been evaluated: the *number of messages Q* and the *response time T*. Q is the total number of exchanged messages in the network, and T is the time a node waited to receive the first response (i.e., the first query hit).

The main system parameters are: N, the number of Grid nodes in the network; R, the number of nodes that concurrently submit query requests; P, the fraction of nodes that possesses the desired resource; and D, the number of first distinct fingers the search is conducted on in parallel. The number of nodes N was ranged from 2000 to 10000, R from 10 to 1000, and P from 0.005 to 0.25. Finally, we used $D = 7$ in all simulations. The system parameter values have been chosen to fit as much as possible with real Grid scenarios. In particular, the wide range of values chosen for P reflects the fact that, in real Grids, discovery tasks can search both for rare resources (e.g., the IRIX operating system) and more popular ones (e.g., Linux).

The time to pass a message from $NodeA$ to $NodeB$ is calculated as the sum of a processing time and a delivery time. The processing time is proportional to the number of queued messages in $NodeA$, while the delivery time is proportional to the number of incoming messages at $NodeB$. In this way, the response time depends on both message traffic and processing load of nodes.

Table 3 shows the number of exchanged messages in both parallel and incremental strategies, with $R = 1$. The parallel strategy always generates $N-1$ messages for each submitted query, which could be prohibitive for large-scale Grids. In the incremental approach, the number of messages is dramatically reduced. Moreover, when the value of P is over a certain limit, the number of messages fluctuates around the value of 2^D and it does not depend from the number of nodes (i.e., network size). This limit is determined by the number of Grid nodes N, the fraction of nodes with matching resources P, and the number of first distinct fingers D.

Table 3.   Comparison on the number of exchanged messages (Q) in parallel and incremental approaches.

N	P	Q (Parallel)	Q (Incremental)
	0.005	1999	279
2000	0.10	1999	127
	0.25	1999	126
	0.005	3999	326
4000	0.10	3999	129
	0.25	3999	124
	0.005	5999	291
6000	0.10	5999	126
	0.25	5999	126
	0.005	7999	282
8000	0.10	7999	128
	0.25	7999	128
	0.005	9999	389
10000	0.10	9999	127
	0.25	9999	125

For example, in a network with $N = 10000$, when $P = 0.1$ the number of matching resources is $N \times P = 1000$. The number of nodes included in the first $D = 7$ fingers is $2^D = 128$, on the average. Obviously, this density is high enough for the incremental strategy to locate the desired resource within the first D fingers. With a lower value of P, nevertheless, the search needs to go beyond the first D fingers; this introduces a fluctuation in the number of exchanged messages, as in the case of $P = 0.005$.

Figure 5 shows the response time in a network composed by 10000 nodes, with $P = 0.10$ and values of R ranging from 10 to 1000. The response time is expressed in time units.

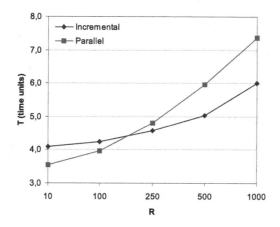

Figure 5.   Response time in parallel and incremental approaches ($N = 10000$).

The main result shown in Figure 5 is that, when the value of R is at the lower end of its range, the parallel approach has a shorter response time. When the value of R increases, the incremental approach outperforms the parallel one. This is because in the parallel approach the overall number of generated messages is much higher than the one in the incremental approach, resulting in increased message traffic and processing load that cause a higher response time.

It is important to recall that in our simulator the processing time is proportional to the number of messages to be processed, and the delivery time is proportional to the number of messages to be delivered. Therefore, the response time increases linearly with message traffic and load of nodes. In a more realistic scenario the processing time and the delivery time may increase exponentially with the load of the network. In this case, the response time in the incremental approach should result significantly better that the parallel one. To better evaluate the effect of high loads in large-scale Grids, we are currently studying the use of more complex processing and delivery time functions in our simulator.

5.   Conclusions

This paper introduced a DHT-based P2P framework to address the variety and dynamism of Grid resources. It exploits multiple DHTs and existing P2P techniques for multiple static resources and implements an "incremental" resource discovery approach for dynamic resources. As compared to the original strategy, the incremental approach generates reduced number of messages and experiences lower response time in large-scale Grids.

Our previous work on Grid resource discovery mainly focused on the use of unstructured P2P protocols and Grid services to address the dynamism of Grid resources [16]. This work improves the previous one by combining the use of structured and unstructured techniques to address arbitrary queries on both static and dynamic Grid resources. We are currently studying how to extend the architecture in this paper to address Grid service discovery, including new features such as dynamic service indexing and XML-based queries support.

Acknowledgements

This research work is carried out under the FP6 Network of Excellence CoreGRID funded by the European Commission (Contract IST-2002-004265).

References

[1] Gnutella Protocol Development. http://rfc-gnutella.sourceforge.net/src/rfc-0_6-draft.html.

[2] C. Gkantsidis, M. Mihail and A. Saberi. Hybrid Search Schemes for Unstructured Peer-to-peer Networks. Proc. of INFOCOM'05, Miami, USA, 2005.

[3] Q. Lv, P. Cao, E. Cohen, K. Li and S. Shenker. Search and Replicating in Unstructured Peer-to-peer Networks. Proc. of the Int. Conf. on Supercomputing (SC'02), New York, USA, 2002.

[4] A. Crespo and H. Garcia-Molina. Routing Indices for Peer-to-peer Systems. Proc. of the Int. Conf. on Distributed Computing Systems (ICDCS'02), Vienna, Austria, 2002.

[5] I. Stoica, R. Morris, D. Karger, M.F. Kaashoek and H. Balakrishnan. Chord: A Scalable Peer-to-peer Lookup Service for Internet Applications. Proc. of SIGCOMM'01, San Diego, USA, 2001.

[6] S. Ratnasany, P. Francis, M. Handley, R.M. Karp and S. Shenker. A Scalable Content-Addressable Network. Proc. of SIGCOMM'01, San Diego, USA, 2001.

[7] A. Rowstron and P. Druschel. Pastry: Scalable, distributed object location and routing for large-scale peer-to-peer systems. Proc. of Middleware 2001, Heidelberg, Germany, 2001.

[8] M. Cai, M. Frank, J. Chen and P. Szekely. MAAN: A Multi-Attribute Addressable Network for Grid Information Services. *Journal of Grid Computing.* 2(1):3-14, 2004.

[9] A. Andrzejak and Z. Xu. Scalable, Efficient Range Queries for Grid Information Services. Proc. of P2P'02, Linköping, Sweden, 2002.

[10] D. Spence and T. Harris. XenoSearch: Distributed Resource Discovery in the XenoServer Open Platform. Proc. of HPDC'03, Washington, USA, 2003.

[11] D. Oppenheimer, J. Albrecht, D. Patterson and A. Vahdat. Scalable Wide-Area Resource Discovery. UC Berkeley Tech. Report, UCB/CSD-04-1334, 2004.

[12] C. Schmidt and M. Parashar. Flexible Information Discovery in Decentralized Distributed Systems. Proc. of the Int. Symp. on High-Performance Distributed Computing (HPDC-12), Seattle, USA, 2003.

[13] A.A. Fisk. Gnutella Dynamic Query Protocol v0.1. http://www.the-gdf.org/wiki/index.php?title=Dynamic_Querying.

[14] S. El-Ansary, L. Alima, P. Brand and S. Haridi. Efficient Broadcast in Structured P2P Networks. Proc. of CCGRID'05, Cardiff, UK, 2005.

[15] S. Andreozzi et al. GLUE Schema Specification Version 1.2. http://infnforge.cnaf.infn.it/glueinfomodel/index.php/Spec/V12.

[16] D. Talia and P. Trunfio. Adapting a Pure Decentralized Peer-to-Peer Protocol for Grid Services Invocation. *Parallel Processing Letters.* **15**(1-2):67-84, 2005.

GRID SUPERSCALAR AND GRICOL: INTEGRATING DIFFERENT PROGRAMMING APPROACHES

Raül Sirvent and Rosa M. Badia
Barcelona Supercomputing Center and UPC, SPAIN
rsirvent@ac.upc.edu
rosab@ac.upc.edu

Natalia Currle-Linde and Michael Resch
High Performance Computing Center Stuttgart (HLRS), University of Stuttgart
linde@hlrs.de
resch@hlrs.de

Abstract   One way to ease the development of Grid applications is to specify and design an Integrated Toolkit which will enable the development of Grid-unaware applications i.e. applications where the Grid is transparent to them but that are able to exploit its resources. Achieving this vision of an Integrated Toolkit requires the investigation and definition of integration between different systems. This paper studies the integration possibilities of GriCoL, a language for the description of complex Grid experiments, and GRID superscalar, a run-time environment which automatically converts sequential program code and deploys it for execution on a Grid. GriCoL operates on a multi-layer paradigm, using both a control flow layer and a data flow layer. We propose integration with GRID superscalar at each of these layers, concluded that integration at the control flow level is difficult to achieve but at the data flow level is possible.

Keywords: Grid programming models, Problem solving environments, GRID superscalar, GriCoL.

1.   Introduction

The difficulty associated with developing applications to be run on the Grid is a major barrier to adoption of this technology by non-expert users. The challenge in this case is to provide programming environments for Grid-unaware applications, defined as applications where the Grid is transparent to them but that are able to exploit its resources. Furthermore, the challenge is to increase the performance of these applications when possible.

To meet these challenges, one research task of the CoreGRID Institute for Grid Systems, Tools and Environments is the development of an Integrated Toolkit [1]. This task aims to specify and design an Integrated Toolkit which will enable the development of Grid-unaware applications. The run-time of such an integrated toolkit would run these applications in a Grid and optimise their performance dynamically.

The CoreGRID STE vision of an Integrated Toolkit is composed of an Integrated Toolkit run-time and of Integrated Toolkit bindings to different programming languages or to graphical tools and portals. For the specification and design of the Integrated Toolkit, the integration between several different systems is being investigated and defined [1]: ProActive, PadicoTM, GRID superscalar, P-GRADE Portal, Satin/Ibis, GAT/SAGA and the monitoring environment OCM-G. In addition, this paper discusses the integration of GriCoL [2], a language for the description of complex Grid experiments, and GRID superscalar, a run-time environment which automatically converts sequential program code and deploys it for execution on a Grid. Several languages (C/C++, Perl, Java and Shell script) are already supported for programming with GRID superscalar [5].

Figure 1 illustrates a vision of how these various components above can interoperate to realistically build an Integrated Toolkit.

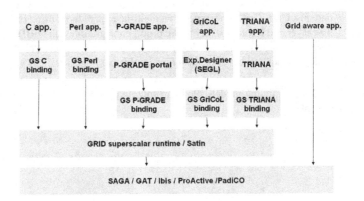

Figure 1.   Integrated Toolkit picture.

The GriCoL language is Grid-unaware. It is a component-based language for describing complex scientific modeling experiments with a sufficient level of abstraction that the user does not require a knowledge of the Grid or parallel programming. GriCoL is currently utilised within the problem solving environment Science Experimental Grid Laboratory (SEGL)[3], which enables the automated creation, start and monitoring of complex scientific experiments and supports their effective execution on the Grid. SEGL has two main parts: a GUI for the design of the experiment, by working with elements of GriCoL, and a run-time system which chooses the necessary computer resources, organises and controls the sequence of execution according to the task flow and the conditions of the experiment program. Sections 2 and 3 of this paper describe respectively GriCoL and GRID superscalar in more detail and section 4 studies the integration possibilities of these two frameworks as a further step in the realisation of the CoreGRID STE Integrated Toolkit.

2. GriCoL

GriCoL is a universal language for programming complex computer- and data-intensive tasks without being tied to a specific application domain.

GriCoL is a graphical-based language with mixed type and is based on a component-structure model. The main elements of this language are blocks and modules, which have a defined internal structure and interact with each other through a defined set of interfaces.

The language is of an entirely parallel nature. It can implement parallel processing of many data sets at all levels, i.e. inside simple language elements (modules); at the level of more complex language structures (blocks) and for the entire experiment. In general, the possibility of parallel execution of operations in all nodes of the experiment program is unlimited.

In order to utilize the capacities of supercomputer applications and to enable interaction with other language elements and structures, it makes use of the principle of wrapping the functionality into components.

Another important property of the language is that it is multi-tiered. This enables the user when describing the experiment to concentrate primarily on the logic of the experiment program and subsequently on the description of the individual parts of the program. The top level of the experiment program is the control flow level, which describes the logical sequence of execution. The main elements of this level are blocks: control blocks and solver blocks. A solver block is the program object which performs some complete operation. The standard example of a solver block can be a simple parameter sweep. The control block is the program object which allows the changing of the sequence of the execution according to a specified criterion. The lower level, the data flow level, provides a detailed description of components at the top level, the control flow level. The main elements of the data flow level are program modules and database sections. The sublayer provides a common description of the database and a section for making additions to the database if necessary. The elements of the language have graphical notation and are represented by icons (for modules and blocks) or as connection lines.

Figure 2 illustrates the above mentioned for an molecular dynamic simulation at the control flow level.

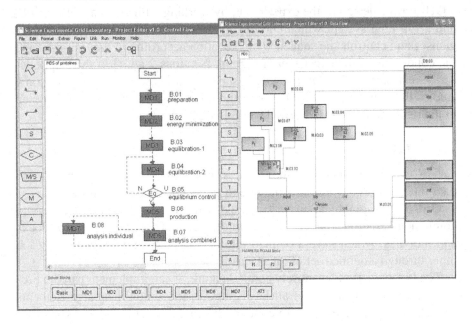

Figure 2.   Screenshots of Molecular Dynamics Simulation ((a) Control flow and (b) Data flow of a solver block.

As can be seen from this figure the language components make it possible to generate multilayer dynamic-control experiment programs with branches. GriCoL offers the user a complete range of control mechanisms on experiment processes: parallelization, testing of conditions and branching, synchronization and fusion, as well as exchange of messages and signals.

Solver blocks represent the nodes of data processing. Control blocks are either nodes of data analysis or nodes for the synchronization of data computation processes. They evaluate results and then choose a path for further experiment development. Another important language element on the control flow level is the connection line. There are two mechanisms of interaction between blocks which are described with the help of connection lines (either red-solid or blue-dashed). If the connection line is blue in colour, the procedure is as follows: each time the computation of an individual data set has been finished, i.e. after completion of a program run within a block, control is transferred to the next block. This process is repeated until all program runs in the block have been completed. That means a pipelined operation on the set of runs. If the connection line is red in colour, control is not passed to the next block before all runs in the previous block have been finished. That means a barrier on the set of runs.

We can illustrate this with an example taken from the field of Molecular Dynamics (MD) simulation, which is a computational method to calculate the time dependent behaviour of a biological molecular system. The left-hand screenshot of figure 2 shows the client visual editor at the control flow level of a large-scale MD simulation study. A total of 3000 different topologies of the system (with different enzyme variants, substrates and starting conditions) are generated in the preparation solver block B.01. The blue-dashed connection lines in figure 2 (e.g. between B.01 and B.02) indicate that as soon as a particular simulation task in B.01 has finished, it can be passed on to the next block B.02. A solid line between blocks (e.g. between B.06 and B.07) means that all tasks have to be finished in the preceding block before the control flow proceeds to the next block.

At the data flow level, a typical example of a solver block program is a modeling program (or a program fragment) which cyclically computes a large number of input data sets. At this level, the user can describe the manipulation of data in a very fine grained way. The solver block consists of computation (C), replacement (R), parameterization (P) modules and a database (Exp.DB). These are connected to each other with lines showing the data transfer between modules and the sequence of execution during the computation process. Each module is a Java object, which has a standard structure and consists of several sections. For example: each computation module (C) consists of four sections. The first section organizes the preparation of input data. The second generates the job and controls its execution. The third initializes and controls the record of the result in the experiment data base. The fourth section controls the execution of module operation. It also informs the main program of the block about the manipulation of certain sets of data and when execution within a block is complete. A typical control block program carries out an iterative analysis of the data sets from previous steps of the experiment program and selects either the direction for the further development of the experiment or examines whether the input data sets are ready for further computation, and subsequently synchronizes their further processing.

This example demonstrates an advantage of GriCoL over the many existing tools such as Nimrod[4] or Condor [4] in carrying out complex parameter investigation studies. Nimrod is able to generate parameter sweeps and jobs, running them in a Grid and collecting the data. However, it is unable to perform the task dynamically by generating new parameter sets through an automated optimization strategy. Condor can be used to launch pre-existing parameter studies using distributed resources but gives no special support for dynamic parameter studies.

The right-hand screenshot of figure 2 shows, at the data flow level, the client visual editor for a particular aspect of the previously described MD simulation. It shows the data flow of the equilibration solver block (B.03) from the left-hand screenshot (control flow level). The computation module (C-Amber) for the simulation program needs the system topology, the coordinates of the system to start from and an input file. Whereas the system topology and the starting coordinates are taken out of the experiment database via the selection module (S2 and S3), the input files are created for each simulation run individually. Therefore three parameterization modules (P1 -P3) provide the values for the replacement module (R1) that puts these values into an input file skeleton taken from the experiment database (via selection module S1). The resulting output form the simulation is put back into the experiment database.

3. GRID superscalar

As a programming model, GRID superscalar is focused on easing the programming of Grid applications. It is clear that the easiest way of programming for a user is with the desired programming language, in which the user is already an expert, and in a sequential fashion, without using complicated parallel schemes where the user must control syncronizations, message passings, and so on. GRID superscalar achieves this by providing bindings to different programming languages (currently C/C++, Perl, Java and Shell script), and a runtime which automatically executes in parallel the user-defined functions that do not have data dependencies between them. From that source code, GRID superscalar builds internally a workflow with the existing data dependencies between functions, as shown in figure 3, and from that workflow the tasks without dependencies are considered to be run on the Grid. GRID superscalar is not only a programming model, but also a set of tools that allows users to easily *gridify* an application.

This programming model has been adapted to several environments, currently: Globus (which can work with versions 2 and 4 of the Globus Toolkit [6]), ssh/scp, Ninf-G [7] , and the next development version, which adds the data dependence detection between scalar parameters.

In order to program an application with GRID superscalar, a developer must provide a main program, the code of the functions in that specific main program to be executed in the Grid, and an IDL file, which describes the interface of these functions (the type of the parameters, and the direction of these parameters). There is a small set of calls that must be added in the main program: *GS_On* for starting the run-time, and *GS_Off* for stopping it. Calls for handling

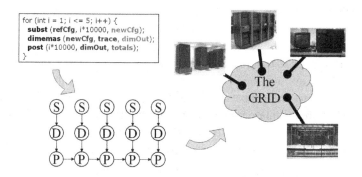

```
for (int i = 1; i <= 5; i++) {
    subst (refCfg, i*10000, newCfg);
    dimemas (newCfg, trace, dimOut);
    post (i*10000, dimOut, totals);
}
```

Figure 3.   GRID superscalar in a nutshell.

local files (*GS_Open/GS_Close, GS_FOpen/GS_FClose*), as the file is the data unit considered for detecting the dependencies between the functions. Also more advanced, but optional, primitives are provided, such as *GS_Barrier* to wait for all generated tasks to finish, and *GS_Speculative_End* to easily create optimization-like algorithms.

GRID superscalar is not only a programming model, but also includes a set of tools in order to ease the porting of the application to the Grid. A tool named *Deployment Center* allows not only to graphically specify and check the Grid configuration, but also to deploy (send and compile) locally and remotelly the code involved in this developer's project. This deployment step is assisted by *gsstubgen*, another tool in charge of generating stubs and skeletons needed for allowing the run-time calls, and *gsbuilder*, responsible for compiling the generated code. This process creates a local client binary and several remote server binaries, which lets a master-worker paradigm application ready to run.

When the user invokes the local binary (the master or client) the run-time comes into action. It starts building a Directed Acyclic Graph containing the data dependencies between the tasks generated till that moment, and at the same time starts submitting the tasks which are ready (with no dependencies) to the available machines, thus achieving its parallel execution. In order to decide which is the most suitable host for a task, an estimation of the task's execution time provided by the user is considered, as well as the time that will be spent to transfer all input files required.

The run-time is also in charge of transferring the files needed by a task to the selected host, submitting the task, and after completion, transfer the results back to the master. The input and output files related to a task are kept in the worker till the end of the execution to try to exploit the locality of files, thus saving file transfers. So the results of a task can be used when the task finishes, without having to wait for the transfer to the master to end. When a task has finished, the data dependence graph is updated (this can generate new ready tasks) and the resource becomes available for executing a new task. And at the end of the execution, the remote files are cleaned up, and the remaining results are transferred back to the master, so leaving everything as if it had been a local execution of the application. Other techniques are used in the run-time, such as file renaming to erase false data dependencies, disk sharing to make GRID superscalar aware of data replicas or real shared file systems, checkpointing in order to restart the computation from where it stopped because of a big failure, and ClassAds [8] constraints specification to filter the resources in the Grid. Also dynamic host reconfiguration is offered to add or remove machines to the computation.

For monitoring the execution, the GRID superscalar Monitor can be used. This tool is very useful to visualize the task dependence graph in order to investigate why the application does not reach the desired parallelism. It also shows the status of the tasks: if a task is running it states the machine where the task is running, and when a task is done, it still holds the information about where it has been run, thus providing a graphical way of determining which hosts are executing more tasks.

Regarding the ssh adaptation of the programming model, one of the objectives was to overcome the overhead detected in some Grid middlewares when submitting small granularity jobs. Also if a user wants to work with GRID superscalar inside a cluster it makes no sense in introducing the overhead of calling to a Grid middleware in order to operate between the different nodes, because all the resources are local. Inside a cluster there is no need of encrypted communication, so an easier task notification mechanism can be used, based on TCP/IP sockets.

The Ninf-G adaptation offered several advantages for GRID superscalar when using a Grid middleware. Ninf-G has an advanced file transfer protocol and the possibility of creating persistent workers. Ninf-G is a GridRPC implementation, thus provides a simpler interface, in contrast to Globus, where the job submission is based on building the corresponding RSL.

The current developments of the programming model have a different general approach for achieving the parallelization of the code. Instead of using generation of intermediate code from the IDL file, the new version is based in code annotations and using a source to source compiler. It offers new features such as full support for scalar variables, support for multidimensional arrays and structs only containing scalars, client side worker threads and tracing for post-mortem analysis.

4. Studying the integration possibilities

The first thing to consider when trying to integrate these two tools is their focus. GirCoL is a graphical language, which is based on a component - structure model. The components of GriCoL, e.g. MPI programs or genetic algorithms, are prepared by the programmer by wrapping the code into the component. The user can then create the experiment using these components by using a tool (such as SEGL), which utilizes GriCoL. The program codes are located in the database and during the execution are sent to the currently available resources In the experiment, a database can be used to get input data and store outputs. In contrast, GRID superscalar needs the source code to be provided (the main code and the functions code), and an IDL to describe the interfaces. Then, using the *deployment center* the code can be automatically sent and compiled in the machines involved in the calculations. This deployment step can be done by the user or by a *Grid administrator*. Once the deployment has finished, all binaries are available on local and remote machines and then the user can execute himself the main program. We must consider also the benefits achieved with the run-time features described in section 3.

From the previous description we can see that each tool misses what the other tool provides. In particular, the graphical programming language of GriCoL offers a very easy way for non Grid expert users to create experiments, and the database capability also fits into user's needs. In GRID superscalar the deployment features are very suitable for Grid environments, because installing a program in a large set of machines can be a tedious task, and the run-time is also a strong point of the tool, with resource management, checkpointing, and other interesting features.

Looking more deeply into both tools, and considering that GriCoL has two levels of work description, we came into two different possibilites of integration:

- Integration at control-flow level.

- Integration at data-flow level.

4.1 Control-flow level integration

In the control-flow integration, GriCoL offers solver blocks and control blocks in order to build the experiment in a higher level vision. So at this level the whole GriCoL experiment (solver blocks and control blocks) can be seen as a GRID superscalar main program where each solver block is a GRID superscalar IDL function, and this main program should describe what the graphical language does (i.e. a translation from graphical to programming language). A solver block can have inside several computing modules (at data-flow level) or even a call to a replacement module (to build a parameter sweep), but this could be seen as different executions inside the same IDL function in the first case, and a call to a more advanced function which performs the parameter sweep in the second.

The main problem we find at this level is that GriCoL only specifies control dependencies, while GRID superscalar is based on data dependencies. The user does not specify at this level the files involved in each solver block, but only the order of these blocks, and conditions or loops to follow with the experiment. Nevertheless, the dependencies between solver blocks could be simulated with dummy files, so GRID superscalar could detect them. By dummy files here we mean files which have nothing to do with the computation, and their only objective is to specify a dependence between two solver blocks.

This can be analysed in more detail. In the case of sequential parts of the experiment, there is no problem for the control of the execution, because GRID superscalar will take into account the dependence generated, and a second solver block will not be executed till the first solver block has finished. So tasks would be generated asynchronously, and a final wait will be performed. The asynchronous task generation scheme also accomplishes the experiment's design in case of solver blocks that can run in parallel.

Although it is possibile to "simulate" the dependencies between different control blocks, the integration at this level will not be natural, because of the different focus of the control-flow level, where data dependencies are not specified. So even being able to generate GRID superscalar tasks, we do not have any information about the files involved in every control block, thus the integration would be very difficult to achieve.

4.2   Data-flow level integration

The second option is an integration at data-flow level, the lowest level from GriCoL. At this level, two different options could be considered:

- Special computing module for a GRID superscalar application.

- Generating tasks from a computing module inside GRID superscalar run-time.

The first possibility will mean a new special type of computing module could be created, and it would be itself a GRID superscalar program. A GriCoL implementation will be responsible for executing the input and output data sections (in charge of transferring the files where needed). This integration will allow final users to build an experiment where some computing blocks use GRID superscalar internally, as it could be done with other special kind of applications (i.e. MPI). The drawback is that GRID superscalar won't have a global view of the computation in the experiment, only inside that computing module, so the benefits from using it would be local. Also a Grid administrator would have to prepare all the different kinds of GRID superscalar applications for making them available to be used from a GriCoL implementation by doing local deployments.

The next option in this data-flow level integration is allowing the generation of GRID superscalar tasks from a computing module. Each computing module's functionality could be encapsulated into a GRID superscalar's IDL function, and be called whenever needed. With this approach, a single instance of a GRID superscalar run-time will have a global view of the computation involved in the experiment, as all tasks would be generated for that single run-time. The single run-time could be in charge of resource brokering (submitting the tasks to the corresponding machines), and will provide the rest of the features available in the run-time. Another particularity of this version is that the GriCoL implementation will call to GRID superscalar run-time directly every time a task must be generated. This is particularly suitable for a specific example of a GriCoL solver block, namely one which carries out a simple *parameter sweep*, because the implementation engine for GriCoL would be responsible for making the calls with the different parameters in this parametric study, so GRID superscalar does not need any extra information to deal with parameter sweep blocks.

4.3   General integrations

From previous discussion we can see that the last option is the most suitable for the objectives of the CoreGRID Task 7.3, that is achieving the creation of an Integrated Toolkit generic enough to handle several programming languages and tools, and making the Grid an invisible layer. There are still other possibilities of integration, but orthogonal to the previous mentioned.

The first one is regarding the code deployment techniques used in GRID superscalar. It is clear that integrating these techniques in the final solution would be very useful for a Grid administrator in order to install the services needed in the machines related to the experiment. Every code or simulator implemented as a solver block could be wrapped into a GRID superscalar IDL function, and then could be easily deployed as it is done in GRID superscalar.

And the second orthogonal integration is about the database support provided in GriCoL. The data unit for GRID superscalar is the file, while GriCoL supports defining interaction with a database in order to get or store the data needed for the experiment. This feature is important, as scientific data is usually stored in databases. So, GRID superscalar must be aware of those databases, and use them as a way to treat data from the different experiments instead of working only with files.

5.   Conclusions and future work

With the proposed integration of these two tools, we achieve a unique solution for several ways of programming the Grid. The first one is GriCoL, focused on graphical design of experiments, and the second is programming from source code, as can be done with GRID superscalar. This paper presents an initial solution for the integration, and establishes a basic step towards the creation of the Integrated Toolkit described in CoreGRID Task 7.3, by simplifying the development of Grid applications and allowing the execution of applications in the Grid in a transparent way.

Regarding future work, a deeper study for integrating the database support in the final solution should be performed. Also the integration of the message passing features specified in GriCoL could be considered.

Acknowledgments

This work has been partially supported by NoE CoreGRID (FP6-004265) and by the Ministry of Science and Technology of Spain under contract TIN2004-07739-C02-01.

References

[1] CoreGRID Institute for Grid Systems, Tools and EnvironmentsRoadmap version 2 on Grid Systems, Tools and Environments. CoreGRID deliverable D.STE.04, 2006.

[2] N. Currle-Linde and M. Resch. Gricol: A Language for Grid Computing. In *Grid2006*, Barcelona, Spain, 2006. To appear.

[3] N. Currle-Linde, U. Kuester, M. Resch, and B. Risio. Science experimental grid laboratory (segl) dynamical parameter study in distributed systems. In *ParCo 2005 - Parallel Computing*, Malaga, Spain, September 2005.

[4] A. de Vivo, M. Yarrow, K. McCann. A comparison of parameter study creation and job submission tools. In *Technical report NAS-01002*, NASA Ames Research Center, Moffet Filed, CA, 2000.

[5] R. M. Badia, J. Labarta, R. Sirvent, J. M. Pérez, J. M. Cela, R. Grima. *Programming Grid Applications with GRID Superscalar*. Journal of Grid Computing, 1(2):151-170, 2003.

[6] I. Foster, C. Kesselman. *Globus: A Metacomputing Infrastructure Toolkit*. Int. Journal of Supercomputer Applications, 11(2):115-12

[7] Y. Tanaka, H. Nakada, S. Sekiguchi, T. Suzumura, S. Matsuoka. *Ninf-G: A Reference Implementation of RPC-based Programming Middleware for Grid Computing*. Journal of Grid Computing, 1(1):41-51, 2003.

[8] R. Raman, M. Livny, M. Solomon. *Matchmaking: Distributed Resource Management for High Throughput Computing*. Proceedings of the Seventh IEEE International Symposium on High Performance Distributed Computing, July 28-31, 1998, Chicago, IL.

DERIVING POLICIES FROM GRID SECURITY REQUIREMENTS MODEL*

Syed Naqvi
Centre of Excellence in Information and Communication Technologies (CETIC), Belgium
STFC Rutherford Appleton Laboratory, United Kingdom
snaqvi@ieee.org

Alvaro E. Arenas
STFC Rutherford Appleton Laboratory, United Kingdom
A.E.Arenas@rl.ac.uk

Philippe Massonet
Centre of Excellence in Information and Communication Technologies (CETIC), Belgium
philippe.massonet@cetic.be

Abstract   The emerging Grid applications require rigorous approaches to handle security management issues as their scale, heterogeneity, and complexity can not be handled with simple examination and monitoring mechanisms. In this paper, we propose a rigorous method of deriving security policies for grid applications. These policies are derived from a security requirements model built using the KAOS requirements engineering methodology. We consider an example grid application of distributed file system; its formal security requirements model is developed followed by its refinement and then the derivation of security policy for this application. The derived policies are refined and transformed into operational policies for their implementation. We developed templates for the security policies to facilitate and formalise the various stages of policy derivation.

Keywords: Grid security, formal requirements modelling, security policies.

---

*This research work is supported by the European Network of Excellence CoreGRID (project reference number 004265). The network aims at strengthening and advanc-ing scientific and technological excellence in the area of Grid and Peer-to-Peer technologies. The CoreGRID webpage is located at www.coregrid.net.

1. Introduction

Security policies define the types of security measures that are used and what scope those measures have, but not how those measures are designed or implemented. System security policies are derived from security requirements that specify the risks and threats that must be countered. These are system-specific policies [12] and reflect the threat environment and the security problems assumed by system designers. We aim at deriving implementable policies from the high level requirements model. These policies are then further refined into operational policies. At the operational stage, it is ready to be implemented in the real systems. In this paper, we have interrelated secu-rity requirements and security policies for grid data management system (GDMS) [9]. It is a part of our ongoing work of a policy-driven approach to security requirements. The implementation of this approach in the real systems requires formal derivation of security policies from the requirements model.

This article is organized in the following manner: Section 2 presents a security requirements model. Derivation of security policies from the requirements model is elaborated in section 3. Section 4 presents related work and a conceptual discussion. Finally, some conclusions are drawn in the section 5 along with an account of our future directions.

2. Security Requirements Model

In this section, we present a case study of a Grid-based distributed file system. The exponential growth in the scale of distributed data management systems and corresponding increase in the amount of data being handled by these systems require efficient management of files by maintaining consistency, ensuring security, fault tolerance and good performance in terms of availability and security [7]. The problem addressed in this section is to assure fault tolerant and secure management of a Grid-based distributed file system. Fault tolerance is attained by keeping an adequate number of replicas at different nodes; whereas secure management is based on the encrypted transfer of files between the nodes. The various parameters involved in attaining in these two broad requirements are illustrated in this section.

2.1 Problem Statement

To understand the fault-tolerance mechanism intended for Grid-based distributed file system, consider a grid storage system shown in the leftside of figure 1. Data elements A and B are distributed over several resources. A_1 and A_2 are the subparts of A; B_1 and B_2 are the subparts of B. Central part of figure 1 depicts a failure situation where a node is broken down.

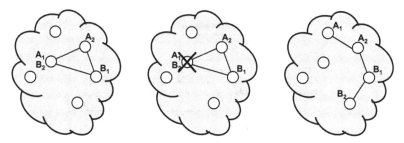

Figure 1. Distributed data elements; storage site is broken down; and redistribution of data-set.

A *Data Manager* will start searching resources that match the storage requirements and preferences of the stakeholders of the data elements. This is a critical phase as security negotiations and the matching of security parameters have to be resolved besides seeking the storage capacities and other performance parameters. The security assurances should be met before moving the data-set to a new node. The rightside figure 1 shows that the resource broker didn't find a node that can host both A_1 and B_2 simultaneously (as was the case before the failure occurred) and hence it found two different nodes - one for A_1 and the other for B_2 - to maintain the same security level of these elements.

2.2   Goal Model

Figure 2 depicts the overall goal model of the security requirements of a distributed file system using the KAOS (Knowledge Acquisition in autOmated Specification) requirement engineering methodology [1]. It illustrates that the main goal of the system is to assure that the files are always secure and available. This overall goal is refined with the sub-goals of availability and security. These sub-goals are further refined to describe the set of auxiliary sub-goals needed to elaborate the upper level goals. Finally a set of requirements is associated with each refined sub-goal to demon-strate the prerequisite of attainment of these goals. In figure 1, the goals and sub-goals are represented by thin-lined parallelograms whereas the requirements of the refined goals are represented by the thick-lined parallelograms. For instance, the goal file redundancy maintained requires move files to new nodes, detect node failures and identify new nodes. A goal model also includes the constraints of attaining certain goals. For example, in figure 1, the goal files readily accessible is constrained by the data confidentiality requirement of encrypted file transfer.

2.3   Responsibility Model

By definition, the responsibility model is derived from the goal model. A responsibility model contains all the responsibility diagrams. A responsibility

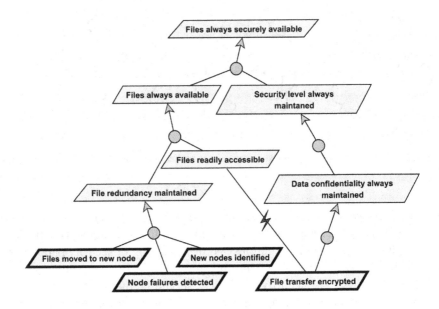

Figure 2.   Goal Model.

diagram describes for each agent, the requirements and expectations that it is responsible for, or that have been assigned to it.

Figure 3 contains the responsibility diagrams of the problem statement considered in this section. It assigns the responsibility of the requirement encrypted file transfer to the data manager. Likewise, the responsibility of the requirement node failures detected is assigned to the data monitor that monitors the object node and employs the monitor and notify operations to keep an eye on the performance. The monitor operation satisfies the requirement of node failure detection [5].

2.4   Object Model

The object model is used to define and document the concepts of the application domain that are relevant with respect to the known requirements and to provide static constraints on the operational systems that will satisfy the requirements. The object model consists of objects pertaining to the stakeholders' domain and objects intro-duced to express requirements or constraints on the operational system. There are three types of entities that can be found in the object model: entities (independent passive objects); agents (independent active objects); and associations (dependent passive objects).

The object model is compliant with UML class diagrams as the entities correspond to UML classes; associations correspond to UML binary association

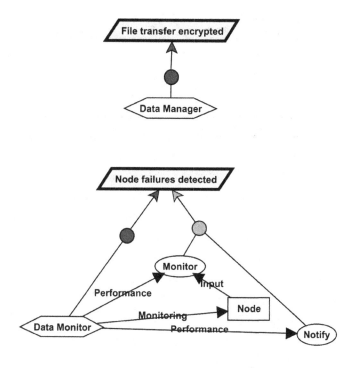

Figure 3. Responsibility Model.

links or n-array association classes. Inheritance is available to all types of ob-jects including associa-tions. Objects can be qualified with attributes.

2.5 Operation Model

The operation model describes all the behaviours that agents need to fulfil their requirements. Behaviours are expressed in terms of operations performed by agents. figure 4 shows the operation model of the problem statement consid-ered in this section. The file transfer requirement (with or without encryption) requires an operation move files. Likewise the requirement of identifying new nodes requires an operation of find available nodes. Another example is the use of monitor and notify operations for the requirement of the detection of node failures.

2.6 Dealing with Obstacles

Obstacles are the situations where a goal, a requirement or an expectation is violated. In such situation, the obstacle is said to obstruct the goal, requirement or expec-tation. Dealing with obstacles allows analysts to identify and address exceptional circumstances.

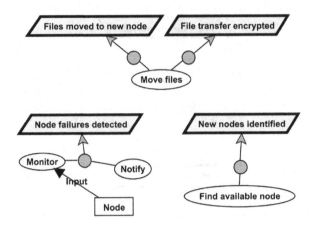

Figure 4.   Operation Model.

Figure 5 depicts the obstacles model of the problem statement considered in this section. It shows that undetected node failures are the obstacles for the requirement of node failure detection.   Obstacles have been used for deriving

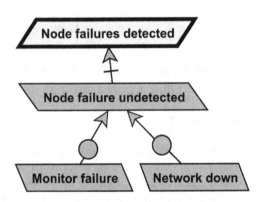

Figure 5.   Obstacles Model.

security requirements previously [6]. Here we are following a complementary approach in which security requirements are mod-elled directly.

3.   Derivation of Policies from Security Requirements Model

An important concept in distributed systems, Grids and large collaborative networks is the concept of Virtual Organisation (VO) [3]. A VO can be seen as a dynamic collection of distributed resources that are shared by a dynamic collection of users from one or more physical organisations. In the case of a Grid-based distributed file system, a VO may consist of a set of physical sites (nodes) providing one or more resources. In our case, resources are mainly storage capabilities, but they can include other capabilities such as computational power.

Following Wasson and Humphrey [11], we can define three types of policies in VOs:

- **VO-wide operational policies** - this type of policies describes the state of the VO as a whole and not any single node or service. These policies are statements about the intended operational state of the VO, such as the following:

  - 75% of the data will be stored following an evenly distribution through the participating nodes. The remaining 25% will be stored into those nodes that have defined themselves as being of high-storage capacity.
  - The computational load of the VO is to be divided equally among all member nodes.

  This type of policies follows mainly from domain invariants, properties know to hold in every state of some domain object [1].

- **VO resource policies** - this type of policies describes the VO's rules for the behaviour of its member resources. These policies correspond to rules that pertain to particular resources within the VO rather than across the entire organisation. Examples of this type of policies for the case of our system include:

  - If a file contains unclassified information then encryption is disabled.
  - Node N_i must provide 1000GB of storage to the VO.
  - Node N_j must provide the VO with dedicated compute time from midnight to 6 am CET every day.

  This type of policies follows directly from the object model, where attributes (properties) associated to particular type of object are defined. VO resource policies are also called resource usage policies, and are the base for defining SLAs (Service Level Agreement) [10].

- **VO agent policies** - this type of policies specifies rules for agents (users) of the VO's resources, from the perspective of the VO itself. These policies include permit/deny action on various possible agent operations, but more importantly they may specify pre-condition for any given operation, as well as obligations that the agent receives for performing an action. Example of this type of policies are:

- In a move files operation, the *Data Manager* agent must disable encryption if the file-transfer path includes trusted domains only.

- The *Data Monitor* agent must notify the *Data Manager* agent when a failure occurs in a node.

The main source of VO agent policies is the operation model, where pre/post conditions are defined for the operations performed by agents.

As mentioned in [11], there is a connection between the various types of VO policies: a VO-wide policy can be specified by applying the same resource and/or agent policy to all resources/agents in the VO. For instance, if each node in a four-site VO has a resource policy that it must perform 25% of the VO's total workload, this is equivalent to a VO-wide policy that all nodes will equally divide the VO's work. This kind of relation can be exploited for refinement general policies into more specific ones.

3.1   Refinement of Requirements Model

We derive security policy from the requirements model and define templates with attributes such as subjects, subject's responsibilities, objects, object's activities, etc. These templates are then populated using natural language to make it more expressive semantically. The first step in the derivation of security policies from the requirements model is to refine the requirements model so that policies templates can be evolved from it. These templates are then populated for the specific system.

The goal model shown in figure 2 is a concise representation of the goals of a Grid-based distributed file system. It only provides a picture of high-level security requirements. It needs further elaboration or the refinement for the derivation of policy.

Figure 6 shows the refined form of the goal model shown in the figure 2. For ex-ample, it refines the goal files readily accessible by defining a sub-goal storage sites always connected and the operations, network faults identified and network faults fixed, to be performed to attain this goal. These refinements enable the designers to identify the operations needed to attain the various goals and they draw clear demarcation of the duties of the various actors involved in the whole system. This demarcation helps not only in the evaluation of the actors' privileges but also to carryout the accountability.

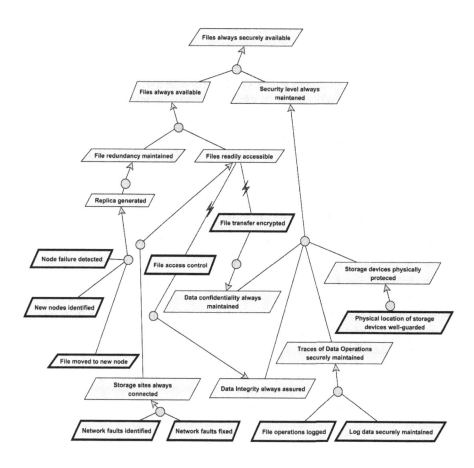

Figure 6. Refined Goal Model.

3.2 Policy Templates

Requirements templates have been used in security requirements models [2]. Here we are following a complementary approach in which security policy templates are developed. Policy templates are designed to formulize policy statements. Every policy must have a core set of attributes and may have a set of optional/additional attributes. An example set of core attributes is given in table 1. These attribute are expressed in a high-level language (plain text). The resulting policies are the draft version of the security policies which require further refinement (cf. section 3.4) and subsequent transformation into operational policies (cf. section 3.5).

Table 1.   Core attributes in a policy template

ID	Policy identifier
Description	Explanation of the policy parameters (optional)
Subject	Active entity that manages object(s) through a set of actions
Object	Passive entity that is managed by subject(s) through a set of actions
Action	Task to be executed by a subject on object(s)
Authorization	Privileges given to the subject to perform actions on the object. Authorization maybe restricted by constraints
Constraint	Conditions that need to be fulfilled before an action is initiated.
Event	Condition that triggers the policy

3.3   Population of Policy Templates

Before populating the policy templates, crude textual policies are derived from the requirements model. For example:

New replica of file is generated when an existing storage node is failed

Now a corresponding policy template can be populated as shown in table 2. This is a structured representation of a policy element; however, it cannot be implemented in this form as it requires refinement and transformation into operational policies.

Table 2.   A populated policy template

ID	NFRG
Description	NFRG: New File Replica Generation
Subject	Data Monitor
Object	Grid data storage nodes
Action	Replica generated
Authorization	Create files replica
Constraint	Availability of nodes
Event	Replica-host node failed

3.4   Refinement of Policies

Policy NFRG can be further refined to provide more realistic security policy. For instance,

> *When the number of available file replicas becomes less than the threshold number, the monitoring agent will generate new replica by negotiating the security compatibility of the nodes with the file security requirements*

Now the policy can be represented as shown in table 3.

The refined policies provide more details, including some object (file replicas), attributes (number of available replicas), and agents (Monitoring agent).

Table 3. Policy example

ID	NFRG
Description	NFRG: New File Replica Generation
Subject	Data Monitoring Agent
Object	Backup/unused Grid data storage nodes
Action	Replica file generated on the compatible nodes
Authorization	Locate compatible storage nodes and create files replica
Constraint	Availability of compatible nodes
Event	Number of available replicas becomes less than threshold value.

However, they still lack the description of exact techniques and technologies to be employed in the real systems. These details are provided in the implementation policies. Implementation policies are specific to a particular system and cannot be directly applied to other systems.

3.5 Implementation of Policies

Unlike generic policies, which are quite abstract, operational policies contain specific details of a particular system. An example operational policy derived from the same example policy could be as:

> *When the number of available replicas of CosmicGravitationalWaves.xls file becomes less than ninety percent of the total number of replicas over the LCS gird, the Grid Data Monitoring Tool will generate new replica by negotiating the security compatibility of the nodes with the security requirements of Cosmic-GravitationalWaves.xls file by using the Web-Service Agreement protocol*

Now the operational policy may look like as shown in table 4.

Table 4. Example of an operational policy

ID	NFRG
Description	NFRG: New File Replica Generation policy is to be implemented in the Laser Interferometer Gravitational-Wave Observatory (LIGO) environment as part of LIGO Scientific Collaboration (LSC) Grid
Subject	Grid-Data Monitoring Tool (DMT)
Object	LSC Grid nodes
Action	Replica of file CosmicGravitationalWaves.xls generated
Authorization	DMT can employ Web-Services Agreement (WSA) protocol to negotiate the security parameters and evaluate the compatibility of the node where replica is to be generated
Constraint	Availability of the nodes that correspond to the storage and security requirements of CosmicGravitationalWaves.xls file
Event	Number of available replica-host nodes becomes less than 90% of the total number of replicas.

This is how the policies are derived from the requirements model and then refined and translated into the operational policies. A comprehensive set of such policies for the example case of LSC will also consist of secure transfer of file contents to the newer nodes. An operational policy for such data transfer will provide low-level details such as encryption algorithm to be employed, key-length to be maintained etc.

4.   Related Work and Discussions

Tropos [4] is a methodology for modelling organizations in terms of actors, goals, and dependencies to early requirements and provides a basis for extending early requirements to late requirements, architectural design, and detailed design. Tropos emphasizes the need to identify organizational concerns, separate them from implementation concerns, and give them first-class treatment. Toward this end, Tropos posits five main classes of concern: actors, resources, goals, soft goals, and tasks. A particular requirements model will contain multiple instances of each of these classes. Properties are not represented directly in the Tropos schema but may be captured in hard or soft goals. Tropos incorporate several types of concern relationship, including decomposition, means-ends, and dependency relationships.

Our KAOS based approach offers a goal-dependency model of requirements and takes a view of concerns that is appropriate to requirements and separated from implementation. It also provides some downstream continuity, from requirements to architectural refinement. In some contrast to Tropos, our approach adopts a more explicitly multidimensional perspective on requirements. Conceptually, requirements in the abstract and elements in a model can be associated with different aspects. Goals are subject to disjunctive and conjunctive refinement. Our approach supports multiple views of the requirements, including refinement, operationalisation, entity-relationship, and agent.

5.   Conclusions and Future Directions

In this paper, we presented our approach for rigorous derivation of security policies from the requirements model. We carried out a case study of Grid based distributed file system to explain our approach. For the same case study, we modelled the VO requirements in term of resources and the actual usage of resources in the VO. Moreover, we also linked our work with the work done with the use of the KAOS methodology. We have already worked for the representation of policies in a policy language [8] and now we have developed a technique for the derivation of security policies from the requirements model.

Our future directions include the exploration the negotiation issues of the QoS parameters in order to reach Service Level Agreements (SLA). This approach of addressing semantic modelling issues by providing requirements for expressing security related quality of service will turn Grid based storage systems into knowledge representation systems

References

[1] A. Dardenne, A. Lamsweerde, and S. Fickas. Goal-directed requirements acquisition. *Science of Computer Programming*, (20):3–50, 1993.

[2] J. Dorr, D. Kerkow, A. Knethen, and B. Paech. Eliciting efficiency requirements with use cases. *9th International Workshop on Requirments Engineering - Foundation for Software Quality, Workshop held at CaiSE'03*, 2003.

[3] I. Foster, C. Kesselman, and S. Tuecke. The anatomy of the grid: Enabling scalable virtual organizations. *International Journal of Supercomputer Applications*, 15(3), 2001.

[4] A. Fuxman, M. Pistore, J. Mylopoulos, and P. Traverso. Model checking early requirements specifications in tropos. *Proceedings of Fifth IEEE International Symposium on Requirements Engineering 2001 (RE'01)*, pages 174–181, 2001.

[5] E. Kalyvianaki and I. Pratt. Building adaptive peer-to-peer systems. *4th International Conference on Peer-to-Peer Computing (P2P 2004)*, (ISBN 0-7695-2156-8), 2004.

[6] A. Lamsweerde. Elaborating security requirements by construction of intentional anti-models. *26th ACM-IEEE International Conference on Software Engineering (ICSE'04)*, pages 148–157, 2004.

[7] S. Naqvi, P. Massonet, and A. Arenas. Security requirements model for grid data management systems. *Proceedings of the International Workshop on Critical Information Infrastructure Security 2006 (CRITIS'06)*, 2006.

[8] S. Naqvi, P. Massonet, and A. Arenas. A study of languages for the specification of grid security policies. *CoreGRID Technical Report TR0037*, 2006.

[9] S. Naqvi, O. Poitou, P. Massonet, and A. Arenas. Security requirements analysis for large-scale distributed file systems. *Proceedings of the CoreGRID Workshop on Middleware*, 2006.

[10] R. Strum and W. Morris. Foundations of service level management. *Book*, (ISBN 0-6723-1743-5):288, 2004.

[11] G. Wasson and M. Humphrey. Toward explicit policy management for virtual organisations. *4th IEEE International Workshop on Policies for Distributed Systems and Networks (POLICY2003)*, 2003.

[12] L. Wills. Security policies: Where to begin. *SANS Whitepaper*, 2002.

DOMAIN-SPECIFIC METADATA FOR MODEL VALIDATION AND PERFORMANCE OPTIMISATION*

Jeyarajan Thiyagalingam, Vladimir Getov
Harrow School of Computer Science
University of Westminster
Watford Road, Northwick Park
Harrow HA1 3TP
UK

V.S.Getov@westminster.ac.uk

Sofia Panagiotidi, Olav Beckmann, John Darlington
Department of Computing
Imperial College London
180 Queen's Gate
London SW7 2AZ
UK

jd@doc.ic.ac.uk

Abstract   Interactive problem solving environments are gaining widespread acceptance within the Grid community. While developing applications and frameworks to support and to integrate with these interactive environments is very important, it is also necessary to treat the legacy applications with the same importance. In this paper, we report an ongoing effort in enabling a legacy application to support, integrate with, and evolve as a scalable problem solving environment for Earth system modelling.

Our strategy has been to componentise the existing legacy framework, augment each component with metadata, and using this metadata address different issues arising when performing component composition. We describe the means for specifying, publishing, and using the metadata in solving two different but crucially important issues when performing component composition – model validation and model efficiency.

Keywords: components, composition, performance, metadata, specialisation

---

*This work has been partially supported by the GENIE and GENIEfy projects, funded by NERC, and later by the FP6 Network of Excellence CoreGRID project, funded by the European Commission.

1.   Introduction

Interactive problem solving environments are gaining increasing interest from end users and finding their widespread acceptance within the Grid community. The intuitive part of such frameworks is how the complexities of solving computationally demanding problems are hidden from the end-users by visually appealing front-ends.

Component-based programming is a suitable methodology for developing applications and frameworks to support, to integrate with and to evolve as a problem solving environment. In the context of component-oriented programming, a framework or an application is seen as a composition of components, on which some of them might have been developed outside the context of the application domain. This raises, at least two interesting issues when composing an application from components: firstly, performing a strict validation on the bindings of interfaces and semantics of the composition are important to guarantee that the composition is functionally valid and secondly ensuring that the overall performance of the composition is optimum. Although the first issue has been relatively simplified with the modern programming languages, the latter issue has not been largely addressed. These issues are further complicated when considering legacy applications or frameworks and a number of issues still remain to be addressed.

Further, the process of validating and optimising compositions is vital for ensuring the scalability of a composition and thus that of the problem solving environment.

Majority of legacy applications do not have any explicit notion of components and performing a composition based on these legacy codes is often complicated. Although functional aspects of legacy code can be componentised without any explicit modernisation (such as rewriting in an object-oriented language), such componentised versions do not match their counterparts in many aspects.

We argue that when each component is augmented with additional information, metadata, the task of performing valid and efficient compositions becomes relatively simplified and can be automated. Such an approach involves appropriately specifying, publishing, extracting and correctly using the metadata for different operations. The (specification of the) metadata for a component highlights all salient features of a component. This information can voluntarily be embedded by developers in the form of annotations [6, 10, 5, 12] or by the compilers. Though compilers may capture and provide substantial amount of information, high-level, domain-specific details are better captured by manual specification or by specialised tools. Metadata for a component can be furnished as part of the binary or externally. For instance, for a selected class of binaries, such as Java bytecode or .NET-based binaries [11], these metadata can examined or extracted using reflective introspection [18, 17]. Where such facilities are infeasible or limited, for instance when the metadata cannot be embedded, the metadata has to be furnished separately. Once the metadata for a component is extracted (either through reflective introspection mechanisms or by examination of external metadata), the information can be staged to address different issues.

However, legacy software pose many challenges in all these aspects. Lack of support for appropriately expressing components, limited techniques for specifying and extracting metadata, and limited availability of well defined mechanisms for using the metadata contribute towards this problem.

In this paper, we report our findings in addressing these issues, using a legacy application as a driving example. Although we use the legacy code-based case study as a motivating example to illustrate our techniques, the techniques are equally applicable to modern component-oriented solutions and across many different application domains. The key step is to find methods for specifying, publishing and extracting the metadata from legacy codes. Techniques for using the metadata to address different issues are the same across legacy and contemporary systems. We illustrate how we plan to use component-specific metadata to address two interesting problems that arise when performing component composition, especially when evolving a legacy code-base into an interactive problem solving environment.

The main contributions of this paper are as follows:

1 We formulate methods for specifying, publishing and extracting metadata for/from legacy software components.

2 We present a number of complementary strategies for verifying the validity of compositional patterns.

3 We discuss our plan in using the metadata for performing efficient component composition by using a real-world component-based application.

We consider this work as part of the advanced design methodology effort within CoreGRID. A problem solving environment dealing with legacy systems is ideally a part of every Grid environment, and thus this joint effort is directly addressing the aims of the CoreGRID project.

The rest of this paper is organised as follows: In Section 2 we describe our underlying example, GENIE (Grid ENabled Integrated Earth system modelling) - a component based modular platform for simulating long term evolution of Earth's climate. Section 3 describes the motivation for our work. The overall mechanism for specifying, publishing and extracting metadata are discussed in Section 4. Section 5 discusses how the metadata could be used to address two different issues: verification of validity of composition and performing

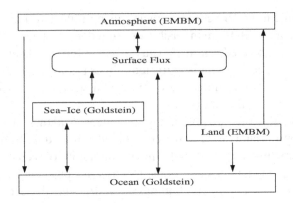

Figure 1.   A sample configuration representing an Earth system model.

efficient component compositions. In Section 6, we discuss previous work immediately related to ours and Section 7 concludes the paper with directions for further research.

2.   GENIE Application

2.1   Overview

GENIE [1] is a scalable modular platform used to produce and simulate a range of Earth system models in order to understand the long-term changes in Earth's climate. The framework includes different variants of *earth modules* such as the atmosphere, ocean, sea-ice, marine sediments, land surface, vegetation and soil and ice sheets. A typical Earth system model is a composition of different variants of these earth modules (or different instances of earth modules), which are in fact different *configurations* suited for different simulation scenarios. Each Earth module is bound to the natural laws of physics that govern the exchange of energy, fluxes, water and other physical or biogeochemical tracers. Further, each Earth module uses their own module-specific computational models and module-specific data representations for representing boundary surfaces where the exchanges occur.

Figure 1 shows a sample Earth system model (or configuration). The model uses different instances of each of the Earth system modules (instance types are shown within parenthesises). Interactions between different (instances of) Earth modules are shown by arrows. In addition to Earth system modules, a configuration may also use modules to represent exchanged or accumulated physical or biogeochemical tracers (for example, the surface flux module in Figure 1).

2.2   The Past, the Present and the Future

In the original implementation, the GENIE was implemented in pure FORTRAN without any explicit notion of components and services. The framework included a driver module for orchestrating the execution, inter- and intra-module communications and data exchanges for a given configuration.

At present, these earth-modules have been componentised. To facilitate interoperatability between different language-specific implementations and to expose these components on the Web services front, these components have been wrapped through Java interfaces [13]. With these wrappers in place, the overall composition of these components (and thus different earth system models) may include remote components and remote services.

Currently, the simulation of a given model could be submitted, managed and executed on the Grid using the Globus Toolkit [7] or Condor [16].

In the context of Grid, problem solving environments or problem solving portals are finding broader range of audience including scientists. Evolving GENIE as a, or as a part of a portal is an interesting challenge. This includes creating component repositories, building automated submission, management, scheduling and execution mechanisms and building/supporting visualisation platforms. In addressing this challenge, although we could potentially make use of existing techniques to handle different issues which may arise within, there are still issues need to be addressed. We use one of these issues, discussed in Section 3 as a key motivation for this paper and to illustrate our techniques.

3.   Motivation

One of our goals in improving the GENIE platform to evolve it as a portal or as a part of a portal where end-users could visually compose a simulation model. Such a visual composition will include different visual components representing various earth modules, which may be Web services or native components. Each component is permitted to have different variants (with varying models, different parameterised configuration, costs, locations, performance and interfaces) whose properties can be configured, at least partially. In effect, the overall properties of a composition, i.e. the configuration of the model, can be configured by end-users. There are at least two immediate issues arising in supporting such user configurable simulation models. Firstly, the validity of a composed simulation model should be verified against the law of physics, or more specifically against the domain-specific facts of Earth system modelling. Secondly, the composition should be made efficient in terms of cost, performance and usage of resources.

The task of verifying the validity of a composition requires inherent knowledge of components (such as applicability information, parameters, their ranges, patterns of interactions and other similar information) and requires substantial exposure to the domain-specific details of Earth system modelling. Although it is possible to embed these information as part of the application, such an approach would prevent the scalability issue to be handled efficiently, i.e. components cannot be added or removed dynamically. Decoupling the platform from possessing any component-specific information (component metadata) leads us to furnish the same metadata through an external source. However, in the current setup of GENIE, components cannot carry any form of metadata on their own.

Secondly, when composing components to build a model, opportunities may arise for improving the efficiency of compositions. Efficiency of a composition is a multivariate function. However, we restricted our cost model to have only one parameter, namely runtime (performance), to simplify the process. Opportunities for optimisation may also arise during runtime and using the metadata may result in significant improvement in performance. For example, performance is highly correlated to the location of Web services and choosing a service whose proximity is closer to the client has desirable advantages on performance.

A closer inspection of these requirements show that if each component is augmented with metadata, it is at least partially possible to overcome some of the challenges. We discuss the nature and specification of the metadata in Section 4 and our means to exploit the metadata in Section 5.

4.   Metadata for Legacy Components

The specification of the metadata should permit information to be equally expressed across different components while permitting salient and domain-specific features of components to be highlighted. Towards this, the metadata should capture any implementation-specific and composition-specific information and details relating to the domain of the application. The organisation of the metadata, in terms of management and usage, is also equally important to the contents of the metadata. We follow the organisational structure outlined in [17] to organise our metadata. Metadata related to components are externally supplied as discussed below (in contrast to the approach of being supplied by the binary itself).

In the case of legacy components, extracting metadata from legacy binaries is a difficult process, unless such metadata have been embedded within the components and explicit extraction is facilitated as in [10], but at higher-level.

In our case, we manually specified the metadata for each componentised version of the legacy code. The metadata is then associated to the matching component and placed in an associated repository. Service enabling our componentised versions results in additional advantage of associated metadata being served as part of the services contract. When not accessed through services, the external metadata is supplied by explicit method calls produced by component wrappers.

The exact information to be captured/specified can be divided in three different groups: basic component-specific information, domain-specific information and experience-specific information as below:

Component-specific information specify the interfaces and interactions to the component such as inputs, outputs, their types and other compositional information (such as containment relationships and parent module information). Additional information, which are specific to legacy components, can also be included as part of this section.

Domain-specific information are often in the form of constraints, specifying valid ranges, valid values, valid units and additional conditions which are fully derived through the knowledge of the component.

Experience-specific information are accumulated across runs, such as performance results on different platforms, or for different configurations.

The metadata at different levels may overlap and then extended across components, wherever applicable, to cover compositions. For example, in the case of composite components, which is a form of composition, the metadata will cover each component in the composition.

5. Staging the Metadata

The next step is to appropriately use the metadata to address different problems. In our case, we are considering two different issues: model validation and efficient composition, which are discussed in the following sub-sections.

5.1 Model Validation

In an Earth simulation model, different instances relating to different Earth modules may coexist. This means, for instance, there may be two different atmospheric models that may coexist inside a single simulation model, perhaps to represent different atmospheric conditions over different regions of the Earth. Each instance interacts with each other for exchanging physical and/or biogeochemical tracers, specifically through their ports. Since different instances may share common interface properties, validating interface-specific details alone may not be sufficient enough to guarantee that the model is valid. We use the different parts of metadata in the process of validating a model.

- **Physical units of ports**: Wherever applicable, each physical tracer (such as speed, energy) and/or biogeochemical tracer (such as CO_2, dust, Alkalinity) is related to a unit (such as K, ms^{-2}). When verifying a coupling between instances of different modules, their physical and bio-geochemical couplings need to be verified to ensure that the connections between tracers of coupled modules are valid.

■ **Resolution/Dimension of computational models**: As outlined earlier, each component may be configured to use a specific computational model, for instance the resolution of spatial grids and/or dimension of the spatial grids. In many cases, these models do not match and this issue is appropriately handled depending on the context. For example, when spatial grids are different, tracer values are appropriately interpolated/extrapolated. However, this often comes with correction factor to guarantee the conservation of energy/fluxes. Validating whether a coupling leads to large deviation in values or corrections may result in verifying whether there are violations of physical laws of conservation.

■ **Number of instances**: An Earth module may mandate an upper or lower bound on number of instances that may be present in a model. Verifying that the instances do not violate this requirement, provides an extra scoring.

■ **Value range**: A possible range of values that an input/output tracer can assume is specified as part of the metadata, for example value range for temperature. Depending on the model, the value range may help in arresting invalid models at pre-simulation stage or during simulation.

■ **Existing models/couplings**: Capturing and recording outcomes of models and couplings as part of the metadata (as part of the experience-specific metadata) may help in using experience-specific data in identifying invalid models/couplings.

■ **Interface- and type-specific information**: In addition to existing details, interface- and type-specific details of coupled tracers need to be matched.

We are continuing our effort in identifying more domain-specific metadata parameters to be used against validation of simulation models. An added advantage of using the component metadata is that it partly guarantees that the application (or component) is free from value specific logics.

5.2   Performance Optimisation

An Earth system model is simulated for a long period, for instance for multi-millennial periods, and it is both time consuming and computationally intensive. Although each module may be optimised for best performance (or for other objective functions), the overall composition cannot be pre-optimised.

One of the reasons for a composition to yield sub-optimal performance is that components are not aware of the overall behaviour of the composition. The use of the metadata in performing efficient component composition has previously been demonstrated by many authors [10, 4]. The key idea in our approach is to tailor the metadata to include domain-specific and experience-specific information in addition to the component/interface-specific details. We use the following metadata for resolving key performance issues.

- **Location/type of component**: As outlined already, a composition may include locally available, native components and remote Web services. Since, the communication latencies are highly correlated to the overall performance of the composition, wherever applicable, locally available components should be preferred to Web services and services in close proximity to services with high latencies. However, this issue may be further complicated if a second optimisation parameter is added, such as cost.

- **Computational models**: Some of the computational models of a given component may have matching computational model such that they all yield almost similar results but exhibiting significant difference in performance. For example, when simulating maximum Atlantic meridional overturning circulation (MOC), resolutions of $36 \times 36 \times 8$ and $72 \times 72 \times 16$ for oceans, results in similar MOC figures for higher flux corrections. Further, the choice of a faster resolution may be justified by subsequent interpolations/extrapolations for corrections.

- **Data from past runs**: Instance of some Earth modules always have similar (or constant) startup or input values. Wherever possible, the past data can be used to save computational time. Very frequently, similar simulation models may overlap in time period and thus the data. For instance, exploring the stability of the ocean thermohaline circulation (THC) is very repetitive in nature and it is possible that the simulation span to overlap with an existing (similar) model.

We are investigating the issue of staging these metadata to improve the overall performance of simulation models, THC in particular.

6. Related Work

Problem solving portals, modular visualisation environments and work-flow editors help exploring the problem and/or solution space by providing an abstract view of the interaction between associated modules [8, 4, 2]. Our work is also partly aligned with providing a similar abstraction while addressing the issues discussed in previous sections. However, one of the key differences in our work is that we make an extensive use of component- and domain-specific metadata in the process.

The Bespoke Framework Generator (BFG) [14] is a prototype implementation of the Flexible Coupling Approach (FCA) and partially being used as a coupling framework within the GENIE application. BFG permits rules relating to compositions to be built and wrapper codes to be generated. Our work has similar goals and results to theirs but we make extensive use of metadata from which the composition rules are inferred. Our work is more suitable in a scalable environment where exact rules are difficult to specify, especially when nature of evolving components are not known in advance. Further, our metadata supports specification of rules where necessary but does not depend upon on them for its operations. In addition to this, our work exploits the runtime correlated metadata to seek optimisation opportunities.

The THEMIS framework [10] demonstrates how component specific metadata can be used to perform cross component optimisations. Using component metadata for optimising resources and applications in the context of Grid is considered in [9]. Organisation of metadata for component-oriented compositions is discussed in [17]. Our work utilises some of their principles and techniques in advancing the solutions. We also make extensive use of some or part of the wrapping techniques outlined in [5, 12, 3]. However, our implementation of wrappers also function as part of the Web service so that the metadata can be published as part of the Web service.

The OASIS framework [15] offers a component model description and configuration mechanism for coupled models. The framework is specifically aligned towards issues related to climate earth system modelling. Although it proposes earth-specific metadata, the metadata does not capture the details which are relevant to our work.

7.   Conclusions

In this paper we have highlighted two issues that arise when performing composition of components, namely validity and efficiency. We also discussed the importance of addressing these two issues both in the context of legacy applications and modern component-oriented programming. We placed a particular emphasis on providing additional information related to components, which we call metadata, and using the same to automate or semi-automate the process of component composition.

Carefully specifying the metadata such that it captures the component and domain-specific information leads to potential benefits, which we outlined in Section 5. We used a legacy application as a driving example to illustrate the details and nature of the metadata for components based on legacy code. We also highlighted our plans in staging the metadata for validating the models and improving the efficiency of models. These two aspects are crucially important for guaranteeing the GENIE platform becomes a scalable problem solving environment by permitting extensive, yet valid and highly performing, range of models to be composed.

However, we discussed only a subset of the issues arising in performing compositions of components. A number of interesting issues remain to be addressed.

- Currently, we do not capture or specify any information as part of the metadata to parallelise the simulation and to improve the performance. This issue is partly addressed and included in the BFG framework through rules. However, we intend to take a different approach where the parallelism can also be inferred from metadata if not specified explicitly.

- The experience-specific metadata may dramatically increase in size and may affect the overall performance. We plan to separate this aspect of the metadata in a separate consolidated storage (such as a common database).

- Manually specifying the metadata for legacy components is a complex process. Diminishing or ageing skills in legacy systems, unavailability of up-to-date documentation, willingness of new programmers to get a deeper understanding of the code are some of the contributing reasons for the difficulty in keeping pace with the changes. However, fortunately, GENIE is based on FORTRAN code-base and it is not entirely impossible to cope with the ageing code exposure — if FORTRAN code is assumed to be not in parallel with modern programming languages.

- One of the interesting outcomes of using the metadata is how the application or component becomes free from value-specific logics. It is possible to take an aggressive approach here to migrate more issues into the metadata from the component/application. For instance, computational models of components may consist of or may have access to alternative solvers/smoothers. This can be captured inside the metadata. However, such an aggressive approach may increase the overheads in handling the metadata. There is an optimum amount of information that can be passed as metadata and rest in the application/component logic. It is interesting to observe the optimality and defining metrics for such optimality.

- As mentioned in Section 3, efficiency of a composition is a multivariate function. We simplified the model and assumed that performance is the primary concern. However, in a real setup, factors such as cost may also need to be considered.

At present, we are investigating means for unifying and generalising the metadata specification across different components and across the whole domain. We are also implementing the framework for extracting and staging the metadata in performing compositions. We are certain that the proposed approach could be used to solve associated issues in other domains of applications and in contemporary component-based systems.

References

[1] Grid ENabled Integrated Earth system model (GENIE). http://www.genie.ac.uk

[2] Parallel Grid Runtime and Application Development Environment (PGRADE). http://www.lpds.sztaki.hu/pgrade/

[3] D.M. Beazley and P.S. Lomdahl. Controlling the Data Glut in Large-scale Molecular-dynamics Simulations. *Comput. Phys.*, 11(3):230–238, 1997.

[4] O. Beckmann, A.J. Field, G. Gorman, A. Huff, M. Hull, and P.H.J. Kelly. Overcoming Barriers to Restructuring in a Modular Visualisation Environment. In *Proc. 7th Workshop on Languages, Compilers, and Run-time Support for Scalable Systems (LCR'04)*, pages 1–7, ACM Press, 2004.

[5] S.H. Edwards. Toward Reflective Metadata Wrappers for Formally Specified Software Components. In *Proc. Workshop on Specification and Verification of Component Based Systems at OOPSLA'01*, 2001. http://people.cs.vt.edu/ edwards/downloads/Edwards-SAVCBS01.pdf

[6] D. Flanagan and B. McLaughlin. *Java 1.5 Tiger: A Developer's Notebook*. O' Reilly & Associates, Inc.. 2004.

[7] I. Foster. Globus Toolkit Version 4: Software for Service-Oriented Systems. In *Proc. IFIP International Conference on Network and Parallel Computing, Lecture Notes in Computer Science*, 3779:2–13, Springer, 2005.

[8] J. Freire, C.T. Silva, S.P. Callahan, E. Santos, C.E. Scheidegger, and H.T. Vo. Managing Rapidly-Evolving Scientific Workflows. In Proc. 2006 International Provenance and Annotation Workshop, Lecture Notes in Computer Science, 4145:10–18, 2006.

[9] N. Furmento, A. Mayer, S. McGough, S. Newhouse, T. Field, and J. Darlington. Optimisation of Component-based Applications Within a Grid Environment. In *Proc. ACM/IEEE Conference on Supercomputing'01 (CDROM)*, pages 30–30, ACM Press, 2001.

[10] P.H.J. Kelly, O. Beckmann, T. Field, and S.B. Baden. THEMIS: Component Dependence Metadata in Adaptive Parallel Applications. *Parallel Processing Letters*, 11(4):455–470, December 2001.

[11] S. Lidin. *Inside Microsoft .NET IL Assembler*. Microsoft Press, 2002.

[12] A. Orso, M.J. Harrold, and D.S. Rosenblum. Component Metadata for Software Engineering Tasks. In W. Emmerich and S. Tai (Eds.), *EDO, Lecture Notes in Computer Science*, 1999:129–144, Springer, 2000.

[13] S. Panagiotidi, J. Cohen, J. Darlington, M. Krznarić, and E. Katsiri. Service-enabling Legacy Applications for the GENIE Project. In *Proc. All Hands Meeting*, Nottingham, September 2006.

[14] M.K. Bane, C.W. Armstrong, R.W. Ford, G.D. Riley, and T.L. Freeman. GCF: A General Coupling Framework. *Concurrency and Computation: Practice and Experience*, 18(2):163–181, 2006.

[15] R. Vogelsang, D. Declat, H. Ritzdorf, S. Valcke, R. Redler, and T. Schoenemeyer. OASIS4 User's Guide. *PRISM Report*, 2004.

[16] D. Thain, T. Tannenbaum, and M. Livny. Condor and the GRID. In F. Berman, G. Fox, and T. Hey (Eds.), *Grid Computing: Making the Global Infrastructure a Reality*, John Wiley & Sons Inc., 2002.

[17] J. Thiyagalingm and V. Getov. A Metadata Extracting Tool for Software Components in Grid Applications. In *Proc. IEEE John Vincent Atanasoft International Symposium on Modern Computing*, pages 189–196, IEEE CS Press, 2006.

[18] R. Vallée-Rai, L. Hendren, V. Sundaresan, P. Lam, E. Gagnon, and P. Co. Soot - A Java Optimization Framework. In *Proc. CASCON 1999*, pages 125–135, IBM, 1999.

A SERVICE FOR RELIABLE EXECUTION OF GRID APPLICATIONS

Elżbieta Krępska and Thilo Kielmann
Dept. of Computer Science
Vrije Universiteit
Amsterdam, The Netherlands
e.krepska@gmail.com
kielmann@cs.vu.nl[*]

Raül Sirvent and Rosa M. Badia
Barcelona Supercomputing Center and
Universitat Politècnica de Catalunya
Barcelona, Spain
rsirvent@ac.upc.edu
rosab@ac.upc.edu

Abstract   In grid environments, with the large number of components (both hardware and software) that are involved in application execution, the overall probability that at least one of these components is (temporarily) non-functional is increasing rapidly. In traditional operating systems, such failures are flagged as fatal and the application will be stopped, relying on a re-start after the problem will have been fixed. In a large grid system, this is not a feasible approach as failures happen too frequently while error diagnostics might not be possible at all.

   This scenario is asking for a different approach to application execution, where detection and circumvention of error conditions become an integral part. We present a service that is keeping track of an application's life cycle, from submission by the user to successful completion of its execution. In a case study, we describe how GRID superscalar, a grid application programming environment, can benefit from our service.

Keywords: Reliable execution service, fault tolerance, mediator component toolkit, GRID superscalar.

---

[*]Contact author

1.   Introduction

Grid environments integrate diverse resources and services. Also, the number of nodes in a grid might be highly variable as, for example, in the LHC Computing Grid (LCG) [26]. Such heterogeneity and churn contribute to the complexity of a grid environment, leading to some degree of unreliability. Geographic dispersion, along with administrative site autonomy [10] further contribute to complexity and thus unreliability. Performance variabilty and sporadic unavailability of the underlying networks complicate matters even further.

Obviously, with a large number of components (both hardware and software) involved in the execution of a grid application, the overall probability that at least one component is (temporarily) non-functional is increasing rapidly. In traditional systems, such failures are flagged as fatal and the application will be stopped, relying on a re-start after the problem will have been fixed.

In a large grid system, this is not a feasible approach as failures happen too frequently while error diagnostics might not be possible at all, either because of the overall system scale, or because logging information might be available only locally at the system that has failed.

This scenario is asking for a different approach to application execution, where detection and circumvention of error conditions become an integral part. In previous work [17], we have identified the need for a persistently running service that is keeping track of an application's life cycle, from submission by the user to successful completion of its execution. In this paper, we present such a service.

In Section 2, we investige failure types and fault-tolerance mechanisms. Design and implementation of our reliable execution service (RES) will be presented in Section 3. Section 4 describes how RES can be used for executing application workflows from the GRID superscalar system. Section 5 concludes.

2.   Failures in Grid Environments

Typically, a user submits his application via a resouce broker to a machine in the grid. Before the job is started, required input files must be pre-staged (copied to the execution host) and afterwards, output files have to be post-staged to the user. Failures might happen during many stages of that process:

1 *Execution services failure.* Services executing the application such as a resource broker or a local scheduler might misbehave/crash or might not be able to satisfy the job requirements.

2 *Local environment failure.* The application might fail locally on the selected machine, for example because of insufficient disk space.

3 *Resource failure.* A resource might fail that the application depends upon, like network outages or unresponsive services.

4 *Application specific failure.* The application might fail due to a problem with its code, like causing memory segmentation faults, numerical errors or deadlocks.

Failure (1) of a resource broker or a scheduler might be masked by trying to start a job on a different site. A failure of grid job manager can be circumvented by submitting directly to a cluster, provided we can discover hosts belonging to a grid. Failure (2) can be masked by restarting a job on a different host. To discover failure type (3), special failure detection and monitoring services are necessary [6, 9, 13, 16, 21]. Only failures of type (4) should not be masked, and feedback about their occurrence should be provided to the user. Fault-tolerance (FT) mechanisms can be implemented on different levels:

Application-level FT. Here, fault tolerance is built directly into the application code. While this approach can provide flexibility and efficiency by exploiting application-level knowledge, it is often perceived as cumbersome by application programmers [19]. Runtime environments like the GAT [1] or Satin [24], or fault-tolerant versions of MPI [8] can lower the burden on the programmer.

Multi-layered FT. Here, each layer handles the errors within its own scope, pass others up the hierarchy [23]. This approach simplifies higher-level layers, however, at the expense of performance penalties as higher layers themselves can not adapt any more [18]. Building FT into each component in a grid is also not practical, due to scale and diversity of components.

External FT services. The grid environment might offer an automatic failure detection service which basically allows building more intelligent fault-tolerant services on top of them. Such services [6, 21], however, suffer from poor integration with application execution and from the necessity to be ubiquitously deployment in a grid.

2.1 Related Work

Phoenix is detecting failures by scanning scheduler log files [18]. It can diagnose execution and data transfer errors. Phoenix can follow different, user-definable failure-handling strategies. Applicability of Phoenix is limited to those systems of which log files can be interpreted.

Application failures can also be handled on workflow level [14]. Here, individual tasks might be run alternatively should another task fail. The system in [14] relies on information from the resource broker only, but can also be combined with heartbeat monitors [13]. The execution service for the NASA Information Power Grid [20] is executing interdependent tasks, restricting error diagnosis to application exit codes.

The Globus GRAM service [25] is frequently criticized for not returning application exit codes, returning its own codes specifying certain types of failures instead. Condor-G [11] uses the GRAM protocol and detects and handles resource failures to provide "exactly once" execution semantics. Unfortunately, this mechanism can not be used without deploying Condor-G as the grid middleware.

The fault tolerant manager proposed in [3] supervises the execution of jobs and in case of a failure a decision maker decides on a recovery scenario. Interestingly, the proposal counts a dramatical decrease in the application performance as a failure, too.

Some systems focus on failure detection only. The Heartbeat Monitor (HBM) [21], is an unreliable, low-level fault detection service for a distributed system. The service bases on unreliable fault detectors [4] which try to discover which system components (machines or processes) *might* have failed and notify the application of that fact. Whether to trust this information, how to interpret it, what to do about it, is left entirely to the application. Défago et al. [6] improves performance and scalability of this scheme by introducing hierarchisation and gossipping between monitors.

However, those services are lower-level, they only inform that they suspects that a component has crashed. The application should decide whether and how to recover from the failure what can be non-trivial, especially that the heartbeat monitors do not know the failure root cause. In the following, we describe a service that implements a rather comprehensive approach to failure detection, diagnosis, and resolution.

3.   A Service for Reliable Application Execution

In previous work, we have identified the need for a persistently running service that is keeping track of an application's life cycle, from submission by the user to successful completion of its execution [17]. Such a service is supposed to become an integral part of a grid application execution environment based on a mediator component toolkit [5]. We will now present design and implementation of RES, our *Reliable Execution Service*, that has been designed to fulfill this purpose.

3.1   Design objectives

The Reliable Execution Service (RES) is a permanent service providing reliable execution of applications submitted to the grid. Permanence means that the service runs all the time. Reliability means handling transient failures transparently to the end user. The user should observe only the very application errors, with the exception of permanent grid environment failures. The RES service will be designed to meet the following requirements:

Application feedback. In an ideal case, there should not be any requirements posed on the executed application. However, having application feedback enhances greatly failure detection capabilities and enables application specific debugging and logging. Therefore, for both service-aware and unaware applications, the reliable execution functionality should be offered. Additionally, an application can talk to the service, for example requesting an application-specific failure or sending a message to the user.

Failure detection. The service should detect submission and execution problems. After the execution is done it should properly detect the exit code and intercept uncaught exceptions whenever possible. If a monitoring service is available, the service might monitor hosts executing the application, the application process or resources that the application depends on.

Failure handling and recovery. The service should offer diverse failure handling strategies. Checkpointing applications must be supported.

User influence. The user might influence failure detection and recovery schemes by specifying policies. Policies should be separated from the application code.

Workflow-level and task-level fault-tolerance techniques. The service will not implement task-level fault tolerance techniques, such as alternative or redundant tasks (see Section 2.1). However, the service's direct API should allow a developer to implement those techniques easily.

Batch-mode application execution. After submitting a job, the user can go offline and access recorded job status information at a later time. Job history is kept during and after job completion. The user should not have to examine output files to check the application status or to see if it exited correctly.

Minimizing administrative overhead. The service should be designed so that special privileges, accounts or certificates are not necessary. The service should use the deployed security framework and require users to delegate their rights for the service to act on their behalf. Also, there should be no need to install anything on each machine in the grid.

Preventing information loss. Masked grid component failures should be transparent to the user but not to grid middleware or to the administrator. Records of failure occurrences should be stored persistently, to allow other components to adapt their behaviour.

Dependability.   The service should be able to sustain a crash of its hosting machine. When the machine is back online, the service should recover and re-acquire jobs activated before the crash.

Portability.   The service should be independent of the specific middleware installed on the grid, the hosting machine platform, the language-binding of an executed application and the environment of targeted machines. The service acts as a grid meta-scheduler (is able to choose a cluster to run a job), so it has to encapsulate specific grid information at least on clusters belonging to the grid. The encapsulation should be clearly separated from the service code and it should be possible to discover this information dynamically.

Job model.   The service is intended for computation intensive, long running applications (long here means for example more than an hour). The application file staging model is simple as well – it consists of two lists of files to pre- and post-stage. Additionally, for checkpointable applications, the application specification might contain a list of names of checkpoint files and a checkpoint files repository location.

3.2   Service design

The architecture of the Reliable Execution Service is presented in Fig. 1. The most important thread of control in the service is the JobController. It handles users' requests, activates jobs and controls them. It saves execution metadata to the JobRepository. Waiting jobs are submitted to the grid via the GATEngine [1], which chooses an appropriate resource brokerage service to submit the job to.

Job's Executors are threads of control active on grid machines. They supervise the execution "locally", give feedback to the service and mediate communication between the service and the application. After the job is done, its Executor detects the exit code and uncaught exceptions, sends a JobDone signal to the service and exits. The service verifies the execution. In case of a failure, the failure agent diagnoses the problem, classifies it into permanent or transient. Permanent failures are reported to the user in the way that shields the user from middleware and hardware details. For transient failures the agent comes up with a suitable recovery scenario executed then by the JobController.

In case of a failure of the machine hosting the service, the service itself might stop working. However, it is designed such that the previously activated jobs are reacquired, even though control over them is weakened, as connections with the resource broker are lost that were created when the jobs had been submitted.

Service behaviour such as the job execution planning phase, failure diagnosis and execution verification might be influenced by users policies, service

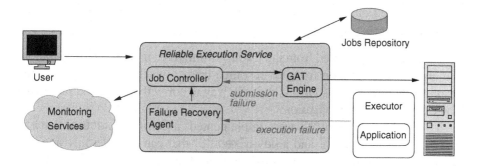

Figure 1. The Reliable Execution Service architecture.

self adaptation based on failures occurrence rates and additional information received from monitoring or information grid services.

As the service is executing on the behalf of its users, it has to use their respective credentials. Our current implementation is using the Globus MyProxy Credential Management System [12]. Using MyProxy, the user can hand over temporary credentials to the RES service, allowing RES to execute the application with the user's credentials. Other security contexts, supported by the GAT engine, could be also used here.

However, delegating POSIX (UNIX) file permissions could not be done easily. Therefore, the user must make sure that the service can access files which are to be pre-staged: the service might be run by a privileged user or the files might be made readable to the appropriate user group or to everybody. An appropriate solution would be accessing files through a grid file system abstraction, as anticipated in [15], with proper grid-wide file permissions.

3.3 Application wrapping

Applications are not executed directly but they are wrapped inside the **Executor** which is responsible for the following tasks:

1 *Controling the application execution.* The wrapper signals to the service when the execution begins, runs the application and after it is done, reports this fact to the service.

2 *Local monitoring of the application execution.* During the execution the wrapper sends heartbeats to the service. When the job is done, it detects the exit code and intercepts uncaught exceptions if possible.

3 *Talking to the application.* The **Executor** mediates the communication between the application and the service. The application might send signals, which are interpreted by the **JobController** according to the user's policy. The signal might be fatal, i.e. describing a failure which

occurred during the execution, or informative, for example debugging and logging signals.

The information received from the Executor might be more accurate and more timely than information from the resource broker which does not control the application directly. Also this is the only way to correctly detect and propagate the exit code of the application.

Two kinds of Executor's were implemented: a GenericExecutor that can execute any application, and a JavaExecutor that can execute only applications implemented in Java but provides more functionalities for them. Communication with the service is done using Java RMI. As executed applications might be developed in any programming language, it was not trivial to implement a generic way to talk to the application. As the JavaExecutor runs the application using the Java's reflection mechanisms, it talks to the application through normal local method invocations. However, the GenericExecutor talks to the application using sockets. To ease the application programmer's task, we have implemented simple language-binding libraries that a user can link to his programs, for in C/C++ and Python languages. If the application is only available as a binary program, it cannot be modified to talk to the Executor. In this case, the Executor can only handle return codes.

Fig. 2 shows some example code of an application that uses the RES programming interface to try an alternative algorithm should the first one fail. The code first tries a supposedly fast implementation. Should this fail, another (possibly slower but less resource hungry) implementation is tried out. This is an example where certain application-level failures can be circumvented using RES.

3.4   Failures detected by the service

The most important detected failures, related to the fact that the application executes in the grid environment, are as follows:

- *Failures prior to the execution.* Before the execution on the target machine takes place at all, numerous types of failures must be anticipated such as pre-staging failures, incorrect job description, security failures and multiple types of submission failures – inability to locate the service, service misconfiguration, not enough resources to execute the job, authorisation/proxy failure, network connection failure, etc.

- *Failures during the execution.* Besides application specific failures such as abrupt termination, throwing an uncaught exception or a failure requested by the application, failures might be caused by other factors such as the inability of the Executor to start the application, security issues, problems with talking to the application or the Executor internal

```
boolean submitAndWait(RESSoftwareDescription sd, RESUserPolicy
   policy) {
   // Locate the service
   RemoteRES res = RESServiceLocator.find();
   // Submit the job
   RESSubmissionResult sr = res.submit(sd, policy);
   // Retrieve the resulting job id
   RESJobId jobId = sr.getJobId();
   // Wait until job is done
   RESQueryResult qr = null;
   while (!(qr = res.query(jobId, true)).isDone());
   // Check if job is done successfully
   return qr.isDoneSuccessfully();
}

// Prepare software descriptions and user policies for both algorithms
// Try the first algorithm
if (!submitAndWait(resSD_fast, userPolicy_fast)) {
   // The first algorithm failed, try the second one
   submitAndWait(resSD_slow, userPolicy_slow);
}
```

Figure 2.   Example code for submitting alternative tasks based on given errors.

problem which should not – but might – occur and in this case should not mislead the user. The service is capable of detecting an abrupt termination of the application basing on the heartbeats received from the Executor. When detecting missing heartbeats the service tries to differentiate between crash of the job process or the Executor, a crash of the machine executing the application, or a transient or permanent network outage.

- *Post execution failures.* After the job execution, the service anticipates post-staging failures and verifies the execution according to the following criteria: heartbeats reception, feedback signals reception, the exit value, presence of output files.

3.5   Recovery techniques

When the FailureRecoveryAgent detects a failure, it must come up with a suitable recovery scenario to resolve the problem. As we cannot prevent grid resources from failing, what we can basically do at the task level is restarting the application in the way that diminishes the probability of the failure recurring. Therefore we mask transient failures using various types of RETRY techniques: retrying on a different cluster (what provides hardware and software diversity), retrying on a machine with certain characteristics, such as a faster processor, more disk space, more memory or with more network bandwidth available or restarting after a certain time.

Another technique used is CHECKPOINTING. It can be used only if the application is developed so that it can write checkpoints or the grid provides system-level generic checkpointing. The stored state information should be enough to restart the process, even on a different resource. This technique is useful for processes which involve significant data manipulation and are unstable or cannot finish data manipulation in a single run.

If the application fails a certain number of times, the failure must be considered permanent. The application FAILURE is reported back to the user. Also in certain cases Executor failures might be worthy to IGNORE, as we may still hope that the application executes successfully.

To select a proper recovery scenario, artificial intelligence techniques might be used, to base the decision also on the job history and overall failure occurrence rates. In the current implementation the history of the job is not taken into account when deciding on a recovery scenario. Misbehaving clusters are detected when failure occurrence rate is near 100% and jobs are not submitted to them provided there are other resources to use.

3.6   Evaluation

The service has been implemented according to the design shown in Fig. 1. We have evaluated it its functionality with a fault-simulating application kernel that we had pre-set to crash with a given probability (between 10 and 20 %). We used up to 100 worker tasks running the fault-simulating application kernel and up to 32 compute nodes. When a worker crashed, it was automatically restarted by the service, transparently to the application. All of the workers completed eventually in spite of the frequent crashes. In a more complete set of tests, we have verified that RES is able to handle the following kinds of failures:

User-related failures: authorisation failures, program binary unavailability, non-zero exit code, pre staging failures due to unavailable files or target directories, catching the application's exceptions, application timeouts, handling of checkpoints.

Grid-related failures: crash of the Executor process, transient network outage, host crash or permanent network outage, cluster/scheduler misbehavior, crash of the RES service itself.

In a separate test, we have evaluated the runtime overhead of submitting jobs via the RES, compared to direct job submission. Fig. 3 shows the results, obtained on the VU cluster of the DAS-2 [7] system. We were experimenting with an application kernel performing prime factorization, written in Java, and

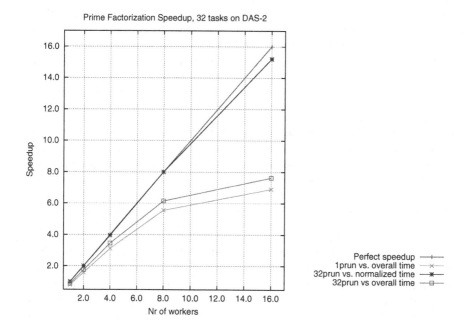

Figure 3. Job submission overhead caused by the RES.

parallelized as a simple task farming program. The program was submitted via the prun job submission tool installed on DAS-2. The RES contacted prun via the Java-GAT. In total, 32 parallel jobs were created per application run. The graphs in Fig. 3 report speedups, relative to sequential execution on a single node of the system.

The purpose of Fig. 3 is to verify the overhead imposed by the RES service, ranging from one up to sixteen worker nodes. In fact, the figure shows two comparisons. The first pair of lines to compare to each other are the ones labelled "1prun vs. overall time" and "32prun vs. overall time." The lines compare submission of the 32 tasks, either as a single job, or by 32 separate job submissions, both to the RES. Notably, differences are only small. The second pair of lines for comparison are "32prun vs. normalized time" and the perfect speedup. Here, the runtimes have been normalized by removing the actual scheduling and waiting times of the underlying prun system. What can be seen is that speedups are (almost) perfect, indicating that RES introduces hardly any runtime overhead to the overall job submission process, while adding failure resilience.

4. Case Study: Reliable Execution for GRID superscalar

GRID superscalar [2] is a grid application programming environment, providing a simple programming model. Its runtime system is parallelizing sequential code, based on the functions defined to be run on the grid, and the data dependencies between the calls in the main program to those functions. The user provides a main program, an IDL file describing the interfaces of the functions which will be executed in the grid, and the function implementations. These can be either coded directly, or wrapped calling to external binaries or scripts. The system has been ported not only to grid environments (using Globus [25] and Ninf-G [22]), but also to work inside clusters with ssh/scp, and as a programming model for multi-core processor platforms, going beyond the boundaries of grid computing.

Recently, GRID superscalar has incorporated a fault-tolerance mechanism for which the user specifies timeout values for individual functions. When a timeout is reached, the runtime system assumes a function to have failed, and tries to cancel and resubmit it. In combination with the RES, GRID superscalar would only need to consider the application-related failures. Also, GRID superscalar can define suitable policies for specific failure scenarios, and, because the RES relies on the GAT framework, it indirectly offers a standard interface for using different grid middlewares transparently. In general, the RES handles the vast majority of grid middleware related errors, and thus simplifies GRID superscalar's task. In addition, the RES provides a uniform interface for worker tasks to report their exit status to the master process, obsoleting the current file-based mechanism that had been introduced to circumvent limitations of current middleware.

GRID superscalar's code generation and deployment techniques perfectly fit the RES framework. Before running an application, different binaries are generated, one for the master part, and several for the worker machines. To the RES, these binaries are like independent applications which must be invoked, along with their input and output files, while GRID superscalar keeps track about all of them, because they belong to the same application.

The checkpointing capabilities of the RES system are focused to offer an intra-task checkpoint mechanism. This is very suitable to the GRID superscalar runtime, which already offers checkpointing techniques, but based on an inter-task approach. So, the combination of the checkpointing inside a task offered by RES, and the checkpointing between tasks offered by GRID superscalar will build a robust framework for the execution of GRID superscalar's applications.

When submitting a job, GRID superscalar maintains information about file locality for input files, aiming to reduce file transfer overhead. This implies that part of the job submission policies (provided by GRID superscalar to RES) have to give preference for execution hosts with good locality of input files.

5. Conclusions

The large number of components being involved in the execution of a grid application raises the probability that at least one of these components is (temporarily) non-functional up to a level where errors can not be neglected any more. This observation calls for an application execution mechanism that has failure detection, diagnosis, and handling as intrinsic functionalities.

We have explored the possible causes of application execution errors, and existing approaches to handle them. We have presented the design and implementation of RES, our *Reliable Execution Service* for grid applications. We have presented a case study in which the GRID superscalar system reliably executes jobs via the RES service, and how the service also helps GRID superscalar to build its own fault tolerance policies. The combination of checkpointing techniques avaliable in both environments creates a strong reliable framework where the computation already performed will be hardly lost.

RES is experimentally being deployed on the DAS-2 system. While we are currently gaining further experience with the system, future work comprises support for parallel jobs as well as more sophisticated failure resolution strategies, possibly based on AI techniques.

Acknowledgments

This research work is carried out under the FP6 Network of Excellence *CoreGRID* funded by the European Commission (Contract IST-2002-004265). It is also partially funded by the Ministry of Science and Technology of Spain (TIN2004-07739-C02-01).

References

[1] G. Allen, K. Davis, T. Goodale, A. Hutanu, H. Kaiser, T. Kielmann, A. Merzky, R. van Nieuwpoort, A. Reinefeld, F. Schintke, T. Schuett, E. Seidel, and B. Ullmer. The grid application toolkit: toward generic and easy application programming interfaces for the grid. *Proceedings of the IEEE*, 93:534–550, 2005.

[2] R. M. Badia, J. Labarta, R. Sirvent, J. M. Pérez, J. M. Cela, and R. Grima. Programming Grid Applications with GRID Superscalar. *Journal of Grid Computing*, 1(2):151–170, 2003.

[3] M. Bubak, T. Szepieniec, and M. Radecki. A proposal of application failure detection and recovery in the Grid, 2003. Cracow, Grid Workshop.

[4] T. D. Chandra and S. Toueg. Unreliable failure detectors for reliable distributed systems. *Journal of the ACM*, 43(2):225–267, 1996.

[5] CoreGRID Institute on Problem Soving Environments Tools and Grid Systems. Proposal for Mediator Component Toolkit. CoreGRID deliverable D.ETS.02, 2005.

[6] X. Défago, N. Hayashibara, and T. Katayama. On the design of a failure detection service for large-scale distributed systems. *Proceedings International Symposium Towards Peta-Bit Ultra-Networks*, pages 88–95, 2003.

[7] The Distributed ASCI Supercomputer DAS-2. http://www.cs.vu.nl/das2.

[8] G. E. Fagg and J. J. Dongarra. FT-MPI: Fault tolerant MPI, supporting dynamic applications in a dynamic world. *Lecture Notes in Computer Science*, 1908:346–354, 2000.

[9] P. Felber, X. Défago, R. Guerraoui, and P. Oser. Failure detectors as first class objects. In *Proceedings of the International Symposium on Distributed Objects and Applications (DOA'99)*, pages 132–141, Edinburgh, Scotland, 1999.

[10] I. Foster. What is the Grid? A three point checklist. *GRID Today*, 2002.

[11] J. Frey, T. Tannenbaum, I. Foster, M. Livny, and S. Tuecke. Condor-G: A Computation Management Agent for Multi-Institutional Grids. In *Tenth IEEE Symposium on High Performance Distributed Computing (HPDC10)*, 2001.

[12] Globus Toolkit. The MyProxy Credential Management Service. http://grid.ncsa.uiuc.edu/myproxy.

[13] S. Hwang and C. Kesselman. A generic failure detection service for the Grid. Information Sciences Institute, University of Southern California. Technical Report ISI-TR-568, 2003.

[14] S. Hwang and C. Kesselman. Grid workflow: A flexible failure handling framework for the Grid. *High Performance Distributed Computing*, 00:126, 2003.

[15] A. Jagatheesan. The GGF Grid File System Architecture Workbook. Grid Forum Document, GFD.61, 2006. Global Grid Forum.

[16] A. Jain and R. K. Shyamasundar. Failure detection and membership management in grid environments. In *Fifth IEEE/ACM International Workshop on Grid Computing*, pages 44–52, Los Alamitos, CA, USA, 2004. IEEE Computer Society.

[17] T. Kielmann, G. Wrzesinska, N. Currle-Linde, and M. Resch. Redesigning the SEGL Problem Solving Environment: A Case Study of Using Mediator Components. In *Integrated Research in Grid Computing*. Springer Verlag, 2006.

[18] G. Kola, T. Kosar, and M. Livny. Phoenix: Making data-intensive grid applications fault-tolerant. In *5th IEEE/ACM International Workshop on Grid Computing*, 2004.

[19] R. Medeiros, W. Cirne, F. Brasileiro, and J. Sauve. Faults in grids: Why are they so bad and what can be done about it? In *Fourth International Workshop on Grid Computing*, page 18, Los Alamitos, CA, USA, 2003. IEEE Computer Society.

[20] W. Smith and C. Hu. An execution service for grid computing. NAS Technical Report NAS-04-004, 2004.

[21] P. Stelling, C. DeMatteis, I. T. Foster, C. Kesselman, C. A. Lee, and G. von Laszewski. A fault detection service for wide area distributed computations. *Cluster Computing*, 2(2):117–128, 1999.

[22] Y. Tanaka, H. Nakada, S. Sekiguchi, T. Suzumura, and S. Matsuoka. Ninf-G: A Reference Implementation of RPC-based Programming Middleware for Grid Computing. *Journal of Grid Computing*, 1(1):41–51, 2003.

[23] D. Thain and M. Livny. Error scope on a computational grid: Theory and practice. In *11th IEEE International Symposium on High Performance Distributed Computing*, Los Alamitos, CA, USA, 2002. IEEE Computer Society.

[24] G. Wrzesinska, R. van Nieuwpoort, J. Maassen, and H. E. Bal. Fault-tolerance, malleability and migration for divide-and-conquer applications on the grid. In *Proc. of 19th International Parallel and Distributed Processing Symposium*, Denver, CO, April 2005.

[25] The Globus project. http://www.globus.org.

[26] LHC Computing Grid (LCG) project. http://lcg.web.cern.ch/LCG.

PERFORMANCE MONITORING OF GRID SUPERSCALAR WITH OCM-G/G-PM: INTEGRATION ISSUES*

Rosa M. Badia and Raül Sirvent
Univ. Politècnica de Catalunya, C/ Jordi Girona, 1-3, E-08034 Barcelona, Spain
rosab@ac.upc.edu
rsirvent@ac.upc.edu

Marian Bubak
Inst. Computer Science, AGH, al. Mickiewicza 30, 30-059 Kraków, Poland
Academic Computer Centre – CYFRONET, Nawojki 11, 30-950 Kraków, Poland
bubak@agh.edu.pl

Wlodzimierz Funika and Piotr Machner
Inst. Computer Science, AGH, al. Mickiewicza 30, 30-059 Kraków, Poland
funika@agh.edu.pl
machner@student.agh.edu.pl

Abstract   In this paper the use of a Grid-enabled system for performance monitoring of GRID superscalar-compliant applications is addressed. Performance monitoring is built on top of the OCM-G monitoring system developed in the EU IST CrossGrid project. A graphical user tool G-PM is used to interpret information received from the monitoring system. We discuss the issues related to the performance analysis of GRID superscalar applications and present the current work progress with focus on the refinement of existing implementation issues and present the required changes to the G-PM and OCM-G architecture. At the end a case study of performance monitoring is presented.

Keywords: grid computing, grid programming models, grid workflows, monitoring tools, performance analysis

---

*This research is partly funded by the EU IST FP6-0004265 CoreGRID project and by the Ministry of Science and Technology of Spain (TIN-2004-07739-C02-01).

1.   Introduction

An important role in any distributed system and especially in Grid environments is played by performance monitoring tools. This is due to the fact that performance information is required not only by the user to get information about the infrastructure and the running applications, but also by most Grid facilities to enable correct job submission, data access optimization services, and scheduling. The complexity and dynamics of Grid environments makes that various entities including infrastructure elements, applications, middleware, and others, need to be monitored and analyzed in order to understand and explain their performance behavior on the Grid.

The GRID superscalar (GS) [1], an approach to Grid computing, supports the development of applications, in a transparent and convenient way for the user. Its aim is to reduce the development complexity of Grid applications to the minimum, in such a way that writing an application for a computational Grid can be as easy as a sequential program. The idea assumes that a lot of applications are based on some repeating actions, e.g. in form of loops. The granularity of these actions is on the level of simulations or programs, and the data objects will be files. The requirements to run the sequential-fashion application on a Grid are expressed as a specification of the interface of the tasks to be executed on the Grid and calls to GS interface functions.

GS provides an underlying run-time environment capable of detecting the inherent parallelism of the sequential application and performs concurrent task submission. In addition to a data-dependence analysis based on these input/output task parameters which are files, techniques such as file renaming and file locality are applied to increase the application performance. The run-time is built upon the Globus Toolkit 2.x APIs [3]. It is also adapted to work with Globus Toolkit 4, Ninf-G [4] and directly with ssh.

The above reasons motivated a design of a monitoring facility that supports the development of applications to be run in the Grid environment using the GS system, to get deeper insight into how an application behaves in such environments, to help in its effective and fault-tolerant execution. The dynamics of a GS application execution necessitates the use of highly reactive tools to catch what is going on with the application. Unfortunately, the existing monitoring systems which provide off-line access to monitoring data do not allow to analyse and react on-line to performance problems arising during the application's execution.

Therefore we have decided to monitor GS applications using a grid-enabled OMIS Compliant Monitoring system (OCM-G), which was developed within the EU IST CrossGrid project [5] for the on-line monitoring of grid applications, thus providing the user with far better knowledge of the application behaviour during runtime. Its features allow to fit it well into the requirements of running an application on the Grid. In order to use this monitoring system, one needs to instrument their libraries so that each time a function is executed or the execution is finished, relevant monitoring data can be sent back to OCM-G. The system gathers all the data acquired, it does not interpret it or show it to the user. This can be done by other tools, which can connect to the monitoring system (an example of such a tool is G-PM), access the data by issuing monitoring requests and visualize it. OCM-G, however, has the biggest support for MPI applications, so making it work with GS is not that straightforward.

In this paper, we focus on the implementation ideas of adapting the OCM-G monitoring system [6] to support GS applications. Its role is to help the user or an automatic facility to decide when a performance problem is encountered. The original concept of performance monitoring for GS applications with OCM-G was described in [8].

We will discuss what metrics are important to assess the performance of the application. These metrics include standard metrics (e.g. *communication time*) as well as application-specific metrics, expressed in a special language which allows the user to define context-meaningful performance indicators. Our next focus is on the further refinement of architectural issues of how OCM-G should operate within GS, and its implementation details.

Our next concern is providing a front-end performance evaluation tool based on the G-PM [7] tool which programs the OCM-G to supply monitoring data and presents them in a meaningful graphical manner. It provides a set of metrics whose values can be shown to the user allowing for easy interpretation of program execution by giving its important details.

This paper is organized as follows: Section 2 describes the requirements needed to be fulfilled to enable monitoring of GRID superscalar applications. Section 3 outlines the current status of work already done, especially w.r.t. library instrumentation and GRID superscalar-specific metrics with G-PM. Section 4 provides an overview of the G-PM tool along with its current limitations. It also shows modifications to the G-PM architecture required to address correctly the nature of the issue. Section 5 presents some of the problems we have encountered integrating OCM-G and GS. In Section 6 we show a case study of the use of the monitoring system for an example application. In Section 7 we overview the functionality of GS Monitor, which is aimed at the monitoring of application execution dependencies, and its integration with G-PM. Section 8 sums up the results and shows plans for further research.

2. Monitoring requirements for and from the GS environment

The GRID superscalar programming paradigm is based on the master-worker model. The user writes the master application in a fashion very similar to writing a sequential application. The main difference is that he/she needs to specify and write functions which will be invoked on the Grid within worker applications. The environment takes care of producing a "glue" between the master and workers. Both the master and worker processes need to register in the OCM-G before doing any real work to be monitored.

In order to monitor the execution of any application, the monitoring system needs to know when specific actions during the runtime take place. This can be achieved through library instrumentation. The libraries used by the monitored application need to be wrapped into additional code which takes care of notifying the monitor about interesting events. This way we can receive all sorts of important data, e.g. the execution time of functions. OCM-G provides facilities for library instrumentation.

The next step is to define GRID superscalar-specific metrics in the G-PM performance tool. These metrics would mainly have to comprise such values as the execution time of GRID superscalar functions and the number of function invocations.

3.   Current status of research

GRID superscalar uses two libraries, `libGS-master` and `libGS-worker`. They are used respectively in the master and worker code. In order to instrument any library in OCM-G, a specific `*.omis` description file has to be written. This file tells the `cg-ocmg-libinstr` tool that performs instrumentation which functions to instrument and in what way.

Therefore we have written, according to the OMIS specification, two files, describing GS libraries. Using these files and the `cg-ocmg-libinstr` tool we perform instrumentation. A question that may arise here is: if we have the GS libraries instrumented, what about the user-defined grid-enabled functions? Well, before every call to a user function there is a call to the `IniWorker()` function and after it there is a call to the `EndWorker()` function. Bothe of them are from the instrumented GS library, so in order to measure the amount of time a user-defined function takes all we have to do is to measure the time between `IniWorker()` and `EndWorker()`. In case the user needs more information, there is one option more - to put the worker functions into a library and instrument this library. To do this, an instrumentation description file needs to be written, where the user can define *event context parameters* of his/her choice. This mechanism gives the ability to send any kind of information to OCM-G (it is usually used to send function parameters). A simple description file can look like this:

```
int user_defined_func(char *pathname, int mode) {
    {
        double var1;
```

```
        double var2;
    }
    START:
    {
        var1 = //... some computations
    }

        string pathname;
        integer mode;
    END:
    {
        var2 = //... some computations
    }
    floating var3 = var1 - var2;
    integer RESULT;
}
```

The above instrumentation sends four event context parameters to OCM-G: function parameters - `pathname` and `mode`, the function result and a user defined event context parameter - `var3`. The computations defined within the `START` tag are performed before the execution of the original function while the computations within the `END` tag - after the original function. Making full use of this information in the case of user-defined worker functions would sometimes require the use of an advanced functionality of G-PM (for instance, to write new, applicationspecific metrics we may need to use the PMSL language [7]), otherwise OCM-G also provides a command-line tool `cg-ocmg-tool` which allows for easy extraction of this data and should be sufficient in some cases.

In order to automate the instrumentation process we have written a script which, using the `GS_HOME environment` variable, finds the GS runtime and its libraries. Then it instruments them using the above description files and the `cg-ocmg-libinstr` tool. The script makes also backup versions of the libraries.

So far we have created "time spent" and count metrics for the following GRID superscalar functions: `GS_{On, Off, Open, Close, FOpen, FClose, Barrier, SpeculativeEnd}`. The *count* metrics represent the number of function invocations in the program and the "time spent" metrics represent the amount of time used by the application to invoke a specific function. Adding new metrics to G-PM is quite easy - usually each one requires just a few lines of code. G-PM also provides an easier way to define new metrics, which does not require modifications of G-PM code - they can be created using PMSL - Performance Measurement Specification Language.

One of the problems we encountered was the fact that Grid Superscalar does not pass command line parameters from the master application to workers. In order to allow the workers to register in OCM-G, they need to have access to some of these parameters such as application name or address of the OCM-G Main Service Manager. The solution we used was writing a script (which we called monGS) through which all monitored GS applications will have to be run. It uses the GS_ENVIRONMENT variable which defines additional data that can be passed to the workers. This variable can be defined on the master side and duplicated in the worker environments so that workers can make use of it.

4.   The G-PM performance tool and its enhancements

G-PM (Grid-enabled Performance Measurement tool) is an application that connects to the OCM-G monitoring system and extracts information on the application being monitored. It allows the user to choose appropriate metrics and display styles in order to observe the execution details of the program.

A problem with G-PM when it comes to the monitoring of GS applications is that it was originally designed for monitoring parallel applications using programming paradigms other than GRID superscalar. Usually, G-PM connects to OCM-G, waits for a specified number of processes to register, attaches to them and starts monitoring them. Afterwards, the list of these processes is never refreshed, thus G-PM cannot attach to new ones. This is presented in Fig. 1.

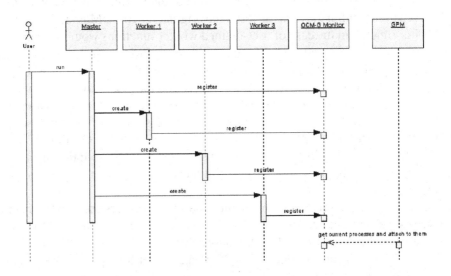

Figure 1.   The original way G-PM attaches to processes.

Whilst being sufficient for the needs of e.g. MPI applications, it is not enough when it comes to monitoring GS applications. The reason for this is that they are much more dynamic. Worker processes are created whenever the user executes one of the grid-enabled functions, they are destroyed once these functions have finished executing. Therefore we may have millions of workers showing up and dying at different moments of a program execution. Also, there are not any limitations on the amount of time workers might live, because their tasks are defined by the user.

A solution to this problem would be to make G-PM subscribe to the events of process registration. The tool would be notified each time a new process has registered to OCM-G. Then the latter would attach to the newly registered process. This would allow to always have an up-to-date list of working processes. This scenario is presented in Fig. 2.

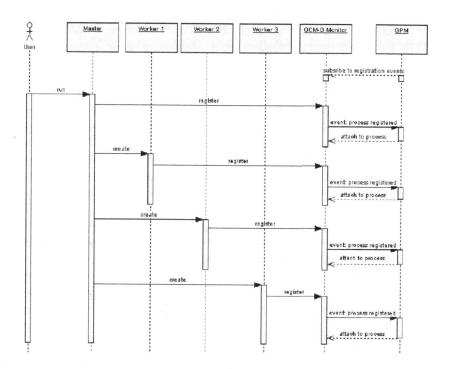

Figure 2. The mode of attaching G-PM to processes modified for GS needs.

There is also a need to enhance G-PM display modes to explicitly visualize the creation and destruction of processes and to be able to show large numbers of processes. One of the new G-PM visualization modes is the space-time diagram [9]. We're currently working on integrating it into the GS-dedicated G-PM version along with adaptation to GS paradigm semantics. A simple screenshot of the new mode can be seen in Fig. 3.

5. Other integration issues

Some of the problems have been solved but new ones arise. One of them is the fact that there might be so many processes in a GS application that

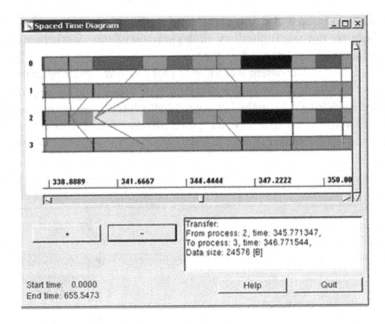

Figure 3.   Space-time diagram.

G-PM becomes incapable of visualizing all of them. The user therefore should have some means to choose which worker processes should be monitored and which need not. This can be solved by disengaging the automatic instrumentation of user functions. The user would add manually one line of the OCM-G registration code in the chosen ones thus choosing not to monitor some of the processes. Another (more automatic and easier from the user's point of view) solution to this problem would allow the user to define a special file, specifying the functions to be instrumented with registration code.

Another problem is the instrumentation of one of the more important GS functions: the Execute() function. It has a variable number of parameters, therefore it cannot be instrumented with any of the available OCM-G instrumentation tools. The only solution we've come up with is to use some low-level assembler instrumentation. Unfortunately, this would be hardware specific, so not very universal.

6.   Case Study

Within our implementation efforts, we made use of a simple example application provided within GS binary distribution. It uses the GS environment to simply add integers on the Grid. Its lack of complexity is not important - we just want to illustrate the process of monitoring. Each GS application needs to invoke the GS_On() and GS_Off() functions at the beginning and at the end of work. These functions are instrumented and their relevant "time spent"[1] and count metrics have been inserted into G-PM so we are going to be able to get information on their execution.

First, we start the OCM-G monitor:

```
cg-ocmg-monitor
```

This starts the monitor and returns its identifier.

Now we start the application. As command line parameters we have to pass the identifier of the monitor and the application name, under which it will be accessible to the OCM-G:

```
./simple --ocmg-appname simple --ocmg-mainsm 959c635d:8bab
```

All we need to do now is to run the G-PM tool in order to observe the application behaviour:

```
cg-gpm simple --ocmg-mainsm 959c635d:8bab
```

Having started G-PM, we can choose some metrics in the measurement definition window, as shown in Fig. 4. We can also decide to limit measurements to specific hosts, nodes, processes, and functions. Let's choose for example the GS_On delay metric (Fig. 4), which will show the time spent in the instrumented GS_On() and GS_Off() functions.

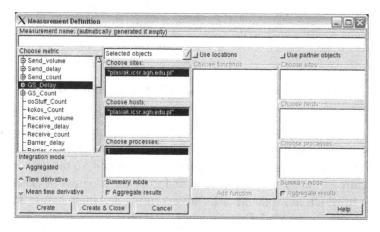

Figure 4.   G-PM: defining a measurement for the instrumented functions.

Now we need to resume the program execution (by default, applications pause their execution after having registered in OCM-G) and have a look at

---

[1]For convenience we call it "delay"

the measurement display. We can observe that the execution of the mentioned functions was spotted by GP-M and the relevant time was calculated and shown in a multicurve display window (Fig. 5). This is of course a simple example, but in a similar way we can monitor the time of any instrumented functions.

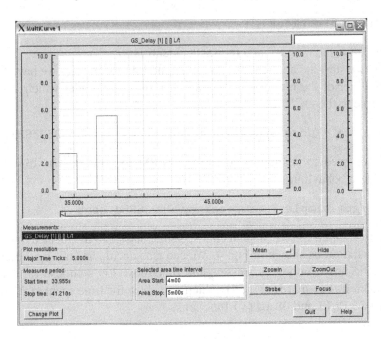

Figure 5.   Measuring the time spent in the GS_On() and GS_Off() functions.

7.   Visualization of GS applications with GSM

When analysing the performance of application execution it is often necessary to correlate it with dependencies within the application. The monitoring infrastructure of GRID superscalar is enhanced by a monitor (GSM) whose aim is to visualize the task dependence graph at runtime, so the user can study the structure of the parallel application and track the progress of execution by knowing in which machine all tasks are executing and their status. The GSM is implemented using the UDrawGraph (UDG) [10], an interactive graph visualization package from the University of Bremen. Just as GRID superscalar, the GSM assumes that the Grid consists of a master machine and worker machines. Additionally, for monitoring purposes, we identify another machine, which does not belong to either of the aforementioned groups, we call it *monitoring machine*. By design, the GSM should run on the monitoring machine, so as not to disturb or affect the Grid computation. The GSM can also be located on the master or on one of the worker machines, if desired.

Figure 6 shows an example of a GSM window, in which the user can resize manually with the graph or even change the order of the nodes for a better understanding of the dependencies between tasks. This is an easy way to find out the degree of parallelism of the algorithm previously programmed with GRID superscalar. As the graph can grow easily for more complex programs, options for stopping the graph generation or for automatically scale / reorder the graph are provided.

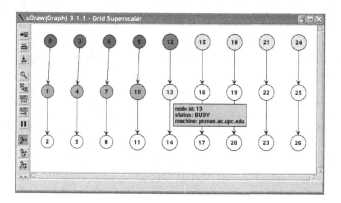

Figure 6. GRID superscalar monitor window.

The nodes representing the tasks in the GSM graph area are coloured in order to visually show the current state of the task, as well as the machine that computes the task. With this colour configuration, the user can easily see which tasks have dependencies, which ones have their dependencies resolved, the tasks currently running, and the tasks that have already finished their computation. This is very important not only to monitor the execution of the GRID superscalar application, but also allowing the user to understand the application cannot achieve more parallelism.

In order to enable correlation between performance measurements and execution progress followed with GSM graphs, some interfaces developed for the needs of GSM are exposed to OCM-G which captures GSM-bound events and reports them to the G-PM tool for measurement purposes.

8. Summary

The work on providing the on-line performance monitoring for GRID superscalar (GS) applications with the OCM-G monitoring system and the G-PM performance evaluation tool is based on a set of requirements posed by GS and feasible to fulfill by the above tools. The OCM-G attaches to the application processes and provides monitoring data and other functionality for the tool using the OMIS interface.

In case of GS applications, we need to make some changes to the way G-PM attaches to processes: whenever a process is created it must be registered in the monitor and a corresponding event sent to the tool, so that it can attach to the newly created process and monitor it. While the OCM-G monitoring system under discussion provides facilities for code instrumentation: a scripting language for describing what and how should be instrumented (using *.omis) and an instrumenting tool which produces an instrumented version of a library, on the front-end level the G-PM performance tool provides a metric definition language PMSL that enables the user to define an own metric most meaningful in the context of the application. This metric can be based on the available metrics provided by the tool and/or so called *probes* inserted into the application code.

So far we have:

- written description files for GS library functions

- created an easy way to instrument GS libraries - the instrumentation script

- added new metrics to G-PM, allowing monitoring of GS functions

- solved the worker registration problem by writing the monGS script.

This work has been carried out without modifications to GRID superscalar code and with very slight modifications to G-PM's code. We are currently working on further extensions to G-PM, which are aimed at making it well adapted to GRID superscalar needs, e.g. an advanced visualization of workers' start-up/destruction.

Acknowledgements. We are grateful to prof. Roland Wismüller from Universität Siegen as well as to our colleagues Bartosz Baliś and Tomasz Szepieniec for valuable discussions.

References

[1] Rosa M. Badia, Jesús Labarta, Raül Sirvent, Josep M. Pérez, José M. Cela and Rogeli Grima. *Programming Grid Applications with GRID superscalar*. Journal of Grid Computing, vol. 1, 2003, pp. 151-170.

[2] T. Ludwig, R. Wismueller, V. Sunderam and A. Bode. *OMIS – On-line Monitoring Interface Specification (Version 2.0)*. Shaker Verlag, Aachen, vol. 9, LRR-TUM Research Report Series, (1997)
http://wwwbode.in.tum.de/Λomis/OMIS/Version-2.0/version-2.0.ps.gz

[3] Globus Project homepage http://www.globus.org/

[4] Y. Tanaka, H. Nakada, S. Sekiguchi, T. Suzumura, S. Matsuoka. *Ninf-G: A Reference Implementation of RPC-based Programming Middleware for Grid Computing*. Journal of Grid Computing, 1(1):41-51, 2003.

[5] EU IST CrossGrid project page http://www.eu-crossgrid.org/

[6] Balis, B., Bubak, M., Funika, W., Wismueller, R., Radecki, M., Szepieniec, T., Arodz, T., Kurdziel, M. *Grid Environment for On-line Application Monitoring and Performance Analysis*. Scientific Pogrammning, vol. 12, no. 4, 2004, pp. 239-251.

[7] R. Wismueller, M. Bubak, W. Funika, and B. Baliś. *A Performance Analysis Tool for Interactive Applications on the Grid*. Intl. Journal of High Performance Computing Applications, 18(3):305-316, Fall 2004.

[8] Badia R.M., Bubak, M., Funika, W., and Smetek, M. *Performance Monitoring of GRID superscalar applications with OCM-G*. In: Sergei Gorlatch, Marco Danelutto (Eds.), Proceedings of the CoreGRID Workshop "Integrated Research in Grid Computing", Pisa, Italy, November 28-30, 2005, pp. 229-236, TR-05-22, University of Pisa, 2005

[9] Funika, W., Duell, J., Jojczyk, P., Strack, R. Enhancing the G-PM Performance Measurement Tool by Space-time Diagram. In: M. Bubak, M. Turala, K. Wiatr (Eds.), Proceedings of Cracow Grid Workshop - CGW'06, October 15-18 2006, ACC-Cyfronet UST, Kraków (to be published).

[10] *uDraw(Graph)*. http://www.informatik.uni-bremen.de/davinci/

IMPROVING WORKFLOW EXECUTION THROUGH SLA-BASED ADVANCE RESERVATION

Philipp Wieder
Central Institute for Applied Mathematics
Research Centre Jülich,
52425 Jülich, Germany
ph.wieder@fz-juelich.de

Oliver Wäldrich and Wolfgang Ziegler
Department of Bioinformatics
Fraunhofer Institute SCAI
53754 Sankt Augustin, Germany
{oliver.waeldrich, wolfgang.ziegler}@scai.fraunhofer.de

Ramin Yahyapour
CEI, University Dortmund
44221 Dortmund, Germany
ramin.yahyapour@udo.edu

Abstract   In SOA-based Grid environments service provider and service consumer usually do not know each other. In order to establish a business relation they must inter alia (i) create a trust relationship, and (ii) set up mechanisms to create reliable, verifiable, and, at least in a commercial environment, also audible agreements with respect to the services requested, delivered and consumed. In this paper we will only briefly address (i) but concentrate on solutions for (ii) based on Service Level Agreements (SLAs). Therefore we will give an overview on the state-of-the-art of SLA usage in Grids, highlight possible obstacles for the deployment of SLAs, and present a detailed example of a service improving the execution of workflows through the use of WS-Agreement to negotiate advance reservation of resources to execute workflow components.

Keywords: SLA, workflow, Grid, advance reservation, UNICORE

1.   Introduction

Workflows have become a common way to describe and organise a sequence of processes, tasks, applications, or services with specific interdependencies to build a complex job e.g. to deliver results of a complex simulation. Today's more stable Grid environments seem to be suitable to allow usage of non-local resources to execute such a workflow if its resource demand exceeds local capacities. However, as the degree of control over resources changes drastically when using resources not belonging to the own administrative domain, additional considerations have to be made and measures to be taken to allow a reliable, efficient, and automatic processing of these workflows. In the following sections we concentrate on these aspects.

In service-oriented Grids service provider and service consumer potentially belong to different administrative domains. In order to enter in a business relation they must among other things (i) establish trust between them, and (ii) set up mechanisms to create reliable and verifiable (in a commercial environment also audible) agreements with respect to the services requested, delivered and consumed. In this paper we describe a research environment where trust is based on the X.509 certificates issued by Certificate Authorities of the cooperating institutions.

The recently increasing number of workshops or conferences with a focus on Grid economics or Grid business models, which are addressing Service Level Agreements (SLA) as one topic reflects the beginning of broader use of SLAs as an instrument to provide and access reliable services. However, SLAs are still far from a regular day by day use for establishing agreements between service provider and service consumer. We will give an overview on the state of the art, highlight possible obstacles for the deployment of SLAs, and present a detailed example of a service improving the execution of workflows through the use of WS-Agreement to negotiate advance reservation of resources to execute the workflow components. The problem we address is relevant for both sides, (i) for the service provider aiming to optimise the use of his services and (ii) for the the service consumer aiming to optimise the workflow execution. However, in this paper we are focusing on (ii), the optimisation of the workflow execution through reduction of the workflow makespan.

1.1   Related work

The solution proposed here uses WS-Agreement [2] as a model to formulate and manage SLAs. Specified by the Grid Resource Allocation Agreement Working Group (GRAAP) of the Open Grid Forum [11] (OGF), the Web Services Agreement Specification version 1.0 will soon be officially released and is already been used in various implementations [16, 14, 4].

One of these implementations is the meta-scheduling environment developed within the VIOLA [23] project. Built around the *MetaScheduling Service (MSS)* [24] a WS-Agreement-based framework has been realised to provide co-allocation of compute and network services for parallel applications that use a message passing interface (MPI [19]) library for communication. As van der Aalst et. al. postulate in [22], patterns can be used to characterise workflow languages from a *control-flow* perspective and a workflow can be described as a set of patterns. According to their classification, the *Parallel Split* pattern describes a *"point in the work flow process where a single thread of control splits into multiple threads of control which can be executed in parallel, thus allowing activities to be executed simultaneously or in any order."* [22]. This is exactly the pattern to be applied in the co-allocation scheduling case, which leads to the conclusion that co-allocation is just a special case of scheduling a workflow. Taking this into account we decided to enhance the MetaScheduling Service to process more general kinds of workflows.

Apart from the MSS, substantial work has been executed with respect to scheduling in Grid environments using SLAs. It is out of scope of this paper to give a detailed overview of the different approaches, but as an example the DI-GRUBER [5] Grid Resource Broker is given here. DI-GRUBER is a solution to store, retrieve, and disseminate so-called usage service level agreements (USLAs) in distributed environments with multiple scheduling decision points. Compared to our work, the paper referenced here concentrates on the performance and scalability of DI-GRUBER in large Grids, whereas we focus on the gain in workflow turnaround time when applying advance resource reservation through SLA negotiation. Therefore, the DI-GRUBER approach is something to be taken into account once the MSS workflow solution is going to be scaled to large environments.

1.2 Remainder of the Paper

The remainder of the paper is organised as follows. In Section 2 we give an overview of the different approaches, use-cases, and state of the art SLA technologies. As an example how SLAs can improve workflow execution we describe in Section 3 the VIOLA MetaScheduling Service, its application and experiences made. In Section 4 we present results of experiments made to evaluate our approach. An overview about further developments for the SLA based service orchestration in Section 5 concludes the paper.

2. Service Level Agreements - State of the art

2.1 Technology Overview

Increasing effort has been put into research and development related to SLAs over the last years, contributions coming from various domains. For the creation of SLAs in Web Services-based business environments Web Service Level Agreements [15] (WSLA) has been proposed as a language to specify SLAs, a system to monitor the compliance of a provided service with a service level agreement, and a workload management system that prioritises requests according to the associated SLAs. A WSLA document contains one *Parties* section; it may contain multiple *Service Definitions* and one *Obligations* section. WSLA supports a distributed model of monitoring the SLA.

Another approach is SLAng [13] being developed at the University College London. SLAng essentially comprises an XML schema which can be used stand-alone for SLA definitions or together with WSDL or BPEL4WS [20]. SLAng includes QoS metrics to describe EPRs of the parties involved by providing contractual information and technical QoS information including the metrics using *Service Level Specification* (SLS). As the metrics are hard-coded in the XML-scheme SLAng is not very flexible. A framework for monitoring SLAs has not yet been defined.

In addition the Grid domain has addressed SLAs over the last years. A framework integrated into the Globus Toolkit has been proposed in [8]. It is based on the SLA negotiation protocol defined within the Service Negotiation and Access Protocol (SNAP) [7] which is based on the General-purpose Architecture for Reservation and Allocation (GARA) [10]. The first implementations used a proprietary format for specification of SLAs. However, it is expected that WS-Agreement will be used in later versions of the Globus Toolkit.

The European NextGRID project believes that the existing approaches to create SLAs do not sufficiently cover business aspects [18]. SLAs should therefore also contain non-functional terms. The authors propose to view the service from different perspectives that distinguish between the customer's and the service provider's view. The shared view is defined by the SLA and will principally contain business terms. SLAs are only to be expressed in terms of business level objectives (BLOs). Non functional terms are used to build the business relationship between customer and provider and help providing a differentiating factor between service providers.

WS-Agreement as proposed by the OGF provides a domain-independent and standard way to establish and monitor Service Level Agreements. We decided to use WS-Agreement as a mechanism for advance reservation of resources for workflow execution for several reasons, the most important being: (i) is the result of the only active standardisation effort for a framework supporting interoperable SLA specification, (ii) it is used or considered to be used in many other projects, (iii) it is extensible and adaptable to arbitrary domains due to pluggable term languages, and (iv) due to the possibility to define guarantee terms and business values it might be used in business or service oriented environments thus allowing an smooth migration from research application to business use. As it is the foundation for our approach we describe it in greater detail in Section 2.3.

2.2   Defining Service Level Objectives and Penalties

Service-level agreements are intended to provide advance knowledge about a certain quality of a service prior to its use. Thus, the definition of the expected or required service-level is an integral part of all SLA approaches. While the SLA will also include additional information like e.g. technical data, provider and consumer information, the actual definition of the guaranteed agreement terms is one of the main aspects for using SLAs [9, 14].

Service Level Objectives (SLO) describe the condition over available service terms (see [2] for details) that must be met. Such objectives can consist of simple conditions for single service attributes (e.g. the guarantee of a minimum bandwidth for a network link). However, also complex service level objectives can be conceived that might require combined, complex conditions (e.g. the combined processing power of several processors and the available main memory must meet minimal requirements).

While these SLOs alone already allow the specification of guaranteed quality requirements, it has to be considered that a single SLA might contain several of these objectives from which only some may apply under certain conditions. Thus, the notion of qualifying conditions or rules can be found under which a certain SLO applies. The definition of several SLOs with corresponding qualifying conditions allows the modelling of complex requirements in SLAs.

While the service-level objectives provide us with the ability to define guaranteed quality of service, it is often necessary to identify the importance of these guarantees. The situation might occur that one party is not able to fulfil a guarantee, either during the negotiation towards an SLA or after a commitment. Thus, a business value might be associated with the requested service level objective to allow either the trade-off between several objectives or the identification of penalties for violating a guarantee. The impact of an SLO violation might differ depending on its importance.

The inclusion of such penalties is crucial for business relevant application scenarios to cover the liability for guarantees. A single SLA might be an important building block in a broader application scenario with complex dependencies and followup-cost if it is broken. As an example one might consider an SLA for a certain network bandwidth which is used in a complex application. Here, a consumer might create a set of SLAs with different providers that guarantee the availability of their resources for a certain time frame for a certain amount of money. The violation of the single SLA by the network provider might render the complete remaining SLAs useless for the consumer, while these independent and bilateral SLAs will require the consumer to pay for them. Therefore, it might be necessary to cover such risk with associating penalties for SLA violation.

For the sake of completeness, we now introduced SLOs and penalties which are considered key aspects for business oriented scenarios. In the following we do not further exploit SLOs and penalties but focus in the next section on the general foundation of supporting SLA management based on WS-Agreement. SLO optimisation and its trade-offs in penalties and risk management is beyond the scope of this paper and an important topic for future research.

2.3   WS-Agreement

The objective of the WS-Agreement draft specification defined by the GRAAP Working Group is to provide a domain-independent and standard way to establish and monitor Service Level Agreements. The specification comprises three major elements: (i) a description format for agreement templates and agreements, (ii) a basic protocol for establishing agreements, and (iii) an interface specification to monitor agreements at runtime.

A service defined in the agreement is specified as a *Service Description Terms* (SDT). Service description terms can be a reference to an existing service, a domain specific description of a service, or a set of observable properties of the service. Multiple SDTs describe different services that are provided within the same agreement. Dependencies between these SDTs can be described by using Guarantee Terms. Guarantee terms specify non-functional characteristics of a service in the service level objectives, an optional qualifying condition under which objectives are met, and an associated business value specifying the importance of meeting these objectives. Additionally, guarantee terms comprise a service scope, which defines a list of services a guarantee term applies to. Thus guarantee terms can be used for defining dependencies between different service description terms within an Agreement, or even to specify dependencies to existing agreements by using *Service References* to address related agreements.

Guarantee terms over multiple STDs can basically be used to model a specific QoS requirement within a *Service Level Agreement*. For example a guarantee term that references multiple service description terms and specifies that these STDs have to be executed in parallel, defines at least a co-allocation of the described services. On the other hand, guarantee terms that incorporate Service References can be used to model decisions based on the outcome of the related SLA. That is, a specific SDT or a set of STDs of an agreement may only become active, if the related agreement was processed successfully. Of course, this can also be done for negative decisions.

Therefore guarantee terms are the key for describing workflows within WS-Agreement. Since the content of the Guarantee Terms is largely free per definition, one can consider every necessary extension for a workflow representation as a part of the Guarantee terms. Therefore the WS-Agreement framework can be used for describing workflows within one SLA, or even to compose workflows from multiple SLAs by using service references.

3. SLA based service provisioning for workflows

In this section we briefly describe the problem and suggest how SLAs can be used to improve the processing of distributed workflows through negotiation and advance reservation of the resources or services required to perform the different tasks of a workflow.

3.1 The workflow resource problem

There are many application scenarios in which not just a single resource is required but a set of resources with certain time dependencies. Assuming that multiple resources are provided by several resource providers, such workflows complicate the management of resources since resource access must be synchronised in advance to allow reliable workflow execution.

SLAs are one instrument which can be used to reserve resources in advance [16]. The time requirements and dependencies can be modelled in the SLA to guarantee the resource availability [17]. The dependency can pose additional importance of single SLAs in a workflow; as the different SLAs may rely on each other, the individual business value of a single SLA might be increased. As mentioned before, this can yield to the need for including higher penalties for individual SLAs.

A main problem for the management of workflows is the negotiation towards the matching SLAs. While the creation of a single SLA might be much easier as both parties can settle on a set of agreement terms, this becomes more complicate if the terms must match or correspond to other SLAs that are in negotiation. For instance, if three resources must be concurrently available in the same time frame, this time frame must be first identified. It then must be assured that all three SLAs are finally committed (or none of them) as it has to be prevented that the consumer gets an eventually unusable subset of SLAs.

On the other hand, if three resources necessary to perform the three tasks of a workflow must be available in a sequential order at different times also three SLAs have to be created. This time, it must be assured that the time dependencies between the tasks of the workflow are reflected in the SLAs leading to the reservations. Figure 1 depicts this situation. The MetaScheduling Service

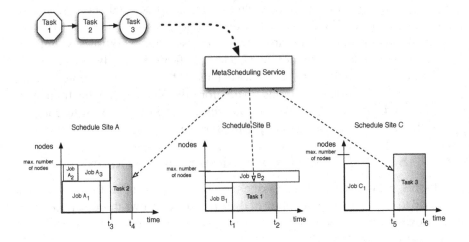

Figure 1.   Mapping of a workflow to three resources respecting the time dependencies.

has to assure that $t_5 >= t_3 >= t_2$ in order to respect the dependencies. At the same time the MSS has to negotiate the individual start times as close as possible to the end times of the respective previous tasks in order to minimise the total duration of the workflow execution (which is a prevalent objective scheduling jobs and workflows).

3.2   Negotiating resource usage

The negotiation required for the resource reservations (as presented in Section 3.1) is based on SLAs describing the requirements of the workflow's tasks and the dependencies between them. The SLAs are derived from the resource requests specified by the user, the format of which depending on the Grid middleware used. In the case of Globus, for example, the user includes resource requirements into a WS GRAM job description, in the case of UNICORE they are embedded into an Abstract Job Object (AJO). These requests are then to be mapped to the respective SDTs. For the specification of the SLA for a workflow WS-Agreement is used (see Section 2.3). In the following description of the negotiation process we refer to the UNICORE environment of the VIOLA project. However, as the MSS is able to communicate with a specific GRAM plug-in in the same way, the process is the same for Globus environments. The following steps are executed to establish an agreement between client and MSS:

1 The UNICORE client requests an agreement template from the MSS.

2 The MSS delivers an EPR of the agreement to the client.

3 The client fills in the template with the workflow-specific details. With respect to the description of resource requests JSDL [3] is used within the SLA and a library to map the UNICORE-specific terms to JSDL.

4 The client sends the completed agreement template back to the MSS.

5 The MSS starts to negotiate the reservation of the resources for the work-flow tasks with the respective local scheduling systems of the resource providing sites according to the SLOs described in the agreement. The negotiations are also based on individual SLAs. This time the MSS plays the role of the client vis-a-vis the resource providers.

6 Once all individual SLAs between the MSS and the different resource providers are in place the MSS accepts the agreement proposed by the client. Otherwise the client is informed that the MSS can not accept the agreement. In this case the user is notified and may modify the requirements for his workflow to adopt to the situation and repeat the negotiation from the beginning.

In case of one or more individual agreements with resource providers fail, the MSS will cancel all other accepted agreements. This is due to the fact that the current version of WS-Agreement does not allow modification of accepted agreements thus all agreements have to be negotiated from the beginning.

3.3   MSS Implementation

As mentioned in Section 3.2 the German VIOLA project develops among other components a meta-scheduling environment providing resource reservations based on WS-Agreement. The immediate objective of this development is to co-allocate computational and network resources in a UNICORE-based Grid, but we designed the environment to support arbitrary types of resources and to be integrated into different Grid middleware systems. The main integration effort to get the MSS working on top of other middleware, like e.g. Globus, is to implement the client-side interface of the MetaScheduling Service. Since it is beyond the scope of this paper to explain the system in detail we refer to [24] for a complete architectural description of it and to [21] for the definition of the negotiation protocol currently implemented.

Figure 2 sketches the basic architecture of the meta-scheduling environment and its integration into the UNICORE Grid middleware. The VIOLA Meta-Scheduling Service communicates with a client application using WS-Agreement, it receives the workflow-specific resource requests as described in Section 3.2 wrapped into a Meta-Scheduling (MS) request, and it returns reservations for all of these resources. To interact with varying types of scheduling systems we use the adapter pattern approach. The role of an Adapter is to

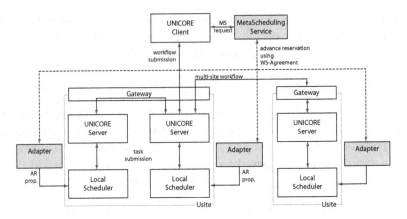

Figure 2.   High-level meta-scheduling architecture.

provide a single interface to the Meta-Scheduling Service by encapsulating the specific interfaces of the different local scheduling systems. Thus the Meta-Scheduling Service can negotiate resource usage by exploiting a single interface independent of the underlying resource type. To achieve this, the Meta-Scheduling Service first queries local scheduling systems for the availability of the requested resources and then negotiates the reservations across all local scheduling systems. These, in order to participate in the negotiation process, have to be capable and willing to let the MetaScheduling Service reserve resources in advance by offering data about job execution start and stop times, and provide at least partial access to their local schedules, e.g. by publishing information about available free time slots.

4.   Results

In order to predict the gain in turnaround time in real world systems by using SLA's for workflows that contain job dependencies we have accomplished a series of experiments. In these experiments we used simple directed acyclic graphs (DAG), where the DAGs were linear lists (node indegree <= 1, outdegree <= 1) and the depth of the graph was 3 (see Figure 3). We evaluated the gain in turnaround time for these DAGs by using best effort jobs and advance reservation jobs for the workflow execution. The test scenario is constructed as follows. As test environment we used a simple MSS setup consisting of 3 independent systems, each utilised with a basic load derived from real world log files [25] before submitting the workflow. Each SLA consists of 3 jobs where each job is scheduled on one system. The resource requirements of the jobs range from [6/8/8] to [48/64/64], where the numbers specify the number of requested nodes (respectively CPUs) for a job. The job runtimes range from 60 minutes up to 240 min. Within one test row all jobs have the same runtime.

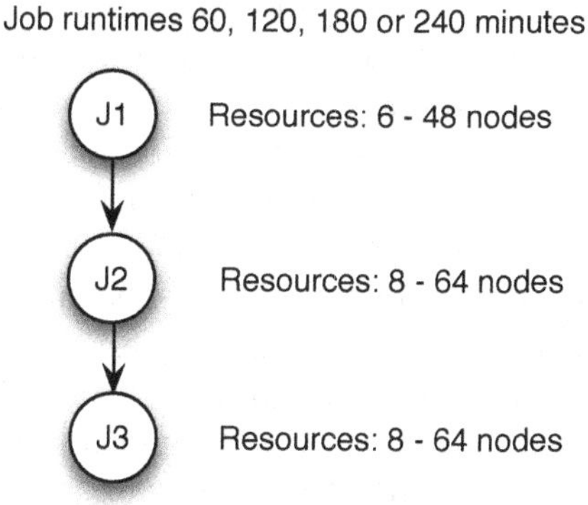

Job runtimes 60, 120, 180 or 240 minutes

J1 Resources: 6 - 48 nodes

J2 Resources: 8 - 64 nodes

J3 Resources: 8 - 64 nodes

Figure 3.   Simple DAG describing the workflows.

For best effort SLAs the first job is submitted to the resource management system and subsequent jobs are scheduled as soon its predecessor has finished. For advance reservation SLAs the jobs are scheduled sequentially at submission time by using the first fixed fit strategy. Once the first job was scheduled the estimated end time of the job is determined and the next subsequent job is scheduled using the determined end time of its predecessor. The start times of a job must not change after it was scheduled. Figure 4 shows the results of our experiments.

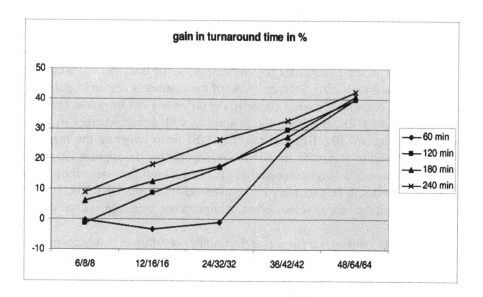

Figure 4.   Gain in turnaround time using Advance Reservation.

At a first glance surprisingly for workflows with low resource requirements and short runtimes it turns out, that the best effort scheduling strategy behaves better in our experiments than the advance reservation strategy. However, this results from the fact that the advance reservation jobs in our test scenario are scheduled at a fixed start time and therefore do not profit from potential back-filling possibilities, e.g. prior jobs that occupied the system resources finish earlier. This problem can be resolved easily if scheduling systems allow back-filling for advance reservation jobs until an requested time (here the estimated end time of the predecessor job) and furthermore provide the functionality to update this time later on. Given that this functionality is in place Grid scheduler can be constructed employing the advance reservation strategy, where the turnaround time is at least as good as for best effort jobs, and the gain in the turnaround time might even increase compared to our test results.

5.   Future Perspectives

Work on performance evaluation for workflow planning with SLAs will be continued considering the observations described above. Future work therefore will mainly focus on the areas:

- further evaluation of the approach based on different DAGs and jobs

- moving to support a standard workflow description language (or a suitable and efficient mechanism to map different languages onto the one selected for the UNICORE environment)

- extending WS-Agreement to allow for a more flexible negotiation process and to support modifications of existing agreements.

Addressing the first aspect we will investigate the ongoing activities related to workflows in the CoreGRID [6] Institute on Grid Information, Resource and Workflow Monitoring Services. One of the institute's research group's is working on *Compatibility and Conversion of different Grid Workflow Description Languages* [12]. Based on the results we will decide whether to adopt a de-facto standard like BPEL (or BPEL4WS) or to integrate the mapping mechanism and to stay with the UNICORE workflow description language. In either case only a single procedure to convert a workflow description to a WS-Agreement will be necessary in the user's client, e.g. a UNICORE client, while allowing the user to select the most appropriate language to describe his workflow.

Experiences made so far show that the number of different resources needed for a complex workflow will often be higher than for a single application that is distributed across several resources, like in the co-allocation scenarios of VI-OLA. The process of negotiating the reservation is based on WS-Agreement version 1.0 which does not support changes of the offer or later re-negotiation.

Thus in case of a service provider not being able to match exactly the requirements of a client now the agreement is cancelled and has to be initiated from the beginning. Even worse, in case of a workflow negotiation including several service providers currently the whole workflow usually will not complete if one of the service providers is unable to deliver the service agreed upon and re-negotiation is not possible.

Extending WS-Agreement to allow for a more flexible negotiation process and to support modifications of existing agreements will help to overcome the potential waste of resources. The GRAAP working group recently started working on these extensions for the next version of WS-Agreement. The group is gathering requirements and contributions, e.g. as drafted in [1] to define a standardised extension of the current protocol.

Acknowledgments

Some of the work reported in this paper is funded by the German Federal Ministry of Education and Research through the VIOLA project under grant #01AK605L. This paper also includes work carried out jointly within the Core-GRID Network of Excellence funded by the European Commission's IST programme under grant #004265.

References

[1] M. Aiello, G. Frankova, and D. Malfatti. What's in an Agreement? A Formal Analysis and an extension of WS-Agreement. In *Service-Oriented Computing – ICSOC 2005*, volume 3826 of *LNCS*, pages 424–436. Springer, December 12–15, 2005.

[2] A. Andrieux, K. Czajkowski, A. Dan, K. Keahey, H. Ludwig, T. Nakata, J. Pruyne, J. Rofrano, S. Tuecke, and M. Xu. WS-Agreement - Web Services Agreement Specification, April 5, 2007. <https://forge.gridforum.org/sf/docman/do/downloadDocument/projects.graap-wg/docman.root.current_drafts/doc6091/50>.

[3] A. Anjomshoaa, F. Brisard, M. Drescher, D. Fellows, A. Ly, S. McGough, D. Pulsipher, and A. Savva. Job Submission Description Language (JSDL) Specification v1.0. Grid Forum Document GFD.56, Global Grid Forum, November 2005.

[4] The Business Grid Project. Web site. 30 Mar 2006 <http://www.ipa.go.jp/english/softdev/sixth.html>.

[5] C. Dumitrescu and I. Raicu and I. Foster. DI-GRUBER: A Distributed Approach to Grid Resource Brokering. In *SC '05: Proceedings of the 2005 ACM/IEEE conference on Supercomputing*, page 38, Washington, DC, USA, 2005. IEEE Computer Society.

[6] CoreGRID. Web site. 14 Aug 2006 <http://www.coregrid.net/>.

[7] K. Czajkowski, I. Foster, C. Kesselman, V. Sander, and S. Tuecke. SNAP: A protocol for negotiating service level agreements and coordinating resource management in distributed systems. In *Job Scheduling Strategies for Parallel Processing (Proceedings of the 8th International JSSPP Workshop)*, volume 2537 of *LNCS*, pages 153 – 158. Springer, 2002.

[8] K. Czajkowski, I. Foster, C. Kesselman, and S. Tuecke. Grid Service Level Agreements. In J. Nabrzyski, J. M. Schopf, and J. Weglarz, editors, *Grid Resource Management*, pages 119–134. Kluwer Academic Publishers, 2004.

[9] A. Dan, K. Keahey, H. Ludwig, and J. Rofrano. Guarantee Terms in WS-Agreement. Technical report, Grid Resource Allocation Agreement Protocol (GRAAP) Working Group Meetings, 2004.

[10] I. Foster, M. Fidler, A. Roy, and V. Sander. End-to-end quality of service for high-end applications. *Computer Communications, Special Issue on Network Support for Grid Computing*, 2002.

[11] Grid Resousource Allocation Agreement Protocol Working Group. Web site. 07 Aug 2006, <https://forge.gridforum.org/sf/projects/graap-wg>.

[12] Compatibility and Conversion of different Grid Work-flow Description Languages. Web site. 14 Aug 2006 <http://www.gridworkflow.org/snips/gridworkflow/space/Workflow+Description+-Languages/Compatibility+and+Conversion/>.

[13] D. Lamanna, J. Skene, and W. Emmerich. SLAng: A Language for Defining Service Level Agreements. In *Proceedings of the 9th IEEE Workshop on Future Trends in Distributed Computing Systems (FTDCS'03)*, pages 100 – 106. IEEE Computer Society Press, 2003.

[14] H. Ludwig, A. Dan, and B. Kearney. Cremona: An Architecture and Library for Creation and Monitoring WS-Agreements. In *ICSOCŠ04, New York*. ACM, 2004.

[15] H. Ludwig, A. Keller, A. Dan, R. P. King, and R. Franck. Web Service Level Agreement (WSLA) Language Specification. IBM, USA. <http://www.research.ibm.com/wsla/WSLASpecV1-20030128.pdf>.

[16] H. Ludwig, T. Nakata, O. Wäldrich, Ph. Wieder, and W. Ziegler. Reliable Orchestration of Resources using WS-Agreement. In *Proc. of the 2006 International Conference on High Performance Computing and Communications (HPCC-06)*, volume 4208 of *LNCS*, pages 753–762. Springer, September 13–15, 2006.

[17] J. MacLaren, R. Sakellariou, K.T. Krishnakumar, J. Garibaldi, and D. Ouelhadj. Towards Service Level Agreement Based Scheduling on the Grid. Workshop on Planning and Scheduling for Web and Grid Services (in conjunction with ICAPS-04), 2004.

[18] P. Masche, P. Mckee, and B. Mitchell. The Increasing Role of Service Level Agreements in B2B Systems. In *2nd international conference on web information systems and technologies*, Setubal, Portugal, April 2006.

[19] MPI: A Message-Passing Interface Standard. Web site. 20 Apr 2007 <http://www.mpi-forum.org/docs/mpi-11-html/mpi-report.html>.

[20] S. Thatte (ed.). Business Process Execution Language for Web Services version 1.1. <ftp://www6.software.ibm.com/software/developer/library/ws-bpel.pdf>.

[21] A. Streit, O. Wäldrich, Ph. Wieder, and W. Ziegler. On Scheduling in UNICORE – Extending the Web Services Agreement based Resource Management Framework. In *Proc. of Parallel Computing 2005 (ParCo 2005)*, September 13–16, 2005. To appear.

[22] W.M.P van der Aalst, A.H.M. ter Hofstede, B. Kiepuszewski, and A.P. Barros. Workflow Patterns. *Distributed and Parallel Databases*, 14(3):5–51, July 2003.

[23] VIOLA – Vertically Integrated Optical Testbed for Large Application in DFN, 2006. Web site. 29 Mar 2006 <http://www.viola-testbed.de/>.

[24] O. Wäldrich, Ph.Wieder, and W. Ziegler. A Meta-scheduling Service for Co-allocating Arbitrary Types of Resources. In *Proc. of the Second Grid Resource Management Workshop (GRMWS'05)*, volume 3911 of *LNCS*, pages 782–791. Springer, 2006.

[25] Parallel Workloads Archive - San Diego Supercomputer Center (SDSC) SP2 log, 2006. Web site. 29 Mar 2006 <http://www.cs.huji.ac.il/labs/parallel/workload/logs.html>.

DEPENDABILITY EVALUATION OF THE OGSA-DAI MIDDLEWARE

William Hoarau and Sébastien Tixeuil
LRI-CNRS 8623 & INRIA Grand Large,
Université Paris Sud XI, France

hoarau,tixeuil@lri.fr

Nuno Rodrigues, Décio Sousa, and Luis Silva
Dep. Engenharia Informática, University of Coimbra,
Polo II, 3030-Coimbra, Portugal

luis@dei.uc.pt

Abstract   One important contribution to the community that is developing Grid middleware is the definition and implementation of benchmarks and tools to assess the performance and dependability of Grid applications and the corresponding middleware. In this paper, we present an experimental study that was conducted with OGSA-DAI, a popular package of middleware that provides access to remote data resources thought a unified Web-service front-end. The results show that OGSA-DAI is quite stable and performed quite well in scalability tests, executed on Grid5000. However, we also demonstrate that OGSA-DAI WSI is currently using a SOAP container (Apache Axis1.2.1) that suffers from severe memory leaks. We show how the default configuration of OGSA-DAI is not affected by that problem, but a small change in the configuration of a Web-service may lead to very unreliable execution of OGSA-DAI.

Keywords: Dependability benchmarking, grid middleware.

1.   Introduction

Grid middleware and grid services are still in its infancy. Until they reach the maturity curve it is important to devise some benchmarks and tools to assess the performance, dependability and security level. These benchmarks and tools should be easily applied to different grid services implementations that follow standard protocols. They should also present some convincing results to the scientists and developers that are working with Grid middleware that was developed in R&D projects. One of the most popular Grid middleware packages is OGSA-DAI, a package that allows the remote access to data-resources (files, relational and XML databases) through a standard front-end based on Web-services specification. In this paper we present an experimental study of the performance and dependability level of OGSA-DAI, by making use of a benchmarking tool, called QUAKE, and running the experiments in the Grid5000 infrastructure. The experiments allowed us to collect some interesting results to the community that is using OGSA-DAI, the team of developers behind it and to the researchers that are studying the dependability metrics of Grid middleware, as is the case of our two groups: INRIA Grand-Large and the University of Coimbra.

2.   Related Works

The idea of dependability benchmarking is now a hot-topic of research and there are already several publications in the literature. The components of a dependability benchmark have been defined in [1]. In [2] is proposed a dependability benchmark for transactional systems (DBench-OLTP). Another dependability benchmark for transactional systems is proposed in [3]. In [20] the authors present a proposal for the classification of dependability in transactional database systems [4]. A dependability benchmark for operating systems was proposed by [5]. That benchmark was targeted for the study of the operating system robustness in the scenario of faulty applications. Another study about the behavior of the operating system in the presence of software faults in OS components was presented in [6]. The research presented in [7] addresses the impact of human errors in system dependability. In [8] is presented a methodology to evaluate human-assisted failure-recovery tools and processes in server systems. Another work was presented in [9] that focus on the availability benchmarking of computer systems. Research work at Sun Microsystems defined a high-level framework targeted to availability benchmarking [10].

At IBM, the Autonomic Computing initiative is also developing benchmarks to quantify the autonomic capability of a system [11]. In that paper they have discussed the requirements of benchmarks to assess the self-* properties of a system and they proposed a set of metrics for evaluation. In [12] is

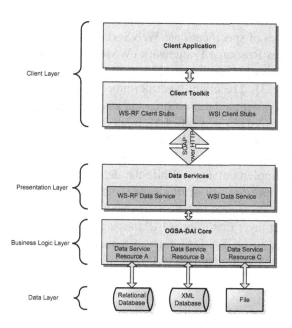

Figure 1. OGSA-DAI Architecture.

presented a further discussion about benchmarking the autonomic capabilities of a system. In [13] is presented an approach to conduct benchmarking of the configuration complexity. A benchmark for assessing the self-healing capabilities of a potential autonomic system was presented in [14]. In [15] the authors present a dependability benchmark for Web-Servers. This tool used the experimental setup, the workload and the performance measures specified in the SPECWeb99 performance benchmark.

The dependability benchmark tool that is presented in this paper is targeted to Grid and Web-services. It has been used to assess the dependability level of SOAP-servers [16], Web-service specifications [17] and tools of Grid middleware. In this paper, we will present a benchmarking study that was conducted with OGSA-DAI middleware.

3. OGSA-DAI Overview

OGSA-DAI [18] is a middleware platform that allows data resources, such as relational or XML databases, to be accessed as Web-services. The software includes a collection of components for querying, transforming and delivering data in different ways, and a simple toolkit for developing client applications. In a short sentence, OGSA-DAI provides a way for users to Grid-enable their data resources.

The presentation layer encapsulates the functionality required to expose data service resources using web service interfaces. The Web-service front-end can run over two types of specifications: Web Services Interoperability (WSI) [19] and Web Services Resource Framework (WSRF) [20]. The WSI version runs over Jakarta Tomcat [21] and Axis [22] while the WSRF version runs with the Globus Toolkit [23]. The client layer permits that every client can interact, in a transparent way, with a data resource via a corresponding Web-service. The front-end of OGSA-DAI is a set of Web-services that in the case of WSI require a SOAP container to handle the incoming requests and translate them to the internal OGSA-DAI engine. Figure 1 presents the main internal modules of OGSA-DAI implementation. While the detailed description of the OGSA-DAI internal is out-of-scope of this paper (more information can be found in [18]) the interesting aspect to take into account is the Web-service that handles the transport layer that uses SOAP messages. Our benchmarking tool can be easily applied to OGSA-DAI since it makes use of standard Web-service specifications. At the moment OGSA-DAI middleware is used in several im-

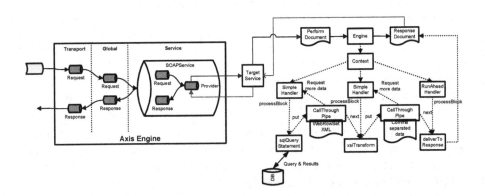

Figure 2.   OGSA-DAI Internals.

portant Grid projects [24], including: AstroGrid, BIoDA, Biogrid, BioSim-Grid, Bridges, caGrid, COBrA-CT, Data Mining Grid, D-Grid, eDiaMoND, ePCRN, ESSE, FirstDIG, GEDDM, GeneGrid, GEODE, GEON, GridMiner, InteliGrid, INWA, ISPIDER, IU-RGRbench, LEAD, MCS, myGrid, N2Grid, OntoGrid, ODD-Genes, OGSA-WebDB, Provenance, SIMDAT, Secure Data Grid, SPIDR, UNIDART and VOTES. This list is clear representative of the importance of OGSA-DAI and the relevance of this particular benchmarking study.

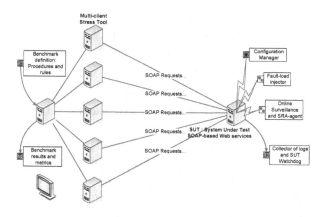

Figure 3. QUAKE Architecture.

4. QUAKE: A Benchmarking Tool for Grid Services

QUAKE [16] is a dependability benchmark tool to assess the performance and dependability level of Grid and Web-services. It is composed by a set of software components, as presented in Figure 3.

The main components are the Benchmark Management System (BMS) and the System-Under-Test (SUT). The SUT consists of a SOAP-server running some Web/Grid service. The application under test is not limited to a SOAP-based application: in fact, the benchmark infrastructure can also be used with other examples of client-server applications that use other different middleware technologies.

There are several client machines that invoke requests in the server using SOAP requests. The Benchmark Management System (BMS) is a collection of software tools that allows the automatic execution of the benchmark. The results generated by each benchmark run are expressed as throughput-over-time, the total turnaround time of the execution, the average latency, the functionality of the services, the occurrence of failures, the characterization of those failures (crash, hang, zombie-server), the correctness of the final results and the failure scenarios that are observed at the client machines (explicit error messages or timeouts). In this study, we used the burst distribution which generates the maximum workload.

There are some other tools in the market that can be used for performance benchmarking of SOAP Web-services, namely: SOAtest [25] and TestMaker [26]. However those tools are mainly targeted for testing the functionality of the SOAP applications and to collect some performance figures. QUAKE has some fundamental differences: it is targeted to study the dependability attributes, it includes a different approach for the workload distributions, a stress-load module to affect the resources of the system-under-test and it is mostly targeted to the collection of dependability metrics.

5.   Experimental Results

In this section, we present a benchmarking study we have conducted with OGSA-DAI by using the QUAKE tool in a large-scale grid infrastructure: the Grid5000.

Grid5000 is an experimental platform dedicated to computer science for the study of grid algorithms, and partly founded by the French incentive action "ACI Grid". Grid5000 consists of 14 clusters located in 9 French cities with 40 to 450 processors each, with a total of 1928 processors. Most of the tests were executed on Grid Explorer (Orsay) which is a major component of the Grid5000 platform. All computers are dual-processors AMD Opterons running at 2.0 GHz with 2 GB of RAM, and each computer has a 80 GB IDE hard drive and a GigaEthernet network interface card. For the scalability experiments, 3 clusters of Grid5000 were used. We used 200 machines of the previously mentioned Orsay's cluster, 50 machines of the Sophia's cluster and 50 machines of the Lille's cluster. Using this configuration, we were able to scale up to 300 clients during our experiments. We deployed a Debian Linux operating system, with a kernel 2.6.13-5, including Java 1.5.0, Tomcat 5.0.28, Axis 1.2.1 and OGSA-DAI WSI 2.2.

5.1   Performance Overhead

The first thing we wanted to know about OGSA-DAI was the price to pay for using it. Since OGSA-DAI is a middleware that stands between users and data-resources it adds complexity to a path that already has some. So, our first experiment was conducted in order to assess performance overhead caused by one more middleware package between data resources and the user application of such resources. Our approach to understand if there was any performance price to pay when using OGSA-DAI was simply comparing performance metrics (Latency and Throughput) with other mechanisms of accessing data resources, namely, direct JDBC connection (1-Tier Model) and a Java Server Page (JSP) accessed by browser making use of the JDBC connector to access the same DB (3-Tier Model). The results are presented in Figure 4.

As expected, in a 10 minute run, we could observe that OGSA-DAI is 315 times slower than JDBC and about 5 times slower than the 3-tier model JSP. In addition, OGSA-DAI has a significantly lower throughput than the other two models. It processes 10 times less request than the direct JDBC access and 5 times less than the JSP. In the presented 10 minute run OGSA-DAI processed 342.827 less request than the JDBC and less 154.320 request than the JSP. The conclusion we must draw from these numbers and figures is that the first price

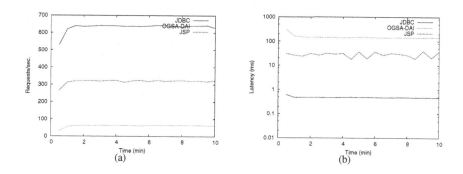

Figure 4. JDBC, JSP, and OGSA-DAI Performance.

to pay when using OGSA-DAI to expose data resources is a significantly short performance when compared to other ways of exposing the same resources.

5.2 Benchmarking Tomcat+Axis

As OGSA-DAI is a middleware on top of Tomcat and Axis, the first study was to measure the dependability level of a simple Web-service application deployed with Tomcat/Axis running in a large-scale cluster of Grid5000. The test was executed with 40 clients and 100,000 requests per client. We used a synthetic application that executes a very simple computation. The versions of the WSI container were: Tomcat 5.0.28 and Axis 1.2.1. The results are presented in Figure 5.

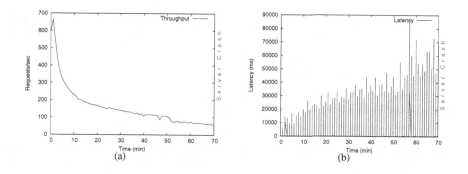

Figure 5. Results with Tomcat/Axis.

In Figure 5(a) we can see that the throughput is decreasing over time until a certain point where the server crashes: at this point only 665,078 requests were executed, instead of the 4,000,000 that were expected. In Figure 5(b) we can see the latency increasing over time until the point where there was a crash (approximately 70.5 minutes of test running). This first study was conducted with a very synthetic application. Then, we decide implement a Web-service on Axis that was working as a front-end to access a database: it receives a SQL query and returns the resulting rows. The results are also taken with 40 clients and are presented in Figure 6. We can see the results are quite similar to the first experiment. The throughput decreases over time until the server has a crash after 80 minutes of execution.

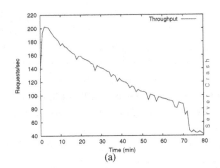 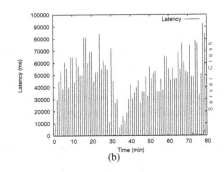

Figure 6.   Second experiments with Tomcat/Axis (database synthetic application).

This was the same behavior we have observed in [16]. In that paper we presented a detailed study of the reliability of SOAP and we have demonstrated that Axis1.3 suffers from severe memory leaks. Some sort of corrective mechanism is mandatory to avoid the failure of the applications that are using that SOAP implementation. It was that particular study that drove our curiosity and our concern to assess the dependability level of OGSA-DAI: if Axis 1.2 and 1.3 suffer from severe memory leaks and OGSA-DAI makes use of Axis 1.2.1 what would be resulting reliability of the applications that make use of OGSA-DAI data grid services? Results are presented in the next subsection.

5.3   Benchmarking OGSA-DAI

Since OGSA-DAI uses the Axis1.2.1 platform to deploy its own Web-services it is legitimate for one to assume that OGSA-DAI should be prone to the severe effects of the memory leaks from Axis. To find evidences, we conducted several tests to the OGSA-DAI platform in a large-scale cluster of Grid5000. The first experiment was conducted with 25 nodes, each one executing 100,000 requests. Figure 7 presents the observed throughput and latency.

As can be clearly seen the performance of OGSA-DAI remained quite stable during all the experiment that was conducted with a maximum burst distribution. The throughput was fairly stable with an average value of 71.43 requests/sec.

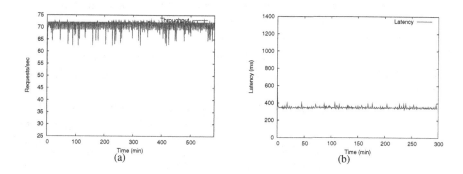

Figure 7. Results with OGSA-DAI (WSI).

The latency had an average value of 349.1 ms. We repeated this benchmark but increasing the number of clients to see the impact of scale on the OGSA-DAI middleware. Different experiments were executed with 25, 100, 200 and 300 clients. The results are presented in Figure 8(a).

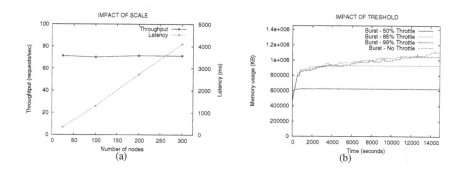

Figure 8. Impact of scale and threshold value on OGSA-DAI (WSI).

We can see that the throughput is the same for every experiment and the latency increases linearly. The server can perfectly handle 300 simultaneous clients requesting accesses to data-services using a burst distribution. It is clear that OGSA-DAI has some congestion-flow control mechanism that sets up the throughput to a fixed value despite the number of simultaneous clients. Although this could explain the impact of scale in the server, it does not explain why the memory leaks present in Axis do not manifest in the OGSA-DAI environment. We then started to look to some of the OGSA-DAI configuration parameters, and in particular to the main parameters that establish some congestion flow mechanism: *(i)* **maximum simultaneous request**: define how many requests can be processed simultaneously, and *(ii)* **request queue length**: this is the queue where the request are stored before being processed.

For all the previous tests the maximum number of simultaneous requests was the same than the number of clients: for example, with 100 clients, the maximum simultaneous request was set up to 100. The queue length was always 20.

We ran the scalability test again but with a value of half to the maximum simultaneous requests and a larger queue to see the impact of these parameters on performance. The results we got were basically the ones presented in Figure 6. So, apparently, these parameters have no influence on the performance, at least at this scale. After this first set of results, we still had no answers to our fundamental question: how OGSA-DAI can be so stable if it uses Axis1.2.1 that suffers from memory leaks?

We conducted some further experiments and some code-inspections to the OGSA-DAI implementation, trying to understand its inner details. One thing that recalled our attention was a method that is called before executing an operation that consumes memory. This method calculates the memory needed for that operation to take place, and then checks if the total consumed memory is above a predefined threshold. If it is not, then the operation can be executed. Otherwise the middleware makes a set of explicit calls to the JVM garbage collector to free up some memory. The default threshold for memory consumption is 85% of the JVM Heap, so all tests we ran previously used this value. We conducted some other tests by changing the threshold value: 50%, 85%, 99% and with the mechanism turned off. The idea was to see if this was the main mechanism responsible for the stability of OGSA-DAI server. The results are presented in Figure 8(b).

This mechanism forces a more frequent usage of the garbage collection mechanism but it is not a mechanism *per se* that provides the robustness to the OGSA-DAI middleware. When we turned off this mechanism we saw some small instability in the memory consumption but the server never crashed. Finally, there was one last thing that caught our attention: the fact that the Web-service deployed with OGSA-DAI was using a scope set to application. This means the WS application is only instantiated once being then shared with every request it receives and by every different client.

This is not the usual way of deploying Web-services unless the Web-service is completely stateless or provides global data that should be shared by all the clients. It is quite usual that a Web-service application needs to store information about a particular session so it can correlate future requests to previous ones made by the same user. These kinds of applications often use scope set to session so that they can manage the information about the clients in a session-based model.

As stated in section 3, OGSA-DAI makes use of Web-services as a front-end layer to the data resources. It really does not need to correlate different requests and the Web-service is completely stateless; it just needs to create an interface which will be the same to every request despite the client where it comes from. This clearly justifies the use of the application scope in the deployed Web-services. But this raises the question: could this be the answer to the stable behavior of OGSA-DAI?

To understand the impact of the scope of the Web-services in the robustness of the applications we conducted two different tests: *(i)* one test with a WS deployed over Axis using an application scope, and *(ii)* another test using OGSA-DAI but the scope was changed to session.

In both tests we used the QUAKE tool, with 10 simultaneous clients that were programmed to make 10 million requests into the server in the overall. Figure 9 shows the results of the synthetic application running on Axis1.2.1 with an application scope Web-service. Figure 10 represent the results of the OGSA-DAI with a session equal to scope.

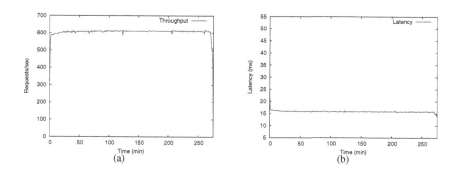

Figure 9.   Experiment with Tomcat/Axis (application scope Web-service).

In Figure 9, we can see that Axis1.2.1 does not suffer from memory leaks if the Web-service is deployed with scope set to application. On the contrary, we can see in Figure 10 that OGSA-DAI runs very unstable if the scope of the Web-service is set to session: the application with OGSA-DAI crashes after 42.5 minutes of test execution and was only able to fulfill 2020 requests. The throughput was very unstable and reached very low values. These results are quite interesting and finally explain why the default configuration of OGSA-DAI was so stable.

The reader should compare the results from Figure 10 with Figures 7 and 8: in these two Figures we could see that OGSA-DAI was very stable and provided a sustained throughput of 70 req/sec, even when we increased the number of clients to 300. In Figure 10 we can see that the throughput is very

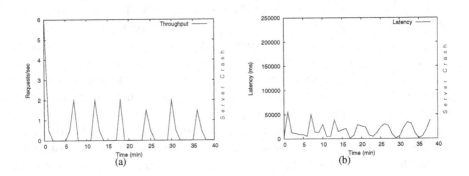

Figure 10.   Experiment with OGSA-DAI (session scope Web-service).

unstable and very low in comparison (average value of 0.78 reqs/sec). Similar observations to the latency of requests: in Figure 8 the results taken with 300 clients have shown an average latency of 4000 msecs. In Figure 10 we can see an average latency of 11.842 msecs (almost 12 seconds) with only 10 simultaneous clients.

All these results are due to the fact the default configuration of OGSA-DAI sets the scope of the Web-service to application. In this case OGSA-DAI does not trigger the memory leaks of Axis1.2.1. If the scope is set to session, the OGSA-DAI will trigger the severe memory leaks of Axis1.2.1 and the resulting reliability will be a major point of concern.

6.   Conclusions

In this paper we have presented the first results from a benchmarking study of OGSA-DAI. The good news from these initial results are the fact that OGSA-DAI is quite stable and performs considerably well in scenarios of scalability and workload testing, as was the case of that experiment with 300 clients in the Grid5000. These are good news for all those Grid Projects that are making use of OGSA-DAI and it is a very positive acknowledge of the good work that has been doing by the OGSA-DAI team. On the other hand, we have proved that the stability of OGSA-DAI is due to the fact it makes of application scope Web-services, which fortunately do not trigger the memory leaks of Axis1.2.1. If by any reason, a programmer needs to implement sessions for the different clients and have to change the scope of the Web-service to session, then there will be a critical problem in terms of reliability of the OGSA-DAI middleware.

This is an interesting lesson that should be taken into account by the team that is developing OGSA-DAI middleware.

In this paper, we have mainly proved that having a dependability benchmarking tool for Web-services and grid-enabled application is crucial for the community. By using our QUAKE tool we were able to detect and understand the reasons for the stability of OGSA-DAI but also the potential leaks that may turn it a very unreliable middleware package, if it triggers the memory leaks of the underlying Axis implementation. Good news for the community is the fact that Axis 2 has already been released and this new version solves most of the problems of the previous versions. However, there are still a lot of software packages (like OGSA-DAI) that make use of the Axis1.2 or 1.3 versions and thereby may potentially suffer from serious memory leaks if they use session scope Web-services. In the future we plan to continue our work on dependability benchmarking for Web-services and we are studying the potential integration of QUAKE with FAIL-FCI [27].

Acknowledgements

This research work is carried out in part under the FP6 Network of Excellence CoreGRID funded by the European Commission (Contract IST-2002-004265). We would like to thank the OGSA-DAI team for their collaboration in this experimental study.

References

[1] P.Koopman, H.Madeira. "Dependability Benchmarking & Prediction: A Grand Challenge Technology Problem", Proc. 1st IEEE Int. Workshop on Real-Time Mission-Critical Systems: Grand Challenge Problems; Phoenix, Arizona, USA, Nov 1999

[2] M. Vieira and H. Madeira, "A Dependability Benchmark for OLTP Application Environments", Proc. 29th Int. Conf. on Very Large Data Bases (VLDB-03), Berlin, 2003.

[3] K. Buchacker and O. Tschaeche, "TPC Benchmark-c version 5.2 Dependability Benchmark Extensions", http://www.faumachine.org/papers/tpcc-depend.pdf, 2003

[4] D. Wilson, B. Murphy and L. Spainhower. "Progress on Defining Standardized Classes for Comparing the Dependability of Computer Systems", Proc. DSN 2002, Workshop on Dependability Benchmarking, Washington, D.C., USA, 2002.

[5] A. Kalakech, K. Kanoun, Y. Crouzet and A. Arlat. "Benchmarking the Dependability of Windows NT, 2000 and XP", Proc. Int. Conf. on Dependable Systems and Networks (DSN 2004), Florence, Italy, 2004.

[6] J. Duraes, H. Madeira, "Characterization of Operating Systems Behaviour in the Presence of Faulty Drivers Through Software Fault Emulation", in Proc. 2002 Pacific Rim Int. Symposium Dependable Computing (PRDC-2002), pp. 201-209, Tsukuba, Japan, 2002.

[7] A. Brown, L. Chung, and D. Patterson. "Including the Human Factor in Dependability Benchmarks", Proc. of the 2002 DSN Workshop on Dependability Benchmarking, Washington, D.C., June 2002.

[8] A. Brown, L. Chung, W. Kakes, C. Ling, D. A. Patterson, "Dependability Benchmarking of Human-Assisted Recovery Processes", Dependable Computing and Communications, DSN 2004, Florence, Italy, June, 2004

[9] A. Brown and D. Patterson, "Towards Availability Benchmarks: A Case Study of Software RAID Systems", Proc. 2000 USENIX Annual Technical Conference, San Diego, June 2000

[10] J. Zhu, J. Mauro, I. Pramanick. "R3 - A Framework for Availability Benchmarking",
      Proc. Int. Conf. on Dependable Systems and Networks (DSN 2003), USA, 2003.

[11] S. Lightstone, J. Hellerstein, W. Tetzlaff, P. Janson, E. Lassettre, C. Norton, B. Rajaraman
      and L. Spainhower. "Towards Benchmarking Autonomic Computing Maturity", 1st IEEE
      Conf. on Industrial Automatics (INDIN-2003), Canada, August 2003.

[12] A.Brown, J.Hellerstein, M.Hogstrom, T.Lau, S.Lightstone, P.Shum, M.P.Yost, "Bench-
      marking Autonomic Capabilities: Promises and Pitfalls", Proc. Int. Conf. on Autonomic
      Computing (ICAC'04), 2004

[13] A. Brown and J. Hellerstein, "An Approach to Benchmarking Configuration Complex-
      ity", Proc. of the 11th ACM SIGOPS European Workshop, Leuven, Belgium, September
      2004

[14] A.Brown, C.Redlin. "Measuring the Effectiveness of Self-Healing Autonomic Systems",
      Proc. 2nd Int. Conf. on Autonomic Computing (ICAC'05), 2005

[15] J. Durães, M. Vieira and H. Madeira. "Dependability Benchmarking of Web-Servers",
      Proc. 23rd International Conference, SAFECOMP 2004, Potsdam, Germany, September
      2004. Lecture Notes in Computer Science, Volume 3219/2004

[16] L.Silva, H.Madeira and J.G.Silva "Software Aging and Rejuvenation in a SOAP-based
      Server", IEEENCA: Network Computing and Applications, Cambridge USA, July 2006

[17] D.Sousa, N.Rodrigues and L.Silva "How Reliable is WS-Reliable Messaging: An Exper-
      imental Study with Apache Sandesha", Submitted for publication, 2006.

[18] OGSA-DAI: http://www.ogsadai.org.uk/

[19] Web Services Interoperability (WS-I) http://www.ws-i.org

[20] WSRF, http://www.oasis-open.org/committees/tc_home.php?wg_abbrev=wsrf

[21] Jakarta Tomcat: http://jakarta.apache.org/tomcat

[22] Apache Axis : http://ws.apache.org/axis/

[23] Globus toolkit: http://www.globus.org/toolkit/

[24] Projects that use OGSA-DAI : http://www.ogsadai.org.uk/about/projects.php

[25] Parasoft SOAtest: http://www.parasoft.com

[26] PushToTest TestMaker: http://www.pushtotest.com

[27] William Hoarau, Sébastien Tixeuil, and Fabien Vauchelles. "Easy fault injection and
      stress testing with FAIL-FCI". Technical Report 1421, Laboratoire de Recherche en In-
      formatique, Université Paris Sud, October 2005

Author Index